ROUTLEDGE LIBRARY EDITIONS:
HISTORY OF MONEY, BANKING AND
FINANCE

Volume 2

BANK BEHAVIOR, REGULATION, AND ECONOMIC DEVELOPMENT: CALIFORNIA, 1860–1910

BANK BEHAVIOR, REGULATION, AND ECONOMIC DEVELOPMENT: CALIFORNIA, 1860–1910

ROGER C. LISTER

Routledge
Taylor & Francis Group

LONDON AND NEW YORK

First published in 1993 by Garland Publishing, Inc.

This edition first published in 2018
by Routledge
2 Park Square, Milton Park, Abingdon, Oxon OX14 4RN

and by Routledge
711 Third Avenue, New York, NY 10017

Routledge is an imprint of the Taylor & Francis Group, an informa business

British Library Cataloguing in Publication Data
A catalogue record for this book is available from the British Library

ISBN: 978-1-138-70169-4 (Set)
ISBN: 978-1-315-10595-6 (Set) (ebk)
ISBN: 978-1-138-05636-7 (Volume 2) (hbk)
ISBN: 978-1-315-16538-7 (Volume 2) (ebk)

Publisher's Note
The publisher has gone to great lengths to ensure the quality of this reprint but
points out that some imperfections in the original copies may be apparent.

Disclaimer
The publisher has made every effort to trace copyright holders and would welcome
correspondence from those they have been unable to trace.

Bank Behavior, Regulation, and Economic Development

California, 1860–1910

BY

ROGER C. LISTER

GARLAND PUBLISHING, INC.
NEW YORK & LONDON
1993

Library of Congress Cataloging-in-Publication Data

Lister, Roger Charles.
    Bank behavior, regulation, and economic development : California,
1860–1910 / by Roger C. Lister.
        p.   cm. — (The Financial sector of the American economy)
    Includes bibliographical references and index.
    ISBN 0–8153–0967–8 (alk. paper)
    1. Banks and banking—California—History.   2. Banking law—
California—History.   I. Title.   II. Series.
HG2611.C2L57   1993
332.1'09794—dc20   92–40629
                                                              CIP

Printed on acid-free, 250-year-life paper
Manufactured in the United States of America

To my parents Daphne and Patrick Lister,
for their loving support over the years,
and by way of congratulations on their fifty golden years;
and to my darling wife Kay C.,
for all her love and excitement about the future.

Contents

Illustrations

xi

Foreword

Lessons From the Past

This study of bank behavior and banking regulation a century ago appears to be far removed from the issues of modern banking, but it provides some valuable insights into current issues. These issues are brought into focus by two contrasting trends around the world in the regulation of the financial sector. In response to various crises, regulatory restrictiveness is being sharply increased in most developed countries. At the same time, rapid liberalization is being introduced to remove structural constraints in many emerging economies. The lesson from California's history is that sharp swings in the restrictiveness of financial regulation are costly. Too rapid liberalization brings a range of excesses. Too quick a reversal brings major adjustment costs. Volatility in regulation adds to the cost of capital for banking by increasing the uncertainty of earnings. Changes in taxation can also be a destabilizing factor. A stable regulatory environment, preferably with minimal regulation, enables the financial sector to contribute to economic development. Yet, this stability is difficult to achieve because major regulatory changes usually result from crises. Policy makers cannot ignore the distortions introduced by new restrictions in their determination to solve current problems.

California's history offers several messages for policy makers involved in liberalizing the regulation of financial institutions. The main goal of supervision is to ensure that bankers behave honestly and competently. A key step is establishing a framework of laws and customs for maintaining fairness in enforcement and sustaining professionalism in regulators. Adequate resources are required for effective supervision.

Banking regulation is more than just legislation. California's history shows how the restrictiveness of regulation depends critically upon the way laws are enforced. Swings in the tightness of supervision can be just as disruptive as changes in laws. The marketplace provides many signals about the health of individual institutions and the financial sector as a whole. Competition between regulators can be valuable, as it lessens the likelihood of an impasse. Ease of entry is a powerful tool because the threat of entry limits the power of existing institutions, a finding that supports branch banking. In making changes, policy makers need to take the public's preferences into account.

Bank failures, capital adequacy, overburdened regulators, ineffective regulation, improper lending, malfeasance, real estate booms and busts. It all sounds familiar. This was California in the late 19th and early 20th centuries, where politicization of the bank regulators, competition between regulatory regimes, and major bank scandals also made appearances. The differences between banking around the turn of the century and banking today are less than might be supposed at first glance. The basic functions of banking were the same: making loans, taking deposits, clearing checks, etc. Bankers then had many of the same concerns as modern bankers: determining the creditworthiness of customers, deciding what rates to charge on loans and pay on deposits, preventing malfeasance by employees, and stopping bank robberies. Real estate loans were just as troublesome to bankers and regulators. Bankers' complaints about government regulation would sound familiar today. There was never the desired amount of the right sort of regulation. Ironically, one common by-product of regulation is the extensive data on banks. The annual reports of California's Bank Commissioners provide a gold mine of information on individual banks.

New Perspectives Ten Years Later

As I have spent the last ten years working largely outside the academic and research world, this foreword does not add information from research that has been completed since I finished my dissertation and I apologize to those scholars who have provided new insights and information. However, I have gained some new perspectives on my research as a participant in the financial sector. At Chase Econometrics, I was involved in a wide range of analyses and consulting for financial institutions. At First Manhattan Consulting Group, I worked with individual institutions as they tackled the business challenges posed by the changing industry. At Citibank, I am now involved in business analysis, assessing credit risk, and portfolio management from a global perspective.

Re-reading my thesis, I was struck by the continued relevance of the issues I addressed ten years ago. In a period of minimal regulation, did banking contribute to the economic development of California? What impact did bank regulation have on the development of banking? What role did financial crises and bank failures play in the evolution of banking regulation? How did regulation change over time? Did free entry lead to excessive bank failures? Did bankers behave like profit maximizing entrepreneurs, with bank capital playing a major role at a time when there was limited regulation? How was bank behavior affected by loan demand, risk and regulation? Was the formation of a new bank a response to the demand for banking services and how did risk or regulation affect bank entry? Did banks possess market power at a time when communications were more limited, yet entry was largely unrestricted? What explains the pattern of bank formations? What explains the pattern of U.S. regional interest rate differentials and the unification of national capital markets? Was it the spread of financial innovation, the changing market power of local banks, evolving regulation, differences in risk and information costs, or disequilibrium between demand and supply in capital markets?

The value of economic history to modern policy makers is to bring order to a myriad of events and provide reference points for the scope of alternative outcomes. One challenge in evaluating policy alternatives is envisioning the full range of possible outcomes. The richness of data from an earlier age provides a stimulating perspective on what might happen by sparking such questions as: what's the same? what's new? how is it different? Taking a longer historical perspective presents more alternative scenarios than recent trends might suggest. A brief summary of the results of this study shows the wealth of insights for modern policy makers in California's banking history.

The Evolution of California's Banking Regulation

A close look at California's banking development reveals a complex pattern of interaction between legislation, regulation, bank behavior and the development of different types of banks during the period 1850 to 1910, as demands for fewer restrictions on banking competed with demands for more safety and soundness. Banking regulation encompassed more than just the rules and legislation governing banks' activities. The enforcement of these restrictions was just as important in determining the extent to which banks chartered under California's laws were regulated. Other laws also affected banks' decisions. In California, property taxes and the methods of taxing banks also affected bank behavior. The competing national banking system added further complexity to the impact of California's regulation on its state-chartered banks. The preferences of bank customers also played a role in the evolution of banking. For example, Californians' dislike of bank notes was responsible for the slow start of national banking in California, in contrast to state incorporated banking's rapid development.

Early legislation in the 1850s banned incorporated banks in California, as they were associated with the issuing of bank notes. Incorporated savings banks, however, were established through a loophole that was subsequently legitimized. With this early start, savings banks established an important role in California's economy that they retained throughout the period. As some of these early savings banks were in fact carrying out commercial banking business, the same loophole was opened up for incorporated commercial banking. By the second half of the 1860s, California had virtually free entry into incorporated banking.

The first attempt to regulate these banks in 1876 was not very successful, as there were no provisions to enforce the requirements of the new law, particularly to establish the veracity of the required bank statements. To be effective, however, laws and regulations required timely supervision of the banks. It was not enough to have just the judicial system enforce the laws; in most cases legal action came too late. As a result, the Board of Bank Commissioners was created in 1878 to supervise and enforce California's banking legislation. The major contribution of banking regulation during the subsequent thirty years was to make it much harder for bankers to behave dishonestly or incompetently by providing for regular examinations by the Bank Commissioners.

California's Bank Commissioners set themselves the major task of providing California with a sound banking industry and reducing bank failures. The reasons for bank failures a hundred years ago appear especially familiar today. Among both state and national banks, many banks failed because of poor management, malfeasance, or both. Some failures were due to large losses on loans, real estate or securities, or alternatively, to reductions in the value of collateral backing bad loans. The Commissioners sought to improve the level of bank management, prevent defalcations and malfeasance, and ensure that any bank's reported financial statements reflected the true state of its affairs. The supervisory process that evolved shows a number of parallels to modern regulation. The essential elements of their examination process would be familiar to modern bankers, particularly their concern with determining the true value of assets. Where assets were overvalued, the Commissioners would insist on a reduction in the assets' recorded value, leading in some cases to the closure of the bank. They then faced the challenging tasks that modern regulators face in closing and then managing failed banks.

The various Commissioners carried out their duties conscientiously during the first two decades of the Board's existence. In the late 1890's, however, the growing burden of inspecting state chartered banks began to limit the effectiveness of the Commissioners, who were unable to obtain additional resources from the Legislature. The introduction of politics into the appointment of the Commissioners also contributed to the decline in the effectiveness of their supervision. To remove the incumbent Commissioners, the Legislature repealed the 1878 Banking Act in 1903. This action permitted the Governor to place his own men on the Board after the law was re-enacted twenty-one days later. The law did not require any Commissioner to have expertise in banking, and only one had to know any accounting. The 1909 Bank Act abolishing the Board and creating the Superintendent of Banks was itself a response to the growing laxity in the Commissioners' supervision in the 1900's. This growing laxity largely offset the impact of additional restrictions that legislation was placing on state chartered banks over this same period and had an impact on the attractiveness of state chartered banks relative to national banks.

Some of the slow growth of national banks in the first twenty-five years of national banking is explained by Californians' distrust of bank notes and the slow growth of banking in southern California in the 1890's, where national banking was more popular. Differences in the burden of regulation between state and national banks was just as important. National banks faced significantly more constraints in the form of minimum capital requirements, a prohibition on real estate lending, a loan limit to a single borrower of ten percent of a bank's capital stock and surplus, and a ban on authorized overdrafts, to name some key restrictions. Moreover, shareholders were liable for up to twice the face value of their shares in the event that the bank failed and the assets were insufficient to pay off the depositors and other creditors.

In the 1900s, the relative advantage of state chartered banks reversed and national banking began to expand. State banks were facing increasing restrictions, while changes in the national banking laws made national banking more profitable. California's property tax laws and its taxation of banks also favored national banks over state banks, particularly savings banks. The growing laxity of state regulation was also a key factor, as the rapid expansion of the economy created an environment where unsound banking practices flourished among state banks. Bankers wishing to be associated with the stronger national system began to switch charters. In response to the weakening of state supervision, self-regulation also appeared, as local clearing houses instituted their own inspections.

These events demonstrate how competition between regulators can limit both the excesses of regulatory control and the extent of regulatory laxity. Competition between regulators provides one avenue for controlling excessive swings in either direction. Depositors were making choices between banks based on their charter. Bankers too had to decide which type of charter provided the right amount of safety and soundness at the cost of additional constraints on their banking activities. In trading off the added cost of more restrictions, bankers were well aware of the externalities of increased likelihood of failure of banks with a particular type of charter. Even borrowers can be concerned with this choice. If a borrower's bank fails during a period of tough times, it may be difficult for the borrower to find a new bank willing or able to provide a new source of funds. Until recently, such borrower concerns were little in evidence in the U.S. Lately, there have been many reported incidents of borrowers being left without lines of credit when their own bank failed and other competing banks did not have the ability or willingness to extend the borrower a new line of credit. Clearly, there are many players in the trade-off between safety and restrictions.

Banking and California's Economic Development

Relatively liberal banking regulation enabled the banking industry to develop in parallel with California's economy. There were no restrictions on the location of a new bank and the minimum capital requirements introduced in the 1890s could be readily circumvented. Even with the minimal regulation of state banking in California, bank failures in California were no more frequent nor significantly higher than in the nation as a whole. This study's findings suggest that banking did contribute to California's economic development by expanding its ability to generate financial capital as the economy's demand for finance grew.

California's economy grew rapidly over the period 1860-1910. This growth, however, was uneven with a period of fast growth being typically followed by a period of slow growth or even stagnation. The pattern of banking's development closely paralleled the state's economy, with both experiencing three periods of growth: the 1860s and 1870s, the 1880s and early 1890s, and the years between 1898 and 1907. Various measures of financial development show that California was one of the top states in the U.S. in terms of banking development from the beginning of this period. California's banking continued to develop as the number of banks and bank deposits grew by more than the state's population, income, and wealth.

The formation of almost a thousand banks in this period shows more clearly the relationship between banking and California's economic development. In 1878, only three of California's more than fifty counties had more than $10 of deposits per $100 of county wealth and twenty four counties had no banks. By 1908, there were thirty-four counties with deposits above this ratio, and only three counties with no banks. This narrowing of differences across the counties demonstrates how banking was supporting local economic development. The pattern of bank entry into local markets in California provides clear evidence that bankers did respond to profitable opportunities offered by market growth and the deficient performance of existing banks. Moreover, the entry of new banks improved the aggregate performance of the banks in the market.

Individual Bank Behavior

A key issue for the modern relevance of this study is the characteristics of the banks that the Commissioners were regulating. The detailed analysis of individual bank behavior shows that banks were generally behaving like profit maximizing modern bankers. One key finding is that they did consider their capital position when determining their loan/asset ratios, at a time when capitalization requirements were minimal or non-existent. This finding on the role of bank capital concurs with the results obtained by some analysts of modern bank behavior, but differs from the findings reported by others who use models that are similar to the one used in this study. The reason for this different result is the use here of separate variables for the bank's capital position and the risk aversion of the bank's management. This separation overcomes the problem that, *ceteris paribus,* more risk averse managements are likely to operate a bank with a higher capital/deposit ratio. The model of individual bank behavior shows that banks did respond to the demand for loans, but the evidence is less consistent than the analysis of the bank entry, which shows banks clearly responding to market growth. One difficulty is accurately measuring loan demand for individual banks.

The behavior of California's banks provides one assessment of regulation's impact. The results for individual banks show that a bank's loan to assets ratio did vary with its charter. National banks had lower loan/asset ratios than state commercial banks, reflecting their more extensive regulation and closer supervision by the U.S. Comptroller of the Currency. These generally lower loan/asset ratios, which are similar to those found by Richard Keehn for national banks in his study of Wisconsin banking over this period, suggest that there was a burden attached to the closer regulation of national banks. If all the banks in California had been national banks, the annual volume of loans would have been five percent less than it was, other things being unchanged. The lack of good substitutes for banks during this period suggests that the regulation of national banks did impose a burden in states where state-chartered banking was restricted. In California, the evidence suggests that the rate of state bank failures was not dramatically higher than that for national banks, certainly not enough to offset the added impact of national banking regulation.

Another issue that is addressed with evidence from California's history is the importance of banks' market power. At a time when entry into the financial services industry has become easier, regulators still concern themselves with banks' market power. Recent examples are the branch divestitures required by the regulators in the approval of major acquisitions of banks with overlapping branch networks. In practice, there is limited evidence that modern banks possess market power. Part of the difficulty is that market power is difficult to measure so the focus turns to the competitive structure of the market. Information costs have been advanced as one source of bank's market power in a concentrated market. Restrictions on entry are often cited as the source of modern bankers' market power. Given the much less developed communications and more limited transportation a century ago, evidence of banks' market power should be visible in their behavior. California's history offers an optimal environment to study whether banks can possess market power in a period when there was de facto free entry into banking, at least for state-chartered banks.

The results of the analysis of bank entry are consistent with the hypothesis that banks possessed market power. However, poor performance, whatever its causes, did not pass unobserved. Market growth and the existing banks' performance were the major determinants of the pace and pattern of bank entry into local markets. Local market concentration and the risk of bank failure slowed entry. The finding that bank formations were a response to the inadequate performance of existing banks suggests that bank entry was a threat that may have kept the performance of existing banks at a higher level, i.e., more loans, lower loan rates and higher deposit rates, than would have been the case if entry had been more restricted. These results support the current recommendations of many analysts for less restrictions on entry into banking, including interstate banking and branching.

At the individual bank level, the market structure results are inconsistent, but the pace of bank entry helps explain these results. In 1890 and 1893, market concentration was positively, not negatively, related to performance, but in 1899 and 1900, it was negatively related to performance. Confirming this pattern, similar results have been reported for Wisconsin for these periods. An important difference between the two time periods is the pace of bank entry in the preceding years. Bank failures, deflation and the lower level of entry in the six years preceding 1899 probably explains the significantly negative effect of market concentration on banks' loan/asset ratios in 1899 and 1900. More than double the number of banks were formed in California in the late 1880s and early 1890s, as compared to the second half of the 1890s. A similar entry pattern is evident in Wisconsin. In both California and Wisconsin, the pace of bank entry can help to explain the changes in the effect of market concentration on bank behavior.

Explaining Regional Interest Rate Differentials

What makes this finding of changing market power particularly interesting is that it helps to explain the pattern of U.S. regional interest rate differentials, as these differentials widened in the 1890s. In studying the evolution of a unified national capital market, economic historians have argued that the pattern of U.S. regional interest rate differentials can be explained by the spread of financial innovations such as the commercial paper market, by regional differences in banks' market power, by regional differences in risk and information costs, and by disequilibrium between demand and supply in capital markets.

California's history shows that these factors were interrelated, so that the pattern cannot be attributed to any single factor. At different times, each of the factors may have played a more important role. Bank entry was related to both economic growth and risk in the form of bank failure. Bank market power was affected by entry. The interrelations among the variables such as bank entry and economic growth tend to confuse the results. If entry was a response to market conditions and the risk of failure, as well as regulation, then market power was also linked to these forces. No single explanation can dominate.

If data on local loan rates can be developed, the differences across California's counties in banking development and the rapid but uneven development of the state's economy might provide an opportunity to study the trends in local interest rate differentials to determine the importance of disequilibrium between demand and supply across California's counties. In the absence of such loan rates, the analysis of bank entry suggest that any interest rate differentials that reflected either market imbalances between supply and demand or the results of local banks exerting their market power would have been gradually eliminated by the formation of new banks. Differences due to risk almost certainly fell as local economies diversified. Financial innovation and improved bank management probably played a role, with the establishment of clearing houses in the major cities across the California being one sign of this trend.

Interest rate differentials are an intriguing issue from a modern perspective. Surprisingly, regional interest rate differentials persist today in the U.S., which raises the question of what determines loan rates. There are several components that drive loan rates: the cost of funds adjusted for maturity, prepayment options and other options, operating expenses, the expected loss rate by type of loan, and a capital charge for the volatility of losses by type of loan. Since loan rates are a mark-up on deposit rates, one indication of imbalance between demand and supply is divergence of deposit rates as well as loan rates. The historical regional interest rate differentials focus on earnings rather than true loan rates or deposit rates. If such rates can be developed, they might show whether widening differentials were due to disequilibrium with higher deposit rates and similar lending margins versus increased market power with lower deposit rates and wider lending margins. Deposit rates do vary regionally.

For example, deposit rates paid by thrifts have differed between the East and West coasts of the U.S. over the past decades. Loan terms can also play a key role in regional differences in rates. For example, differences in the likelihood of prepayment means Californians probably pay more for fixed rate mortgages, because they are more likely to move than U.S. residents generally. Prepayment risk is included in the up-front points and the mortgage rate, rather than being made explicit in the form of specific prepayment penalties.

Perhaps the most critical factor in modern loan rates is the cost of credit risk. In developing models of modern credit problems, I have gained a much greater understanding of how regional diversity affects credit problems. A related issue is the additional cost for the uncertainty of these credit losses. The role of capital is to protect a bank from an extreme level of credit losses. Bankers have to charge not only for expected losses, but also for the capital that has to be allocated to each loan based on the volatility of its expected losses. In my analysis of bank capital in this thesis, I did not address the issue of what was the optimal level of capital given the risk exposure of individual banks. A major avenue for further research is to look more closely at loan losses and their impact on bank capital and loan rates. Such analysis may show that changes in regional economies, by affecting the level and volatility of loan losses, may have played an important role in determining regional interest rates.

The question of how well bankers assess risk and manage their risk exposure has become a much more important issue over the past decade. Regulators have long made capital adequacy a key factor in their rating of banks. However, closer regulation of bank capital has recently become a major focus of U.S. regulators in seeking better protection for the U.S. deposit insurance fund and to ensure a level playing field among financial institutions. California's history suggests that the challenge for regulators in applying more specific capital requirements is to solve one problem without generating new problems. Require too much capital for low risk assets, and banks will have to increase returns from presumably riskier activities to compensate. For example, the current regulatory capital requirements set the same capital ratio for loans that would be rated single "B" as for loans that would be rated triple "A." Overall capital requirements may also drive banks to undertake more risky activities to generate the earnings needed to support the capital base that the regulators require rather than the capital base consistent with the bank's strategy and a true assessment of the risks of the associated activities. The second-guessing of management and the marketplace with imperfect tools such as the broad risk classes for assets is bound to be distorting. The question is what will be the unintended impact of these requirements. Management has to view regulatory capital as a constraint on the attainable set of portfolios for any given level of capital. Changes at the margin will be driven by both their risk/return parameters and their impact on regulatory capital, not the way bank management needs to manage their capital in relation to the riskiness of their portfolios and their chosen strategies.

R.C.L.
October 1992

Acknowledgements

I would like to acknowledge the many people who helped me complete the original thesis. I am very grateful to the members of my thesis committee for all their work. Tom Mayer provided discerning criticism and helpful suggestions. Alan Olmstead supplied challenging counterfactuals and much needed editorial assistance. Richard Green kept me from making econometric errors. My special thanks go to Julie Arnoldo for deciphering my hieroglyphics to produce the first complete draft, and to Linda Reyes for her masterful use of the word processor in many subsequent revisions and her continued cheerfulness in the face of "just one more change." I am also grateful to the numerous other people who willingly gave advice, typed earlier versions, ran regressions, and obtained copies of obscure works, and to my family and many friends who encouraged me to persevere and get it done.

To these acknowledgements, I now have some more to add with this publication of my thesis. My thanks to Garland Publishing Company for the opportunity to give my research exposure to a broader audience at a particularly interesting time in the evolution of the financial services industry worldwide. The views presented here remain my own and do not represent those of my current or former employers. My thanks also to Brian Mitchell and others at Trinity College, Cambridge for stimulating my early interest in economic history many years ago. My appreciation to my family for all those discussions that gave me an interest in both academic and practical matters which made this effort so rewarding. I am especially indebted to Doreen Ottavinia whose dedicated assistance and editorial skills have created a book from my original thesis. Finally, my love and special gratitude to my wife Kay C. for all her encouragement and support through many lost weekends.

Chapter 1

Introduction

Regulation, the Financial Sector, and Economic Growth

In a developing economy, the financial sector can play an important role in furthering economic development.[1] For an economy to grow, resources must be channeled from income into capital accumulation. Economic development requires that this new capital be allocated to new products, new enterprises, new industries, and new regions. Development of the economy brings complexity to the transfer of resources from savers to borrowers, stimulating financial development. New forms of financial instruments are introduced, new financial enterprises are started in new locations, and financial institutions become more important in the functioning of the economy. In particular, the extent of financial intermediation between ultimate lenders and ultimate borrowers increases. Financial development in turn fosters economic development by increasing the efficiency of capital markets.

The process, however, is not inevitable. For a variety of reasons, such as the patterns of trade, the power of entrenched interest groups, the role of foreign institutions, and established business practices, the level and direction of financial activity may not enhance development. Government regulation, some form of which is almost universal in the financial affairs of nations, and other government activities are the most often cited reasons for inadequate financial development. To explore the role that banking plays in economic development, this study analyzes the behavior of individual banks in a period in the development of

1

California's economy when banking was largely unrestricted and entry into banking was essentially "free."

The rapid development of California's economy between 1860 and 1910 makes this state an appropriate subject for studying the relationship between banking and economic development. From producing mainly gold and wheat, California rapidly diversified its economic activities over these five decades. Diversification of the economy was not just the outcome of growth of manufacturing in San Francisco and Los Angeles; in agriculture, the variations of soil and climate were also exploited through the introduction and development of many different crops. What made the role of financial intermediaries so important in this diversification of agriculture was the capital intensity of California agriculture. Not only were machines very much in evidence in cultivating and harvesting the crops, but many of the crops were also capital intensive by their nature requiring considerable capital for processing and packaging.

By comparison with later years, banking in California was largely unrestricted in the period 1860-1910. There were minimal regulations on state commercial bank portfolios; for example, reserve requirements were not introduced until 1905, and even after 1905 there were no provisions to enforce the requirements until 1909. With no significant capital requirements or other charter restrictions, entry for state banks was virtually free. Though national banks faced minimum capital requirements and were generally more heavily regulated than state banks, there were no limitations on the location of either state or national banks in this period. Under these conditions of virtually free entry, banking flourished in California. This period of free entry in California ended around 1909 with the passage of the more restrictive 1909 Bank Act and the creation of the Superintendent of Banks. The U.S. Comptrollers of the Currency also began to make the formation of new national banks more difficult after the numerous bank failures of 1907 and 1908.

The analysis employed in the study ranges from evaluating the aggregate performance of the banking industry to analyzing the behavior of individual banks. This study looks at the changing structure and location of banking activities and investigates the impact of regulation on bank behavior. Most importantly, it investigates the relationship between the formation of new banks and the demand for banking services in local banking markets. This detailed analysis of bank behavior is made possible by a useful by-product of government regulation: data. The annual reports of the California State Board of Bank Commissioners contain individual bank balance sheets for most of California's banks for most years between 1878 and 1908. Only limited aggregate data are available for earlier years. Assessments for property taxes provide a way of measuring the demand for banking services at the local market level. The results of this analysis contribute directly to the ongoing debate among economic historians over the development of national capital markets in the United States in the nineteenth century. They also add to our knowledge of the relationship between market structure and bank performance in local banking markets. This relationship currently plays a key role in the decisions of the courts and bank regulatory agencies regarding bank mergers and acquisitions.[2]

The differences between banking around the turn of the century and banking today are less than might be supposed at first glance, suggesting that there are lessons to be learnt from the past. The basic functions of banking were the same: making loans, providing deposits, clearing checks, etc. Bankers had many of the same concerns as modern bankers: determining the creditworthiness of customers, deciding what rates to charge on loans and pay on deposits, preventing malfeasance by employees, and stopping bank robberies. Bankers' complaints about government regulation would sound familiar today; there was never the desired amount of the right sort. One important difference, particularly for the locational decision of new banks, is the extent of branch banking. Although branch banking was not prohibited by state law, there were very few branches during most of this period in California. While the number of branches began to increase in 1907 and 1908, these branches were mostly located in the same city as the head office. Thereafter, led by A.P. Giannini and the Bank of Italy, bankers began to use branch offices to enter new markets.

Renewed interest in the contribution of the financial sector to economic growth, and the effect on this contribution of the regulation of financial institutions, gives this study an added measure of importance. Dissatisfaction with slow economic growth and concern over persistent inflation has led to a widespread reassessment by economists and governments of national policies towards the financial sectors in a variety of countries. Support for the liberalization of the regulations restricting the financial sector has been growing lately, and more countries have recently been removing some of the restrictions on their financial sectors, particularly those on financial intermediaries.[3]

The financial sector has always been an attractive target for government regulation because of the pervasiveness of financial activity in all but the most undeveloped economies. To hasten economic development, governments in developing countries have typically regulated financial markets, usually with the objective of gaining control over the flow of loanable funds in the economy. As part of a development strategy, governments frequently distorted the relative price of capital to favor particular sectors of the economy. For example, capital would be made relatively cheaper for favored enterprises such as those in the capital-intensive industries, in the export sector, or in industries producing substitutes for certain imports. Maintaining these policies, however, has often required very extensive government control over the financial sector, ranging from regulating banks to severely restricting foreign exchange dealings. Unfortunately, the results of the strategies were not as favorable as anticipated, and the side-effects of the required financial repression appear to have inhibited economic development. Some economists now argue that liberation of the financial sectors in many countries would lead to faster economic growth.[4]

Reassessment of the regulation of financial institutions has also been occurring in developed countries. In the United States, pressure for the deregulation of financial intermediaries has recently resulted in legislation and regulatory action that are now liberating depository institutions from the straight jacket of interest-rate ceilings and other allied regulations. In part, these restrictions were intended to aid housing finance and home ownership by distorting the relative price of capital, but they had become untenable in the face of a steadily rising rate of inflation and a quickening pace of financial innovation. Criticism of other restrictions on depository institutions is also gathering momentum. Prohibitions on interstate branching, limitations on bank holding company acquisitions, and the constraints imposed by the Glass-Steagall Act on bank activities are all being questioned. Support for deregulation comes not only from those who believe the existing regulations are inequitable, but also from those who believe these regulations are inefficient. Deregulation of depository institutions is anticipated to improve the allocation of capital and, some argue, increase the rate of savings, leading to faster economic growth.[5]

Regulatory decisions on bank charter requests, bank merger proposals, and applications for bank holding company acquisitions continue to draw attention to various issues surrounding bank entry. These issues include: the nature and strength of potential competition and probable future competition, the attractiveness of markets to new banks, and the impact of bank entry on competition and the performance of existing banks. Research on bank entry, however, faces a major problem in that the variability of banking regulation over time, across states, and among agencies imparts an often unknown bias to the observed pattern of bank entry. Because restrictions on bank entry were minimal in California between 1884 and 1908, the state offers an interesting opportunity to study the economic determinants of bank entry.[6] In particular, during this period, neither California's Board of Bank Commissioners nor the U.S. Comptrollers of the Currency denied bank charter applications because a local community did not need a new bank. Besides adding to our knowledge of the factors that make markets attractive to a new bank, analysis of entry in this period also contributes to the broader question of whether bank entry should be restricted at all.

Banking, Financial Intermediation and Economic Development

For economic growth to be sustained, capital must be accumulated and invested, preferably in the most productive activity. Financial intermediaries contribute to this process by facilitating the transfer of resources from surplus economic units to deficit economic units, i.e., from lenders to borrowers. Financial intermediaries buy direct claims from deficit units by selling their indirect claims to surplus units. The attractiveness of the liabilities of financial intermediaries is derived from the features of this transformation. Financial intermediaries can take advantage of economies of scale such as in gathering information, in incurring brokerage costs, and in centralizing activity. By pooling the funds of many lenders, they can diversify risk across enterprises, industries, locations, and maturities. This pooling also permits them to offer liabilities with more varied size and maturity than lenders could find among primary securities at the same cost. In combination, these features enable financial intermediaries as a whole to offer lenders a wider choice of attractive financial assets than exists among direct claims, ranging from life insurance, to shares in mutual funds, to checking account deposits. Borrowers also benefit from this process. Financial intermediaries can offer deficit units easier access to funds, at lower rates, and with more variety of terms, than deficit units could obtain if they all issued their own direct claims.[7]

In order to be profitable, financial intermediaries must seek to maximize the spread between the cost of their liabilities and the yield on their assets. By searching for higher yielding outlets for their funds, financial intermediaries contribute directly to economic growth. Loanable funds are more likely to be invested in the projects with the highest marginal products in an economy with a developed financial sector than in an economy where capital accumulation is entirely self-financed by the individual economic units. Theoretically, the search for the most profitable investment will result in the financing of projects with the highest marginal product. In practice, however, a variety of factors may intervene, most notably government regulations that distort relative returns to different investments. The most profitable choice for the financial intermediary then ceases to be the optimal choice for the economy.

Banks are probably still the most important form of financial intermediary. They perform the typical function of a financial intermediary by issuing deposits to surplus units and using the funds to make loans to deficit units. Banks, however, are unique among financial intermediaries in that some of their liability instruments are used as a means of payment. In the nineteenth century, banks often issued their own bank notes; in the twentieth century, note issues have been largely limited to central banks. In any case, in most countries the use of bank notes for payment is now far exceeded by the use of deposit accounts subject to check or other transfer mechanisms to effect payments. Banks perform a valuable service in providing a medium of exchange and a payment mechanism so essential for the functioning of a market economy. Excessive expansion of bank credit, however, financed by increases in bank deposits will generate inflation. While this inflation may create forced savings that are productively invested, it is more likely to disrupt economic activity.[8]

Through their role as the major suppliers of short-term credit, and credit in general, banks can be especially important in furthering economic development through the financing of industry and trade. Some have argued, principally Gerschenkron, that banks can play a very active role in furthering industrial development by also supplying entrepreneurial ability to industrial enterprises. This active role has been attributed to German and Japanese banks in the nineteenth and twentieth centuries respectively. More recently, development banks in various countries have been established to pursue this active role.[9]

While financial intermediation increases the productivity of accumulated capital by improving its allocation, the effect of financial intermediation on the level of savings is theoretically ambiguous. On the one hand, financial development and the resulting higher real yield available on the financial instruments offered by intermediaries encourages savers to substitute future consumption for present consumption. On the other hand, this higher yield increases the income of savers enabling them to consume more now or, alternatively, to save less now to achieve a given level of accumulated wealth in the future. The issue is an empirical one. There is some evidence to suggest that the elasticity of savings with respect to the real interest rate is positive. The problems in testing for this effect lie partly in the inadequacy of the data, and partly in the complexity of economic development. Along with financial development, many other characteristics of the economy are also changing, which makes it difficult to isolate the relationship between savings and real interest rates.[10]

The change that is inherent in economic development creates disequilibrium in the demand and supply of credit. If new activities and new regions are to grow, sources of finance must be developed. The financial sector must expand through the creation of new types of financial intermediaries, new forms of financial instruments, new firms in existing financial activities, as well as new firms in developing regions. In this way, funds in areas or activities with surplus savings and low yields on investment are channelled to those areas or activities with insufficient savings and high yields on investment. While differences in interest rates among regions could persist in an economy with an undeveloped financial sector, such differences in an economy with a developed financial sector would elicit a flow of capital from the low rate region to the high rate region that would equalize rates, other things being equal. Financial intermediaries can increase the efficiency of this transfer of resources by reducing the cost of the transfer.

Financial intermediaries can thus in theory contribute to economic growth by raising the rate of savings, improving the allocation of capital that is accumulated, and increasing the efficiency of capital markets. This contribution can be especially important in an economy experiencing the disequilibrium inherent in rapid economic development. But, as history demonstrates, the results are not guaranteed.

Lessons From the Past

Taking a wide variety of approaches, economic historians have devoted considerable resources to investigating the role and contribution of financial intermediaries to economic growth and development. Banking has received special attention in this effort as the most common, and probably most important, type of financial intermediary, particularly during the period when today's advanced countries were developing. This research, however, has not yielded any firm conclusions. After analyzing the most comprehensive set of data yet assembled, Goldsmith (1969) finds that comparison of financial development among a wide variety of countries reveals only that financial development is associated with economic development. Though he cannot establish causation, Goldsmith does conclude that financial development is a necessary, but not a sufficient, condition for economic growth.[11]

At some point in a country's development, Goldsmith finds its financial sector develops more rapidly than its real economy. In his analysis, Goldsmith employs a broad measure of the relative size of the financial superstructure. He defines this measure as the value of all financial assets divided by the value of all tangible assets or national wealth, and calls it the Financial Interrelations Ratio, or FIR. In general, less developed countries have lower FIRs. Growth in a country's FIR appears to reach a limit for developed countries of around 1 to 1-1/2. The level of a country's FIR depends upon the separation of savings and investing among economics units; greater use of external financing by economic units is associated with financial development. As financial development proceeds, the share of financial institutions in the issuance and ownership of financial assets increases, though the emphasis is more on debt issues than equity.[12]

Goldsmith finds that everywhere the banking system has been the initiator of financial development, first spreading script money and then checking deposits through a developing country's economy. Banking's share of financial institutions' assets gradually declines as new financial institutions grow; somewhat later, banking's share of all financial assets declines. Foreign financial capital and foreign financial outlets for domestic capital have been important in some, but not all, countries. The introduction of foreign technology and entrepreneurship has been easier in financial activities than in many other activities. As might be expected, the financing costs are distinctly lower in countries with developed financial sectors than in countries with underdeveloped financial sectors.

In most countries, financial development has paralleled economic development with the size and complexity of the financial structure increasing as income and wealth per capita grew, at least over periods of several decades. In some countries, above-average financial development accompanied rapid economic growth, but the direction of causation cannot be determined.[13]

The role of banking in the economic development of a variety of countries is the subject of the studies contained in Cameron (1967; 1971). A central theme of the research in these studies is testing Gerschenkron's hypothesis that banking plays an active role in advancing industrial development in moderately backward countries. Though Cameron does supply some quantitative measures of relative banking development and uses them to compare banking development among different countries, in summarizing the studies he concentrates on qualitative comparison of the role of banking in the different countries studied.[14] The conclusion Cameron draws from these studies is that banking can contribute to economic growth, but it can also distort or thwart economic growth. No single optimal path of financial development emerges from these studies. Instead, Cameron suggests that the best policy for governments is to leave the financial sector as free as possible to develop in response to the demand for financial services.[15] He favors policies that permit free entry and stimulate competition.

While the lack of a common approach limits the conclusions that can be drawn from these studies, it is apparent that government regulation and government financial policies were commonly the cause of weak or distorted banking development, and hence lessened the contribution of banking to economic growth. For example, persistent government deficits and the resulting demand for funds are reported to have diverted banks' attention away from more productive investments, in industry for example, in such countries as Austria, Italy, and Spain.[16] Limits on bank entry are exemplified by the lack of free incorporation for joint-stock companies in Austria before 1899. In the United States, however, bank regulation and restrictions on bank entry are found by Sylla (1971) to have favored economic development by furthering manufacturing growth in the northeastern states at the expense of agriculture and economic growth in western and southern states.

According to Sylla, the National Banking System, created in 1863, restricted entry into banking through minimum capital requirements for national banks and limitations on the issuing of national bank notes combined with the taxation of state bank notes.[17] Entry restrictions gave country banks market power which they exploited by discriminating between local borrowers, who paid high loan rates, and the competitive national money market, in which the bank received the going rate. Sylla's evidence for this market power is the higher earnings of non-reserve city national banks in the South and West. Participation in the nation's money market was a product of the required reserve system for national banks. Reserves on deposits, which were required of all national banks, were pyramided up from non-reserve city banks, to reserve city banks, and on to the central reserve city banks in New York City. In general, banks received interest on these reserves giving them an incentive to maintain them. Thus, Sylla argues, the combination of the monopolistic position of national banks, the enhanced connections of country banks with the nation's money centers in the East, and the prohibition of mortgage lending by national banks resulted in funds being diverted from agriculture, and from states in the South and West to the northeastern states to finance industrial growth. Industrialization did indeed proceed very rapidly in the United States over the fifty years following 1863, but some have questioned Sylla's assessment of the role of the National Banking System. These critics hold different views on the development of the nation's capital markets.

A key issue in U.S. economic history continues to be the development of national capital markets. Much of the research on the issue investigates exactly when and why a national market for short-term capital evolved during the period 1870-1910. Attention is focused on the pattern of regional interest rate differentials, which are derived from national bank earnings in different regions. There appears to be a consensus among economic historians that these differentials had narrowed by the end of the first decade of the twentieth century. However, both the pattern of these differentials and the explanation for this pattern remain the subject of debate.[18]

In the first study to employ national bank data, Davis (1965) derives the average annual net rates of return and gross rates of return on earning assets by region from statistics for national banks. The gross rate, he argues, is an approximation for the average regional rate that banks were charging for short-term capital. Unfortunately, the U.S. Comptroller of the Currency only reported this series by state for the period 1888-1914. The net earnings series is available by state for a longer period, 1870-1914, but it nets out national banks' losses and operating expenses.

Assuming that losses are a short-run phenomenon and operating expenses are similar across regions, Davis argues that the net rate of return series identifies the trends in regional interest rate differentials. Employing the U.S. Comptroller of the Currency's regional definitions for the states, he finds that the regional differentials in these six regions declined over the period 1870-1914.

Criticism of Davis' interest rate proxies comes from Smiley (1973, 1975, 1976 and 1977) and James (1974, 1976b, 1976c and 1978), who provide their own alternatives. Neither agrees with Davis' use of the net earnings series, because it leaves out factors that might explain regional interest rate differentials. Instead, each modifies the gross earnings rate series so that it becomes a better proxy in their eyes for national banks' loan rates. Because they base their estimates on the gross earnings series, their interest rate series only begin in 1888, but they do provide other extensions on Davis' rates. Smiley derives an annual average rate on private earnings assets by state for the period 1888-1914. James derives a semi-annual average rate on loans by state for the period 1888-1911. The outcome of these alternative approaches is to challenge Davis' conclusion that regional rate differences narrowed over the whole period. Both Smiley and James provide evidence that regional rates diverged in the middle to late 1890s, before narrowing again after the turn of the century.[19] While Davis does not find this pattern for his short-term rates, he does suggest that the evolution of a national long-term capital market may have been retarded after 1890.[20] Thus, a rough pattern does appear to have emerged from this research.

Even more diversity is to be found among the explanations offered for the pattern of these differentials. Davis attributes the decline he sees in the differentials between 1870 and 1914 to the rise of the commercial paper market, an institution that specialized in the transfer of short-term capital.[21] Other writers argue that the timing is wrong as commercial paper did not become important in many areas until some years after 1900.[22] Sylla finds support for his view that national banks exploited their market power at the expense of local borrowers in the higher net returns of country banks. According to Sylla, the narrowing of regional differentials after 1900 was due to a decline in this market power. Sylla argues it was the lower minimum capital requirements for national banks, introduced by the Gold Standard Act of 1900, that stimulated entry and increased competition among banks in precisely those regions where national banks were exploiting their market power; the South and the

West. James (1976b; 1976c) provides support for the hypothesis that regional differentials depended on banks' market power. Using the number of banks per capita as a measure of the level of banks' market power in a state, James finds market power to be one important factor that explains the movement of his interest rate series over time for each state. According to James, however, it was not the entrance of new national banks that led to declining market power and narrowing differentials, but rather, it was the entry of new state-chartered banks following the liberalization of state banking laws in the 1880s.

The results of a detailed study of Wisconsin banking by Keehn (1972; 1980), however, provide no support for the market power hypothesis. Keehn investigates bank behavior in local banking markets, rather than the regional approach of Sylla or the statewide approach used by James, but finds no evidence that the concentration of banking in these local markets affected bank behavior. Though he has no measure of the effect of entry or the threat of entry, Keehn concludes that the threat of entry by new banks exerted a pro-competitive effect on existing banks, and prevented these banks from exercising any market power during the 1880s and 1890s. Instead of changes in banks' market power, he suggests that improvements in communications, broadly defined, brought about the decline in the interest rate differentials between Wisconsin and more financially developed regions.

From a perfect capital market perspective, Stigler (1967) points out that regional differentials in interest rates could be explained by differences among regions in risk and transactions costs. Rockoff (1977) provides support for this perfect market hypothesis with evidence that average rates of return on national bank capital were higher in those areas where national banks were more prone to fail. Since shareholders in regions with higher failure rates required compensation in the form of higher earnings to compensate them for the greater risks they incurred, loan rates would also have to be higher in these regions. Sylla (1977) questions whether the differences in risk found by Rockoff were enough to warrant the large differences in average yield since the rates of failure were relatively small. Using the sample variance of banks' loan loss rates, James (1976a) tests directly for the impact of risks on his estimated rates of return, but finds that variations in this measure of risk across states, though significant, were much less important in explaining the pattern of rates across states than variations in his measure of market power. Smiley (1977) reports a similar result for the effect of the standard deviation of loan loss rates on his interest rates.

As several authors have observed, these hypotheses all focus on the supply side of the capital market. The demand side has received much less attention with only one study focusing on the importance of demand factors. Using a regional model of the U.S. economy, Williamson (1974) finds that Davis' pattern of regional interest rate differentials can be explained by disequilibrium in capital markets. According to Williamson, excess demand for funds in the Midwest combined with market imperfections to generate higher interest rates than in the East in the 1870s. The differential between rates in the Midwest and East narrowed in the 1880s and early 1890s, Williamson argues, because agriculture was generating a savings surplus. In the 1890s, the situation changed as industrialization accelerated in the Midwest, increasing the demand for funds. This pattern of development, says Williamson, accounts for widening regional differentials in the 1890s. Thus, forces exogenous to the capital markets, not market imperfections or solutions to these imperfections, can explain the pattern of regional differentials. Williamson tests this conclusion by simulating his model under the assumption that capital markets were perfect. Allowing savings to respond to real interest rates, he finds that agriculture would have had a higher share of employment and output under his simulation. Though Williamson hedges his model with caveats and others have criticized the model, the conclusion drawn from the model is interesting because it agrees with Sylla's conclusion that market imperfections favored industrialization, despite the model's being based on a radically different analysis of the U.S. economy in this period.[23]

This limited survey of the literature reveals many unresolved issues in the relationship of banking and financial development to economic development. While Goldsmith's comparative method identifies a broad pattern of financial development, it does not establish an optimal path, nor the consequences of deviating from such a path. The studies in Cameron (1967; 1972) pay considerable attention to banking's role in allocating resources, and explore how government policies often limit banks' ability to perform this role. Not all government regulation, however, was detrimental. In some cases, regulation and government policies were beneficial, preventing financial panics, limiting bank failures and furthering economic development. Focusing on a developed economy's need for a unified capital market, several economic historians

have evaluated the contribution of financial institutions to the evolution
of a national short-term capital market in the U.S. economy between 1870
and 1914. Regulation of banking by both the federal government and the
various states plays an important part in the conclusions these historians
draw from their research.

Broadly speaking, they have argued that the pattern of regional
interest rate differentials can be explained by the spread of financial
innovations such as the commercial paper market, by regional differences
in banks' market power, by regional differences in risk and information
costs, and by disequilibrium between demand and supply in capital
markets. While no single explanation has proved superior, the market
power hypothesis has received the most support. Proponents of this
hypothesis argue that government regulations restricting bank formations
were the major source of this market power, but disagree over the
importance of the national banking laws versus state banking laws in
bringing about changes in this market power. Many unresolved issues
thus remain.

Banking, Regulation and California's Economic Development

The research reviewed above raises a variety of unresolved issues
that warrant further investigation with data from California's history.
How well did banking do in relation to the growth and development of
California's economy? What impact did bank regulation have on the
development of banking? Did this change over time? Was bank behavior
affected by the demand for loans, market power, risk or regulation? What
explains the pattern of bank formations? Was the formation of a new bank
a response to the demand for banking services? How did risk or
regulation affect bank entry? Did free entry lead to excessive bank
failures? And, finally, can the pattern of interest rate differentials between
California and New York City be explained by any of the four hypotheses
offered by economic historians? Answers to these questions should
provide us with a better understanding of the role banking played in
California's economic development and offer a comparative basis for
evaluating bank behavior and government policies in other regions and
economies.

To answer some of these questions, this study employs three
quantitative approaches to analyze bank behavior in California. The first
approach is to evaluate the aggregate development of banking in

California both over time and in relation to other states. The second approach is to develop and then estimate a linear regression model of individual bank behavior that can assess the influence of various factors on the individual bank's lending decision. The third approach is to estimate a model of bank formations in local markets to see what factors determined bank entry. In addition, banking regulation and its enforcement are explored in some detail.

This study covers the five decades between 1860 and 1910. The beginning year is the earliest for which reliable aggregate banking data are available to compare California with other states. The ending year is another census year that permits comparisons to be made between states. There are two principal reasons for ending the period covered in 1910 rather than later, say in 1920. First, the regulatory regime changed in California in 1909 with the passage of the 1909 Bank Act creating the Superintendent of Banks. Moreover, at this time, in response to the 1907 panic and subsequent bank failures, both California's Superintendent of Banks and the U.S. Comptroller of the Currency began to consider a community's need for a new bank when reviewing bank charter applications, thereby ending an era of *de facto* free entry. Second, branch banking expanded rapidly from 1908 onwards, and branches ceased to be in the same city as their head office. Accordingly, bank balance sheets for multi-office banks began to reflect conditions in several local markets, and thus are not amenable to analysis with the model developed in Chapter 4.

Government policies and the regulation of banking can play a major role in determining bank behavior, but first, the nature of this regulation must be explored. The advantage of studying just one state is that close attention can be paid to the details of banking regulation. This close attention can yield important discoveries. As Chapter 2 documents, banking legislation in California was only half the story of banking regulation. The enforcement of banking laws played an almost equal part in determining the restrictiveness of banking regulation. As Cameron (1972) has noted, banking regulation in the United States during the nineteenth century comprised $n + 1$ regimes where n was the number of states. The common factor in all states was the National Banking System, but its role in each state clearly depended on its interaction with the state's banking system. In California, national banking developed slowly. As late as 1900, only one bank in eight in California was a national bank, as compared to about one bank in three in the United State as a whole.

Chapter 2 provides various explanations for this slow development ranging from Californians' dislike of bank notes to differences in regulation and the unequal tax treatment of different types of banks.

In the absence of an agreed-upon optimal path for an economy's financial development, the comparative approach provides one alternative method of assessing banking's development in California. In Chapter 3, quantitative measures of banking's development relative to the economy are used to compare the development of banking in California both over time and with other states. This method of assessment draws on work by Goldsmith and Cameron. In exploring the role of banking in economic development, Cameron has paid particular attention to the type of activity banking financed. While many of California's bankers were active in the development of new and existing activities both in industry and agriculture, there is insufficient data for quantitative analysis.[24] Chapter 3 does contain some discussion of how banking's growth was tied to the changing pattern of economic activity, but the direction of causation is not established.

In an economy whose development is bound up with the settlement and development of its regions, the spread of banking is important for sustaining development. That banking did spread and grow with the developing regions of California's economy is demonstrated in Chapter 3 by the narrowing of differences among California's counties in the level of banking relative to the local economy. This narrowing suggests that banking was generally following rather than leading economic growth. The testing of this hypothesis with a model of bank entry is discussed below.

The availability of bank balance sheets for most of the banks in California for all but a few years between 1878 and 1908 means that a model of individual bank behavior can be estimated for these years. With this second quantitative method, the effect on bank behavior of regulation and other factors can be gauged directly. The single period model developed in Chapter 4 is based on a model of the multi-product, price discriminating bank originally presented by Shull (1963), and subsequently refined by Broaddus (1971; 1974), Klein (1970; 1971), and Miller (1975). Sylla (1969) and Keehn (1972; 1980) also use variations of Shull's basic model. One innovative feature of the model developed in this study is the direct incorporation of the risk aversion of the bank's management into the lending decision. The results of the estimation of the model using multiple regression analysis are presented in Chapter 5.

These results show how the individual bank's lending decision was influenced by loan demand, market structure, bank entry, management's aversion to risk, the bank's capital position, and the bank's age and size. Differences in behavior are found for banks of different types: national banks, state commercial banks, and state savings banks.

Almost a thousand banks of all types were formed in California between 1884 and 1908. The third quantitative method used in this study is the development and estimation of a model in Chapter 6 to explain the pattern of these bank formations as new banks entered local banking markets across California during this period. Economic theory argues that entry of new firms in a competitive economy is a response to differences in expected profit rates. In the absence of barriers to entry, such as economies of scale, entrepreneurs maximize the return to capital by forming firms in those industries or locations where they expect newly invested capital to earn the highest rate of profit. In theory, predicting entry is simple; in practice, what is difficult is determining the expected rate of profit, which perhaps explains the paucity of empirical studies on the entry of new firms in any industry. In this case, since the profitability of a new bank is closely linked to its deposit growth, the model focuses on the potential for deposit growth for a new bank in each local market. Estimation of the model using California's counties as proxies for local banking markets yields the important result that bank entry was a response not only to expectations about market growth, but also to the current level of banking relative to the local economy. Thus, the spread of banking and hence financial intermediation in California can be generally explained as a response to the demand for banking services.

In the final chapter, the role of banking in U.S. economic development is discussed in light of this study's findings for bank behavior in California. A review of the evidence offered to explain the evolution of a national short-term capital market reveals no superior explanation among the four hypotheses offered to date. While other studies have favored particular hypotheses, this study finds direct support for three of the four hypotheses, and does not reject the fourth. California's history reveals that bank behavior was a function of risk, market demand, and market power. The lack of a single dominant factor suggests that the evolution of a national capital market was a more complicated process than some have concluded. One example of this complexity is the nature of bank regulation and the impact it had on bank behavior. In California, the restrictiveness of the State's regulation of its banks depended not only on the State's rules and laws, but also on their enforcement. Under these circumstances, a simple comparison between state and national bank regulations may be misleading, if the national bank regulations were enforced more stringently.

Notes

1. A variety of views on the role of the financial sector in economic development are offered by Cameron (1967; 1972), Cheng (1980), Fry (1980), Goldsmith (1958, 1969), McKinnon (1973; 1976), and Shaw (1973).
2. See, for example, Austin (1977), Kareken (1981) and Scott (1980).
3. Fry (1980); McKinnon (1973; 1976), and McKinnon and Mathieson (1981).
4. Fry (1980); McKinnon (1976); Shaw (1973).
5. See, for example, Federal Reserve Bank of Boston (1972).
6. Prior to 1909, the only significant regulatory hurdle faced by applicants for a state bank charter was fulfilling the legal requirements for incorporation, which were easily met in this period. Minimum capital requirements, introduced in 1895, appear to have been circumvented by the simple expedient of making loans to shareholders. After the panic of 1907, both the Comptroller of the Currency, and the newly-created (1909) Superintendent of Banks for the State of California began to consider a local community's need for a new bank.
7. Benston (1973); Black (1975); Pringle (1974).
8. Goldsmith (1969), Table D-33 pp. 548-49 shows that commercial banks owned two-thirds of the assets of financial institutions in 1880, 1900 and 1912. Cameron (1967, 1972); Davis (1972) discuss banks' ability to generate forced savings.
9. Gerschenkron (1962) argues that the banking sector played a leading role in the economic development of moderately backward countries in nineteenth century Europe. Cameron (1967; 1972) provides detailed studies of various countries which shed some light on this issue.
10. Fry (1980); Goldsmith (1969); Motley (1982); and Wright (1967).
11. Goldsmith (1969), p. 408.
12. Ibid., Chapter 2.
13. Ibid., Chapters 1 and 9.
14. Cameron (1967), Chapter 9, and Cameron (1972), Chapter 1.
15. Cameron (1972), pp. 24-25.
16. See the studies on each of these countries in Cameron (1972).
17. Sylla has expressed this view most recently in Sylla (1977).

18. Keehn (1980) and the discussion of this paper by Sylla (1980), are the most recent contributions to this debate.
19. James (1976c) and Smiley (1976).
20. Davis (1965), p. 393.
21. Davis' most recent opinions on this issue are in Davis (1975).
22. James (1976c; 1978); Smiley (1975); and Sylla (1977).
23. Sylla (1977) criticizes Williamson's model because his simulated results for interest rates differ substantially in Sylla's eyes from the historical rates. Williamson's model also implicitly assumes that financial intermediaries and financial development played no role in improving the flow of funds between regions, and had no impact on the rate of saving or investing.
24. There is evidence that bankers were actively involved in business enterprises with many bankers owning other businesses. Some bankers were involved in various leading sector activities such as the construction of railroads and the development of oil production. Evidence of these types of links between bankers and business is scattered among autobiographies, company histories, and history books, awaiting comprehensive analysis by a future scholar of banks and business.

Chapter 2

Regulation and Banking Development in California, 1853-1909

Introduction

Economic historians have argued that government actions are a major factor determining the contribution of banking to economic development. In this chapter, the regulation of banking in California is explored to see how regulation affected the development of banking in the state. The first important issue addressed in this chapter is the extent to which banking was regulated. Banks today are subject to a wide variety of restrictions ranging from minimum capital requirements to reserve requirements, from ceilings on interest rates on deposits to limits on a bank's portfolio choices. In analyzing the evolution of banking regulation in California, this chapter will explore the origins of these modern restrictions. The regulation of banking is more than just rules and legislation. The supervision of banks and the enforcement of the laws are also important. After all, legislated restrictions on bank behavior are of little value unless they are enforced. As it turns out, banking legislation in California did increase the constraints on state-chartered banks' behavior over the period 1860-1910, though they remained relatively minimal until 1909, but these constraints were largely offset after 1900 by weaker enforcement of the banking laws and more relaxed supervision of state-chartered banks until the 1909 Bank Act.

Just as the extent of regulation currently varies among the different types of banks in the United States, so too in nineteenth century California, the regulations a bank faced varied with its charter. Four types of banks existed in California during this period: national banks, state-chartered commercial banks, state-chartered savings banks, and private (unincorporated) banks. The distribution of California's banks by type in terms of numbers and deposits are given in Tables 2-1, 2-2, 2-3 and 2-4. Comparison of the regulations governing different types of banks highlights the extent of bank regulation. Differences of this kind also provide insights into the relationship between regulation and the development of banking. On the one hand, one would expect banks of the type with the least onerous regulations to expand at the expense of more regulated banks. On the other hand, the least regulated banks may also be perceived as being the most unsound, limiting the expansion of such banks. This chapter explores the differences in regulation among banks of different types and shows that both aspects played a part in determining how banking developed in California.

One notable feature of banking's development in California was the persistent importance of state-chartered savings banks. As late as 1905, California's 110 savings banks had more deposits than the 377 commercial banks in the state (see Table 2-4). Unlike savings banks elsewhere, however, these savings banks were joint-stock and membership savings banks rather than mutual banks; in membership banks, depositors pay a one-time fee to join.[1] Moreover, many of these savings banks legally carried on a commercial banking business, even though some were called savings and loan societies. In view of the important role that savings banks played in other states, such as New York, the position of California's savings banks warrants elaboration. One of the issues explored in this chapter is the basis for the position of savings banks in California's banking industry.

In contrast to the early importance of savings banks, national banks developed slowly in California. Even special legislation creating national gold banks failed to spur on national banking in the 1870s. As late as 1900, there were still only 35 national banks as compared with 250 state banks (see Table 2-2). In the nation as a whole, there were 2,076 national banks and 1,279 non-national banks in 1880. By 1900, there were 3,731 national banks and 9,322 non-national banks, but the national banks had assets of $4,944 million and non-national banks had assets of $6,444 million.[2] Only after 1900 in California did national banks begin to rival state commercial banks in number or size. The third section of this chapter seeks to explain this pattern of development. One possible cause is that under the dual-banking system, which persists today, national banks may have faced more burdensome regulations than state banks. Ironically, national banks' right to issue relatively tax-free bank notes, their major initial advantage over state banks in the United States generally, was of little value in California because of Californians' widespread distrust of bank notes.

For Cameron (1967), the soundness of a banking system is an important feature that helps to determine the contribution banking can make to economic growth. With fewer of the stops and starts associated with financial panics and bank failures, a sound banking system can further economic growth. While banking regulation reduces the number and extent of bank failures, it also imposes costs on the economy by restricting bank behavior and generating the kinds of inefficiencies that are widely criticized today. These inefficiencies can take various forms, such as banks making fewer, safer loans than they would in the absence of regulations, or adopting new, more expensive business methods to sidestep regulations. A prime example from the present is a product of the ceilings imposed on the interest rates that banks can pay depositors: banks are currently selling certificates of deposit to money market mutual funds that are in turn selling their shares to individuals who once held deposits at the banks. In the process, another layer of intermediation has been added to circumvent banking regulations. Relegating the analysis of how banking regulation affected individual bank behavior to subsequent chapters, the discussion in the fourth section of this chapter focuses on the relationship between banking regulation and the number and nature of bank failures of different types as banking regulation evolved.

California's Regulation of its State-Chartered Banks

California's Constitution of 1849 imposed the earliest restrictions on banking activities in the state by prohibiting the issuing of any form of bank notes and the formation of any type of banking corporation.[3] These prohibitions were enacted into law by the Corporation Act passed in 1850. With an abundance of gold in coin and other forms, the prohibition on issuing notes was no deterrent, and unincorporated banking flourished as numerous private banks as well as a few branches of foreign and out-of-state banks were opened to service California's rapidly developing economy (see Table 2-1).[4] Entering by a side door, the earliest incorporated banks were savings banks that were formed under the Corporation Act of 1853 with charters that allowed them to engage in any species of commerce; the first such bank was organized in 1857. While clearly formed to carry out a banking business, as nominal savings and loan societies, these institutions managed to avoid the prohibition contained in the Corporation Act of 1850, but no commercial banks could be organized in this way. This curious state of affairs persisted until 1862, by which time four such savings institutions had been chartered. In that year, the first step towards regulation of the banking industry was taken with the passage of the Savings Bank Act. This Act was the product of dissatisfaction with the lack of control over private banking and a desire to encourage thrift.[5]

To further the growth of sound and stable savings banks, the Act required savings banks, also called savings and loan associations in the Act, to have adequate security on all loans, and prohibited all loans on personal security. The maximum maturity for loans was limited to six years, but there were no restrictions on the renewal of loans. These banks were permitted to invest no more than $100,000 in bank premises, and could not hold real property taken for debt for more than five years. They could not borrow funds except via deposits, and had to accumulate a reserve of $100,000.

Whatever impact these restrictions had on savings banks' activities, the lack of any regulatory agency to enforce the restrictions clearly reduced it. Moreover, a major constraint on savings bank behavior was lifted in 1864 by an amendment that allowed savings banks with no less than $300,000 in capital and reserve funds to make unsecured loans. This amendment had a major impact on banking in California for it legitimized such lending not only for savings banks with the necessary capital, but also for commercial banks.

With the legitimacy of commercial banking established for state-chartered banks, numerous incorporated commercial banks were formed under the Corporation Act of 1853, the same side-door used by the early savings banks. Their number rose from 1 in 1864 to 12 in 1870, and reached 41 by 1875, while the number of savings banks increased from 5 in 1864 to 29 in 1875 (see Table 2-1). What dictated whether a bank was a commercial bank or a savings bank was the Act under which the bank incorporated, rather than the actual activity undertaken by each bank.[6] Though the number of state commercial banks increased more rapidly than the number of savings banks, the latter retained an initial advantage in size that was maintained into the 1900s.

Although the objective of the 1862 Act was to encourage thrift in California, the Act itself makes no mention of mutual savings banks despite their importance in the East at this time. According to Crumb (1935), while some California banks have been called mutuals, it is doubtful if they were ever true mutuals. In a mutual bank, each depositor owns a share in the bank equal to his share of the deposits. Many California banks, however, were started with a membership plan whereby each depositor became a member by paying a fee; in one case, the fee was one dollar. When the bank was considered launched, the fee was dropped, and the existing members owned the bank. In some cases, control of the bank passed to a few individuals as they acquired others' memberships. Some of these banks were converted to fully-fledged stock savings banks by issuing stock. In California, at least, savings banks were not mutuals, despite the absence of paid-in capital in some of their balance sheets and their use of names such as the Hibernia Savings and Loan Society.[7]

The suspension of payment by the Bank of California in 1875 ushered in a period of financial difficulties for California. Though the Bank of California was rescued at some cost to its stockholders, other banks did not survive the results of bad management and financial pressures.[8] While efforts to increase banking regulation in the early 1870s had met with little success, these financial difficulties finally generated sufficient political pressure in 1876 for the passage of an Act that required every state-chartered bank to publish a semi-annual statement of the bank's condition in a local newspaper, and file a statement with the county recorder, accompanied by a sworn statement attesting to the value of the bank's assets and liabilities.[9] As in the past, attempts to introduce state examinations of banks were unsuccessful, but this Act did make bank directors responsible for the results of any false statement.

The failure of several banks in 1876 and 1877 quickly revealed the inadequacy of these provisions and led to the passage of an Act in 1878 that created a Board of Bank Commissioners to regulate California's state-chartered banks. This Act required the three appointed Commissioners to license all state incorporated banks, to make unheralded semi-annual inspections of each bank, and to obtain sworn statements of condition semi-annually from each bank for the purposes of tabulation. Failure to obtain a license or provide a statement resulted in

a daily fine of $100 until corrected. Section 11 detailed the reasons and
process for the closing of a bank:

> If such commissioners, on examination of the affairs of any
> corporation mentioned in this Act, shall find that any of said
> corporations or persons have been guilty of violating its charter or
> law, or is conducting business in an unsafe manner, they shall, by
> an order addressed to the corporation so offending, direct
> discontinuance of such illegal and unsafe practices and a conformity
> with the requirements of its charter and of law, and with safety and
> security in its transactions; and if any of said corporations or
> persons shall refuse or neglect to comply with such order, or when
> it shall appear to these Commissioners that it is unsafe for any of
> the said corporations to continue to transact business, they shall
> communicate with the Attorney-General, who shall immediately
> commence suit in the proper Court against such corporation to
> enjoin and prohibit it from transacting any further business; and
> upon the hearing of the case, if the Judge of the Court where the
> case is tried shall be of the opinion that it is unsafe for the parties
> interested for such corporation or person to continue to transact
> business, and that such corporation or person is insolvent, he shall
> issue the injunction applied for by the said Commissioners, who
> shall cause said injunction to be served according to law; and he
> shall further direct said Commissioners to take such proceedings
> against such corporation or person as may be decided upon by its
> creditors.[10]

Thus, the Board of Bank Commissioners was made responsible for
the supervision and regulation of all state incorporated banks.

The Commissioners took their responsibilities seriously. Ten
incorporated state banks were closed following the first examinations by
the Bank Commissioners. Included among these banks were some of the
largest savings banks in San Francisco. Unfortunately, there was no
provision in the law for the Commissioners to supervise the liquidation
process. They were not even authorized to examine banks in liquidation.
Instead, it was up to the directors of the closed bank to appoint a
receiver. Not surprisingly, and much to the dismay of successive
Commissioners, the liquidation process caused numerous problems,
continuing in some cases for many years.

The provisions of the 1878 Act requiring the Commissioners to
inspect every bank in the state did not extend to national banks or private

banks. By federal statute, only the U.S. Comptroller of the Currency had any visitorial powers over national banks. Private banks escaped licensing because the 1878 Act referred to incorporated banks, though other parts of the law did not distinguish among banks. Needless to say, private banks neither filed sworn statements, nor submitted to examination. The Commissioners complained about this omission, which was partly remedied in 1887 by an amendment that required private banks to file sworn statements of condition. Not until 1905, however, were private banks subject to examination. After 1913, only incorporated banking was permitted in the state.

Despite many sound recommendations by the Bank Commissioners, there were only a few substantive changes in the banking law before 1895. In 1887, the legislature extended the requirement of sworn statements of condition to private banks, but stopped short of authorizing examination. To improve the effectiveness of the Commissioners, examination was made annual rather than semi-annual, giving the Commissioners more time to examine each bank, and banks in liquidation were made subject to examination. However, the Commissioners still had no say in the appointment of a receiver or in the disposition of an insolvent bank's assets. An amendment in 1891 brought trust companies under the Board's control. Building and loan associations were also brought under the Board's control, but only for two years, 1891 and 1982, until a Commissioner was created to supervise these institutions. The success of California's economy and the absence of serious banking problems stalled any more fundamental amendments.

Financial panic, bank failures, and depositor losses in 1893 and 1894, however, gave impetus for the passage of various amendments in 1895. In many of their reports up to this time, the Commissioners had complained about the small capital stock of several banks, a situation which they were unable to control because there were no minimum capital requirements. One section of the amended Act of 1895 responded to these complaints by imposing a minimum capital requirement for banks that increased with the population of the town in which the bank was located. For banks in towns with a population of less than 5,000, the minimum was $25,000. The other ranges were: $50,000 of capital for towns with population between 5,000 and 10,000; $100,000 of capital for towns with population between 10,000 and 25,000; and $200,000 of capital for towns with population above 25,000. Half of a new bank's capital had to be paid in at the time of opening with the balance due before the end of two years. Banks had to build up a surplus (or reserve fund) equal to twenty-five percent of paid-in-capital by transferring to surplus ten percent of net profits each year until this required ratio was established. Advertising and publishing of a bank's authorized capital stock without stating the money actually paid-in was made a misdemeanor; this met another of the Board's complaints.

These capital requirements were less imposing than they appear. By lending to bank shareholders on the security of their bank stock, it was possible for bank owners to raise the necessary capital without any actual cash being paid-in. Until 1903, a bank was permitted to make loans secured with its own stock.[11] There were no restrictions on the amount of loans to any single firm or individual. This contrasted sharply with the national bank regulations, which prohibited loans by a national bank that were secured with its own stock, and limited loans to any single individual or firm to ten percent of a national bank's paid-in capital.[12] A key implication of these differences is that minimum capital requirements on state banks were not the sole determinant of the barriers to bank formation.

Another weakness of the 1878 Act, about which the Bank Commissioners and others complained, was the lengthy process required to close a bank found to be insolvent or in wilful violation of the law. To prevent any dissipation or waste of the assets of such banks, an amendment was passed in 1895 that authorized the Board to take control of the bank before proceeding with the injunction process. According to Crumb (1935), this was a potent stick which subsequent Bank Commissioners failed to use. The suspension of any bank was "tantamount to permanent closing," whatever the court's final ruling.[13] Modern bank examiners, however, would view this stick as too powerful in most cases; the penalty is so great that they would hesitate to use it, preferring instead to exert pressure in other ways (hold up a branch application or levy fines) before going to the extreme of taking over the bank. The Bank Commissioners had no fines to impose, and exerting moral suasion or other pressure was difficult in view of their inadequate resources, which are discussed below.

Various permissive amendments were passed in 1901. Savings banks were allowed to make mortgage loans for a maximum of ten years (increased from six years), and they could hold real estate taken for debt for up to ten years (increased from five years). The limit on the premises of savings banks was raised to $250,000. One restrictive measure was the prohibition of loans secured by a bank's own stock. Any such stock acquired by foreclosure was to be sold within six months.

To remove the incumbent Commissioners, the legislature repealed the 1878 Banking Act in 1903. This action permitted the Governor to place his own men on the Board after the law was re-enacted twenty-one days later. Believing that they would not be subject to regulation, entrepreneurs formed some fifty banks in this period, many of them with little or no capital stock. However, only a minority transacted any business, and barely a handful survived beyond 1905. Besides recreating the Banking Act of 1878, the Act of 1903 also increased the number of Commissioners to four, and restricted savings banks to making loans that did not exceed sixty percent of the value of any real estate held for security. In addition, the Act required that any receiver of a failed or suspended bank would now be appointed by a court, not the bank's directors, a change that earlier bank commissioners had fought for since 1878.[14]

No reserves against deposits were required of any banks until 1905, when a twenty percent ratio of reserves to deposits was imposed on commercial banks in cities with population in excess of 200,000, and a fifteen percent ratio was imposed on all other commercial banks. One-half of these reserves had to be in cash-on-hand; the remainder could be deposited elsewhere. Since private banks were included under the same rules and regulations governing state incorporated commercial banks, these reserve requirements applied to all commercial banks in the state other than national banks, which had their own requirements. There were, however, no special provisions such as fines for enforcing these reserve ratios.[15]

A part of the law that had been enforced to some degree, namely, the minimum capital requirements, was successfully challenged in 1907, when a California superior court judge ruled such capital requirements were unconstitutional. This unfavorable ruling was handed down despite the similar Federal law applying to national banks. The California legislature, however, promptly passed a new section of the Bank Act requiring all banks, except savings banks, to have a paid-up capital stock and surplus fund of at least ten percent of all liabilities to depositors, banks, and creditors with a $25,000 minimum and a $100,000 maximum. This law was made retroactive, causing several private banks to retire.[16]

By 1908, there were only 16 private banks in California, with just 2.1 million dollars in deposits, less than 0.5 percent of all deposits in

California's banks (see Tables 2-2 and 2-4). While this last legislative change heralded the end of unregulated private banks, in fact, private banks had been relatively unimportant in California's development since the 1880s. One explanation of this lack of importance is the advantage that incorporation and limited liability conferred on the owners of a joint-stock bank over the owners of an unincorporated bank. The latter had substantially more at risk since all the assets they owned, not just their investment in their bank, could be attached to pay the creditors of the private bank if it failed. Offsetting this added risk was the advantage of no regulation. Up to this time, the burden of California's regulation on its state banks does not appear to have been so heavy that the option of unregulated banking was a profitable one. As the next section demonstrates, the burden of regulation was less than might be inferred from the banking legislation discussed in this section, because the Bank Commissioners relaxed their supervision of state banks in the 1900s. Private banks may also have become less attractive to depositors in the 1900s because of a higher failure rate than state banks; this factor is discussed in more detail below.

Stimulated by the bank failures and financial crisis of 1907, the state legislature passed a completely new Act in 1909 "to define and regulate the business of banking."[17] The most notable feature introduced by the new Act was the separation of banking activities. Any bank could undertake commercial, savings and trust activities, but was now required to have a department for each activity it engaged in. Though many of its provisions had precedents in the Bank Act of 1878 and subsequent amendments, the new Act was more detailed and comprehensive than earlier legislation. Not only were state banks subject to more regulation, particularly on their asset portfolios, but the regulators were also given the authority and manpower to enforce the new law. Enforcement of the bank law was now the responsibility of the Superintendent of Banks with ten examiners at his disposal. The difficulties bankers experienced in meeting the new requirements suggest that their behavior was affected significantly by the new Act.[18]

By specifically authorizing branch banking, the new act also took a step with far reaching consequences. The preceding Bank Act of 1878 had neither authorized nor prohibited bank branches. According to the Attorney General of California in a response to a question from the Bank Commissioners in 1903, the few branches, or agencies as they were known, were legal under the general incorporation laws of the state. In

1900, there were only four agencies, all located outside San Francisco and Los Angeles. All this changed in 1906 when the earthquake in San Francisco gave a major impetus to branch banking, as major banks were forced to seek temporary quarters by the destruction of the financial district. While many of these temporary branches were closed when the new or rebuilt main offices were re-opened, branch banking was firmly established in San Francisco. The number of branches statewide increased from 5 in 1905, to 11 in 1906, and then 29 in 1908. The two requirements of the 1909 Bank Act were not particularly onerous, and were generally the same as faced new banks under the Act. A new branch had to have at least $25,000 in capital, and obtain written permission from the Superintendent of Banks, who had to determine that public convenience and advantage would be promoted by the new branch. Branch banking expanded both in San Francisco and Los Angeles. It also grew among the small towns and cities as country banks used this vehicle to enter new markets. By 1910, there were 36 branches in California, and by 1913, there were 80. From these beginnings, were to grow the statewide branch networks that characterized California's banking industry in recent decades.[19]

Reviewing California's banking legislation over this period, it is readily apparent that the constraints this legislation imposed on bank behavior were very limited, not only in comparison to present banking regulations, but also in comparison to regulations governing national banks in the years 1863-1910, which are discussed below. Though California's banks faced such restrictions as minimal capital requirements, these restrictions did not constrain the typical bank from achieving a profit-maximizing portfolio. The major contribution of banking legislation in this period was to make it harder for banks to behave dishonestly or incompetently by providing for regular examinations by the state. As California found in the 1870s, it was not enough to have just the judicial system enforce the laws; in most cases, legal action came too late. In practice, however, there was a major flaw even in this limited regulation of banks: to be effective, the banking laws had to be enforced by the Bank Commissioners.

The Enforcement of California's Banking Laws

Prior to the 1878 Act creating the Board of Bank Commissioners, there was no regulatory agency enforcing the laws governing banking. What enforcement there was originated in the courts, usually after a bank had failed. From the start, the Bank Commissioners, however, took their responsibilities seriously, closing several banks and admonishing others after their first round of inspections. Thereafter, at least until the end of the century, the Commissioners endeavored to provide California with a sound banking industry. Evidence of this is to be found in their annual reports, which are full of recommendations for bankers and legislators. The Bank Commissioners suggested ways that bankers could improve their operations, and pleaded for legislative changes that would increase the soundness of banking in the state. Almost all the legislative changes described in the previous section appeared in the Bank Commissioners' annual reports before being acted upon by the Legislature. Until the turn of the century, it was not a lack of motivation, but inadequate resources and insufficient authority that prevented the Bank Commissioners from being more effective.

Opposition to more stringent regulations typically came from both bankers and businessmen. Rural areas, in particular, opposed the prohibition of overdrafts, minimum capital requirement, required reserves against deposits, and separate departments for commercial, savings, and trust activities. Larger and older banks, and members of the clearinghouse associations in San Francisco and Los Angeles generally favored legislation that would reduce bank failures and improve banking's image, but these banks' support for further restrictions usually waned when economic conditions improved. Bank failures, or the increased probability of such failures, produced the original 1878 Bank Act, and the amendments of 1895 and 1905. Reacting to the poor state of California's banking in the 1900s, the California Bankers Association played an active role in the formulation of the 1909 Bank Act.[20]

The Bank Commissioners were in a unique position to influence banking operations through their examinations and their annual reports. Most of their reports up to 1898 contain a variety of exhortations and suggestions directed at the shareholders, directors, and officers of state banks. Shareholders were reminded that they were ultimately responsible for the operation of the bank. They should therefore have an expert accountant inspect the bank every two years. In addition, all loans to directors and officers of the bank should be reviewed and the value of any security checked. Directors must guard against dishonest employees. Various methods could prevent defalcations. A daily balance was considered essential, and cash on hand should be counted at the opening and closing of business each day. The certificate of deposit register required close monitoring with all proper entries checked by a second employee. All payments of interest and capital on outstanding notes ought to be recorded on the back of the note. This allowed both the directors and the examiners to evaluate the note at a glance.

In their report of 1886, the Bank Commissioners gave an account of their "manner of examination."[21] After arriving unannounced at the bank before it had opened, the Commissioners (usually two) administered an oath to the officers present. First, the cash-on-hand was counted. Then, they "carefully canvassed" the market value of all bonds, stocks or warrants held as security for loans or owned by the bank. They reviewed the bills receivable, personal notes, mortgage notes, and notes secured by collateral, looking at the actual value and status of possession of these assets and comparing these values to those on the bank's books. If they were dissatisfied with the value of any assets, the Commissioners made enquiries outside the bank. Any assets found to be worthless or very doubtful were written off and the officers informed. After an investigation of the bank's liabilities, the Commissioners declared the bank to be solvent as long as the value of the assets that were passed as good exceeded the value of all liabilities to depositors, banks, and creditors. The Commissioners also checked the certificate-of-stock book to ensure that there was no overissue of stock. They also remarked that these visits provided them with the opportunity to discuss banking operations and pass on the knowledge they had acquired from examining other banks.

The examining process highlights the importance of a bank's paid-in capital stock and reserve fund. Decisions to close a bank hinged on the difference between a bank's liabilities to depositors, bankers, and creditors, and its assets found good by the examining Commissioners. Reductions in the value of assets held by the bank, particularly those due to loan defaults, were a major cause of bank failures. Once a bank was closed by order of the court, it usually remained closed. Thus, the size of a bank's capital stock and reserve fund relative to other liabilities affected the risks a bank could take with its asset portfolio. The structure of a bank's liabilities thus affected the risks a bank's management could afford to take with the bank's asset portfolio. In Chapter 4, this factor is incorporated into a model of individual bank behavior. The empirical results obtained with this model suggest that the structure of a bank's liabilities did influence the risk taken by the bank's management during this period.

Around 1900, the Bank Commissioners ceased to carry out their responsibilities with the same zeal they had shown in earlier years. Their examinations were less rigorous than before, and in some cases were little more than a glance at the books.[22] Their reports contained fewer recommendations, and, after 1903, became purely perfunctory.

One reason for this decline was the burden on the Bank Commissioners of actually making the bank examinations. In 1900, only three Commissioners examined 290 banks, a demanding task at a time when transportation was still rather limited in such a large state.[23] The examination of a large savings bank took two Commissioners five to ten days in 1886. By the 1900s the large banks had substantially more assets to inspect. Amendments did add a fourth Commissioner in 1903 and a secretary in 1905, authorized to make examinations, but the number of state banks had meanwhile increased to 297 by 1903, and reached 404 in 1905. During these years, there was also a high turnover of banks through failure, retirement and change of system. The task of examining all these banks would have daunted even the most dedicated of public servants. The Legislature was hardly supportive, being unwilling to provide the Commissioners with the necessary resources to carry out their duties; it would not even allocate any funds for the printing of the annual report in the years 1897, 1898 and 1901-1904.

The introduction of politics into the appointment of the Bank Commissioners also contributed to the decline in their reputation and stature.[24] In 1903, the Legislature repealed the 1878 Bank Act. This move enabled the newly-elected governor to replace the incumbent Commissioners with his own political cronies. The law did not require any Commissioner to have expertise in banking, and only one had to know any accounting. Thus, when the Act was reenacted twenty-one days later, there were no constraints on the governor's appointments. Whereas previous Commissioners demonstrated their grasp of banking by the numerous recommendations appearing in their reports, the reports of the new Commissioners contained no such suggestions. For example, neither the 1907 nor the 1908 Reports contained any discussion of the bank failures and financial panic of those years. The 1909 Bank Act, which abolished the Board of Bank Commissioners, was itself a response to this growing laxity. Its provisions carefully detailed the restrictions placed on banks' behavior and the responsibilities of the newly created Superintendent of Banks.[25]

In practice, the increase in the legislated restrictions on banking, especially after 1895, was counterbalanced by less supervision. For while the various Bank Commissioners carried out their duties conscientiously during the first two decades of the Board's existence, thereafter they performed these duties with less diligence. Thus, the behavior of state banks may have been even less constrained than the laws in principle would indicate, a finding that has implications for a variety of issues, including the development of national banking California.

The Development of National Banking in California: Slow Growth to 1900

The most obvious explanation of national banking's slow growth in California is that national banks were more heavily regulated than state banks. In fact, differences in regulatory regimes did play an important part in determining the pattern of development of national banking as is made clear below. There is, however, more to the issue than the bank laws and how they were enforced. While more regulation may make banks of a particular type less attractive to bankers or entrepreneurs, the same regulation may make this type of banking more attractive to bank customers. Just as an individual bank's reputation is an important factor affecting its success, so too the reputation of a type of bank affects the success of all banks of this type. Unfortunately for national banking, Californians had an intense distrust of bank notes, which not only negated the major initial advantage of national banks over state banks, but also tainted all national banks in Californians' eyes as following unsound banking practices.

Given the availability of gold coins in California and the poor reputation of state bank notes, it is perhaps not surprising that California banned all note issues by banks in its 1849 Constitution.[26] For other states this might have been a serious handicap, but California had a ready supply of gold coins from the U.S. Treasury's mint in San Francisco, which opened in 1853. Before that, the coins of many countries circulated in combination with gold dust and nuggets. By the time of the 1863 Act creating national banks, Californians' distrust for bank notes was well established, having been confirmed by the depreciation of greenbacks.[27] Under these circumstances, national bank formation was generally deemed impossible as it was widely believed that their success hinged on the acceptability of their note issue.[28]

The treatment of greenbacks, whose value in gold fluctuated about a declining trend, gives some idea of the opposition to bank notes in California. Although issued by the Federal Government, the courts determined that state taxes could not be paid in greenbacks in either California or Oregon.[29] A California law was passed to allow a contract to specify the form of payment in either coin or greenbacks. Pacific Coast businessmen blacklisted those who paid with greenbacks, and banks refused to accept greenbacks for deposit. These actions indicate the value the commercial community placed on a stable medium of exchange. Their actions appear to have been successful since greenbacks failed to displace gold coin, in some sense violating Gresham's law. Social pressures prevented the bad money from driving out the good.[30]

Responding to Californians' dislike of the notes issued by national currency banks, Congress passed legislation in 1870 creating national gold banks.[31] These banks were identical to national currency banks, with the exception of the notes they issued. For every $100 of U.S. bonds deposited with the Treasury, each national gold bank could issue $80 of notes as compared to $90 of notes for national currency banks.[32] These notes were redeemable for gold only at the counter of their issuing bank, and were receivable at par at all other national banks. Each national gold bank had to have at least twenty-five percent of its outstanding circulation on hand in the form of gold and silver coin. A ceiling of one million dollars was placed on each bank's circulation. During 1871, the year the first national gold bank opened, the notes of national currency banks averaged 90 cents on the dollar. Some thirteen national gold banks were formed before the resumption of specie payments in 1880 and the passage of an act permitting their conversion to national currency banks. Three national gold banks were formed in Massachusetts, but they soon converted. The remaining ten were located in California, though only one was in San Francisco. The combined note issue of all these banks only reached three and a half million dollars.

Ironically, their major characteristic proved to be a liability. Because they were redeemable only at the bank of issue, they were discounted in the East by the cost of telegraphic transfer and interest for seven days, presumably the time taken for the Eastern bank to recover its funds. In addition, the higher reserve requirements made the issuing of these notes unprofitable as compared with the issuing of national bank notes. By 1884, all national gold banks had converted to national currency banks. In any case, the national gold bank notes were only being gradually accepted by Californians despite being redeemable in gold.

In the mid-1880s, the influx of immigrants and tourists from the East began to change the perception of national banks in California, as these newcomers had predominantly favorable experiences with national banking and national bank notes.[33] In 1885, there were 17 national banks in California, of which 6 were in the southern counties, but only one was in San Francisco. This number was far fewer than the 73 state commercial banks in California (see Table 2-2). Seven more national banks had incorporated by 1886, five being located in the south. An additional 14 national banks formed over the next two years, bringing the total number of national banks to 38 in 1888, up from only nine in 1878, yet still far fewer than the 110 state commercial banks. Many of these new national banks were in fact conversions of existing state banks; in some cases, this conversion was a device to obtain a charter as the bank was first incorporated under the state's laws, and then converted.

The collapse of the real estate boom in southern California in 1887-1888 brought widespread financial problems to southern California.[34] The popularity of national banking in the south now became a liability. With banking in the area experiencing difficulties, the expansion of national banking ceased despite the growing acceptance of national bank notes and national banking itself. In 1892, there were only 36 national banks, one less than in 1888, as compared with 161 state commercial banks. Between 1885 and 1892, two national banks failed, one retired voluntarily, one merged voluntarily with another national bank, and two banks converted to state banks.[35] The panic of 1893 brought about bank failures and retirements in Los Angeles and San Diego, further impairing the reputation of banking in the south. The 1890s were a decade of consolidation for banking in southern California, and banking in the state as a whole made little progress after the 1893 panic. National banking failed to gain ground in the decade as there were only 37 national banks in California in 1900, the same number as in 1890. Between 1893 and 1900, only three new national banks were formed, while three national banks failed and one retired. The four state banks that converted to national charters were offset by four national banks switching to state charters.

While some of the slow growth of national banking is explained by California's distrust of national banks in the first 25 years of national banking, and by the slow growth of banking in the 1890s in southern

California where national banking was more popular, differences in the burden of regulation between state and national banks were probably just as important. Prior to the 1878 Bank Act, there is no doubt that state commercial banks were far less burdened by regulation than national banks, since the state banks faced virtually no restrictions on their activities, and there was no state agency to enforce the laws that did exist. Even with the passage of the 1878 Bank Act, however, national banks were still at a substantial disadvantage.

The rapid growth of national banking during the 1880s led the Bank Commissioners to compare national banking with state incorporated banking in their 1889 report. They emphasized the disadvantages of the national system. Prospective national bank owners had to submit to the U.S. Comptroller an application with the bank's title, location, proposed capital, and the names of at least five prospective shareholders endorsed by a Representative in Congress or "accompanied by letters from other persons of prominence, vouching for the character and responsibility of the parties, and the necessities of the community where the bank (was) to be located."[36] While the minimum capital stock was $50,000, a capital stock of less than $100,000 required special permission. All the initial capital stock had to be paid in regular installments within six months. Directors were required to own at least ten shares. Owners of national bank shares were liable for up to twice the face value of their shares in the event that the bank failed and the assets were insufficient to pay off the depositors and other creditors. State bank shareholders, on the other hand, faced no minimum capital requirements, and were liable only for the percentage of debts and liabilities in excess of the liquidated assets equal to the proportion of the face value of the bank's capital stock they held when the debts were incurred. In addition, the California Bank Commissioners could not refuse to license any duly incorporated bank, regardless of its owner's character or its location.

Various constraints were also imposed on the portfolios of national banks, the most important being the restrictions on mortgages on real estate.[37] Loans to any single borrower could not exceed ten percent of a bank's capital stock and surplus. This limited the amount any national bank could deposit with a state bank. Overdrafts were not allowed to be authorized by a bank's officers, but customers appear to have been able to overdraw their accounts since overdrawn accounts were reported for some national banks in the U.S. Comptroller's annual reports. Shareholders could borrow from their own banks provided they did not use their shares as collateral. National banks not in reserve cities had to have a reserve equal to fifteen percent of their deposits of which two-fifths had to be in cash, with the remainder due from national banks in reserve cities. Since there were only three national banks in San Francisco, the nearest reserve city, the choice was severely limited in 1889.[38] By and large, state commercial banks faced none of these restrictions until 1895, but even those restrictions introduced in that year, such as minimum capital requirements, were not enforced to the same degree as the national bank laws. The burden of regulation on national banks was even greater than these comparisons might suggest. The U.S. Comptroller's annual reports are full of rules adopted to enforce the national banking laws, the steps taken to enforce the laws, and court cases arising from both these activities. In contrast, the California Bank Commissioners' reports contain very few references to these kinds of activities, indicating a much lighter burden of regulation on state banks.

Even in the case of the more highly regulated national banks, however, the letter of the law occasionally turns out to have been less restrictive in practice than some have supposed. In a recent study of national banks' mortgage lending, Keehn and Smiley (1976) show that the law did permit lending on real estate under certain circumstances. They suggest that such lending was much more common than has been supposed. There were various methods by which national banks obeyed the law and yet were able to loan on real estate. For example, while it was illegal to make a mortgage loan initially, a national bank could renew a personal loan with real estate as security. A limit of five years was placed on the duration of these loans and on the length of time any national bank could hold real estate besides its building and lot. However, these time limits may not have been important constraints, since there is considerable evidence that loans were typically of five years or less in duration, often being repaid in a lump sum at the end of the contract. In California, savings banks faced similar time limits; no loan could last for more than six years. Under California's Second Constitution, no corporation was allowed to hold real estate not needed for business purposes for longer than five years, which restricted the maturity of state commercial bank loans. There was, however, no prohibition on the renewal of loans.

Other methods by which national banks avoided restrictions on mortgage lending were noted by the Bank Commissioners in their 1889 report.[39] One method was for a national bank to lend to a solvent agent who would then make the mortgage loan. Alternatively, shareholders of national banks could establish a savings bank to be operated in conjunction with the national bank. According to the Commissioners, such banks were sometimes operated by the same management in the same office.[40] The savings banks provided the national bank with funds requiring no reserves (the funds were booked as due-to the savings bank), and permitted the national bank to offer mortgage loans to its customers. The Commissioners opposed this practice because the depositors of the savings bank could be exploited, and the savings bank put in jeopardy by furnishing funds to the national bank. Through their regulatory control over the savings bank, the Bank Commissioners could curtail such abuses. In one case, when pressure failed to bring results, the Bank Commissioners brought about the failure in 1892 of the California National Bank of San Diego because it was unable to repay deposits of the California Savings of San Diego upon their insistence.[41] State commercial banks also had affiliations with savings banks, primarily to obtain additional funds, but because the Commissioners had regulatory power over both types of bank, abuses by state banks were more easily curtailed.

What then were the advantages of national banks in 1890? By this time the right to issue bank notes had ceased to be their major advantage; the use of checks was well established; and other assets offered better rates of return than issuing notes.[42] The important attraction was the name "National Bank" standing for reliable regulated banking. Some people even believed that national banks' deposits were backed by the Federal Government, and such banks would not be allowed to fail.[43] Though this belief had no legal foundation, it was true that fewer national banks failed, and that national banks were more closely regulated than state banks in many states besides California. The rate of failure, however, was not always lower, as is discussed in the next section. Federal regulation of national banking did offer investors a uniformity that was not available from the shares of state banks. One survey of national bank stock holdings made in 1876 suggests that out-of-state ownership of bank stock was common; it also suggests, somewhat surprisingly, a flow of funds from the West and the South to the East.[44] In California, the growth of national banking in the 1880s appears to have been the result of familiarity with this system among newcomers, including tourists, who deposited their money and invested their funds in such banks.[45] Slower growth of these banks in the 1890s was probably a function of the slow growth of banking in the state generally, combined with more stringent regulation of national banks.

The Rapid Growth of National Banking in California in the 1900s

After the stagnation of the 1890s, the expansion of national banking in California in the 1900s was dramatic. The number of national banks rose almost fourfold from 37 in 1900 to 143 in 1908, while the number of state commercial banks doubled from 178 to 329. More importantly, the share of national bank deposits out of the deposits at all banks in California almost doubled from 12.5 percent to 23.8 percent in the same period (see Table 2-4). A third of the 120 national banks organized between 1900 and 1908 were conversions of state banks, which included some large state banks in San Francisco (see Table 2-5). In these years, national banking not only shared in the growth of banking in California, but also expanded at the expense of state banking.

Why did the advantage shift to national banking in the 1900s? Historians have given two reasons for the expansion of national banking that occurred nationwide in the 1900s: the growing regulation by states of their own banks, and changes in the national bank laws which encouraged national banking. In California, there were two additional reasons for the expansion of national banking: the discrimination of California's property tax laws in favor of national banks, and the declining reputation of state banks. The growing regulation of state banking in California has been described above. The remaining reasons are discussed below.

In the Gold Standard Act of 1900, Congress took steps to redress the balance between national and state banking by lowering the minimum capital requirement for national banks in small towns to $25,000 from $50,000 and by making the issuance of national bank notes more profitable.[46] Under this Act, the minimum capital requirements were:

$25,000 for banks in towns with less than 3,000 inhabitants,
$50,000 for banks in towns with between 6,000 and 3,000 inhabitants,
$100,000 for banks in towns with between 6,000 and 50,000 inhabitants, and
$200,000 for banks in towns with more than $50,000 inhabitants.

Previously, the minimum capital stock for banks located in towns with less than 3,000 inhabitants was $50,000; the other requirements were unchanged.

Up to 1895, the national bank requirements were clearly more onerous than those on California's state banks, since no capital requirements existed for state banks in California. From 1895 until 1907, the minimum capital requirements for California's state banks were:

$25,000 for banks in towns with less than 5,000 inhabitants,

$50,000 for banks in towns with between 5,000 and 10,000 inhabitants,

$100,000 for banks in towns with between 10,000 and 25,000 inhabitants, and

$200,000 for banks in towns with over 25,000 inhabitants.

When compared with national banking requirements, the state's do not appear to be consistently lower or higher. It all depends on the number of inhabitants. For example, California had higher capital requirements for banks in towns between 25,000 and 50,000 inhabitants. This provides an example of the care which must be taken in analyzing the impact of state banking laws. Legislation enacted in 1907 required every state bank to have a capital stock equal to ten percent of all liabilities, with a $25,000 minimum and a $100,000 maximum. This Act made entry into towns with more than 3,000 inhabitants easier for state banks. Only if a bank had more than $250,000 in deposits, a sizeable bank, would it face more onerous requirements than a national bank in a very small town.

State banks also had certain advantages over national banks, which significantly reduced the impact of capital requirements on state banks. While national banks were required to have their capital paid up within six months, state banks had two years. In addition, loans could be made to individuals to enable them to buy the bank's stock. No national bank could lend on its own bank stock. In 1903, such loans were also prohibited for state banks, but there were no restrictions on the amount that could be loaned to any individual or firm.

It is not clear what impact these changes in capital requirements did have. In the four years after the imposition of a minimum capital requirement in 1895, 22 state banks were formed, but only one national bank was organized. Apparently the new state requirements did not limit the formation of state banks, at least not so as to favor national banking in these years. In the period 1900-1904, 136 state banks and 45 new national banks were formed. Of the latter, 14 had less than $50,000 in capital stock (the average was $26,786), and 20 were conversions from state banks. Between 1905 and 1908, 205 state banks and 74 national banks were organized. The latter included 41 banks with capital stock less than $50,000 (the average was $25,455), and 39 conversions from state banks. These numbers suggest the reduction in national banks capital requirements did increase the number of national banks. However, in the absence of a reduction in the minimum capital requirement for national banks, it is probable that there would have been more state banks, but not fewer banks overall. In any case, the national banks with the minimum capital stock had a small impact on the aggregate level of national banking in California. These 52 small national banks added only $1.4 million in bank capital, while the remaining 64 national banks added $13 million.

The profitability of the note issue was also increased as banks could now issue currency up to 100 percent of the bonds deposited with the Treasury. In addition, the tax on notes issued by national banks was reduced from one-half to one-quarter of one percent. By this time, bank notes were much less important for the banking business than they had been in earlier years (some considered the main use for national bank notes to be advertising), and these changes probably had a minor impact on the attractiveness of national bank charters to bankers in California.[47]

As in many other aspects of its banking history, California's manner of taxing national banks was unique. According to the U.S. Comptroller's annual report in 1880 and California's Commission on Revenue and Taxation, national bank shareholders were liable for taxes based on either the market value or the book value of their bank stock in all states except California and Nevada.[48] The valuation method varied from state to state, as did the location where the tax was to be paid, with some states making the bank liable for taxes where the bank was located, others where the shareholder was located. Since federal law required that national banks be taxed no more than state banks, state banks were generally taxed equally in each state, though the rates of taxation varied among states, at least in 1880.[49] In California, however, banks, like individuals, were taxed on their real and personal property. Real property consisted of real estate, including buildings and improvements, and mortgages; personal property for a bank included furniture and fixtures, stocks, bonds, warrants, money on hand on the first Monday of March, and solvent credits less debts.

Up to 1899, California taxed national banks on their real estate, but not on their mortgages or their personal property. By federal law, national banks were liable for taxes on real estate provided all banks in the state were subject to the same tax rules, but national banks could not be taxed on other property. This discrepancy gave an apparently large advantage to national banks that was mitigated in practice. In the first place, national banks made fewer mortgages than state banks because of the severe restrictions on mortgage lending by national banks. Moreover, the burden of this tax varied across the state. By custom, mortgages in the southern counties were written net of property taxes with the mortgagor paying the tax, while the property tax on mortgages in the northern counties was paid by the banks, with the mortgagor paying a correspondingly higher interest rate.[50] The incidence of the tax was thus divided between the borrowers and the bank somewhat differently in each case.

State banks could reduce their tax liabilities in several ways. They could hold only stocks and bonds that were issued by the Federal Government or by a corporation, city or county located in California, which were all tax-exempt on the grounds that the property of these entities was already being taxed. As a result of this law, state banks held only tax-exempt securities according to the Commission on Revenue and Taxation. The tax laws, thus, had the same effect on California's development that New York's restrictions on the portfolios of its mutual savings banks had on New York's economic development.[51] While the tax laws added to the demand for securities issued in California, they also made California more susceptible to financial panics and business failures. In periods of financial stringency in California, the market for securities was presumably thinner and more depressed because Californians' portfolios were much less diversified than they would have been without the tax laws. The California Commission on Revenue and Taxation notes the added susceptibility of state banks under the tax laws, and argued that a change to a tax on bank capital would allow banks to diversify.[52] The Commission also favored the change to eliminate other techniques used by banks to lower their taxes. Banks typically reduced their cash on hand and disposed of any warrants before tax day. Another technique, though not one reported by the Commission, would have been for banks to lease their bank building rather than own it in order to reduce their holdings of real property. This would have reduced the banks' tax liability, but they would still be paying some tax indirectly through their rent.

For commercial banks, both state-chartered and private, the most important feature of the property tax was that debts could be used to offset solvent credits. Solvent credits constituted "all of a bank's loans and discounts and the deposits it keeps with its correspondents and with other bankers within or without the state except mortgages."[53] All banks were allowed to deduct debts from these credits. Commercial banks, but not savings banks, were permitted to include deposits in their debts. Few commercial banks had solvent credits in excess of their debts, and thus, commercial banks largely avoided paying any tax on solvent credits. In theory, the owners of commercial banks' deposits were liable for property tax, but in practice, they often failed to report their commercial bank deposits as part of their personal property. The owners of savings bank deposits, however, owed no taxes on these deposits as they were considered interest in the property of savings and loan associations, rather than the debt of a bank. Under this provision, which originated in legislators' desire to facilitate the ownership of savings deposits and encourage thrift, savings banks could not deduct their deposits from their solvent credits to determine their tax liability. As the savings banks duly noted, there was little basis for the provision since California's savings banks were joint stock, not mutual banks.[54] The end result was that savings banks were liable for substantially more taxes than commercial banks were liable for either directly or indirectly because of the evasion of taxes by the owners of commercial bank deposits. This burden of taxation on the banks is explored below.

Until the 1890s, there is no readily available evidence to show that the relative burden of the tax laws was a major factor in a bank's choice of charter. In 1880, national banks in California were paying state banks taxes at a lower rate on their capital than national banks in all other states; they paid on average only 0.3 percent, while the average for the national was 1.7 percent.[55] There is, however, no comparable figure for California's state banks, and the relative advantage of national banks cannot be determined simply. In the 1890s, the Commission on Revenue and Taxation reported that some state banks converted and some new banks chose national charters to reduce their property tax liability.[56] Further evidence of the growing importance of taxes was the amending of the state's revenue laws that made owners of national bank stocks liable for tax on the market value of their shares as part of their personal property. The tax was due in the county where the bank was located. Certain deductions from the market value of these shares were allowed that were similar to those permitted on solvent credits. The new tax law resulted in a sharp increase in the taxes paid by national banks in 1900 according to the Commission, though it did not provide statistics for all banks.[57] This tax increase might have reduced the demand for national bank charters, but it did not last.

By 1904, virtually no taxes were being paid by national banks as they had increased the amount of the deductions from the market value of bank stocks so as to eliminate their shareholders' tax liability. The issue ended up in the federal courts where the state lost in 1905 on the grounds that the new tax on national banks discriminated against national banks by taxing not only property owned by such banks, but the banks' goodwill as well. State banks were not taxed on the value of their franchise. The Legislature failed to pass a new law, and instead referred the question to the Commission on Revenue and Taxation. Between 1905 and 1911, national banks paid property tax solely on the real estate they held. An act passed in 1911 instituted a tax of one percent on the capital stock, the accumulated surplus, and undivided profits of all banks.[58] By treating all banks equally, this act ended the tax advantages of national banking in California.

There is empirical evidence to show that national banks had an advantage in the 1900s. The average rate of all state taxes paid by national banks in California in 1905 was 0.23 percent of their capital and surplus, less than a quarter of the rate of 1.1 percent paid by state commercial banks.[59] Since national banks' net earnings in California for 1905 averaged 5.1 percent of their capital and surplus, this tax advantage appears relatively significant.[60] Unfortunately, there are no earnings figures for state commercial banks to make a comparison. Savings banks in California paid an average dividend rate of 8.5 percent of their capital stock. Adjusting this dividend rate for transfers to surplus, and for the ratio of capital to capital plus surplus suggests that savings banks were also earning net income of about 5 percent of capital plus surplus. That their net earnings rate matched the national banks' is surprising since they were paying taxes at a rate of 7.5 percent of their capital plus surplus. Their high tax rate was due in large part to the predominance of mortgages in their portfolios, which was presumably counterbalanced by savings banks charging higher interest rates on mortgages. Even on non-mortgage property, however, savings banks were paying taxes at a higher rate of 1.1 percent, as compared to the 0.7 percent paid by state commercial banks, and the 0.2 percent paid by national banks on their holdings of non-mortgage property. Because any taxes paid by holders of commercial bank deposits, whether national or state-chartered, are ignored for lack of data, the relative tax burden on the savings banks is overstated, though probably not by enough to eliminate it.

The differences in the tax rates suggest that California's tax laws did give national banking a significant edge over state banking. This edge probably helps to explain the growth of national banking in California in the 1900s, especially with the sharp drop in taxes on national banks after 1900 cited by the Commission on Revenue and Taxation. The actual burden of this unequal taxation, however, does not appear to have left savings banks' earnings below those of national banks. In practice, state banks presumably offset the tax on mortgages by charging higher rates on mortgages than on other loans; national banks could not undercut state banks' rates because of the limitations on mortgage lending by national banks.

Three reasons have been offered so far in this study for the advance of national banking in California in the 1900s: the increasing regulation of state banks relative to national banks, changes in the national banking laws that made national banking more profitable, and the heavier burden of taxation on state banks. A fourth reason is the declining reputation of state banking in the 1900s. The politicization of the Board of Bank Commissioners in 1903 confirmed the falling standards of supervision induced by insufficient examining power. Lax supervision and rapid growth of both banking and the economy created a good environment for unsound banking practices to flourish.

This process culminated in the failure of nine state banks in 1907 and 1908, including the largest state bank failure in California during the period 1860-1910.[61] The California Safe Deposit and Trust Company had over $13 million in assets when it failed. The Bank Commissioners closed 16 banks, of which 7 subsequently reopened.[62] Numerous other banks retired before the Bank Commissioners could close them. Dissatisfied with the Commissioners' examinations, the San Francisco Clearing House Association introduced its own examinations in 1908, which resulted in various commercial banks closing in San Francisco. Even in 1910, the newly-created Superintendent of Banks closed several banks and reduced the capital and surplus of others, complaining in his first report of the poor condition of many banks in the state. In contrast to these state bank closings and retirements, only one national bank failed (in 1904), and just four national banks retired voluntarily between 1900 and 1908 (see Table 2-5). There is little doubt that national banks enjoyed a better reputation in the 1900s as a result of their better record of failures. In the next section, the relationship between regulation and bank failures is explored in more detail.

Regulation and Bank Failures

A major objective of California's regulation of its banks was to reduce the extent of bank failures. At the same time, various groups including bankers opposed any increases in regulation because they feared such increases would restrict the ability of the banking industry to provide the economy with what they saw as necessary, and profitable, services. In some sense, the actual pattern of banking regulation in California was an experiment in determining the least amount of restrictions on banks that would provide the desired level of banking services while keeping the extent of bank failures at an acceptable level. Over time, the acceptable number of bank failures appears to have fallen, resulting in a growing number of restrictions on bank behavior. The question explored in this section is whether banking regulation made any difference to the extent of bank failures over the period 1860-1910.

As a preliminary to answering this question, a brief discussion of the causes of bank failures in this period is appropriate. While the Bank Commissioners usually identified failing banks in their annual reports, a complete record of the causes of these failures cannot be compiled because the Commissioners only occasionally identified the causes of these failures; much work still remains to be done with other sources to establish a complete record. A rough picture, however, can be gleaned from the Commissioners' reports and other sources. Many, perhaps most, bank failures were due to poor management or malfeasance or both. Some failures were due to large losses on loans, real estate or securities, or alternatively to reductions in the value of the collateral backing bad loans. A few banks failed due to insufficient liquidity, either because of poor communications or the lack of a lender of last resort. Bad management and malfeasance caused the largest, and most troublesome, bank failures in California's history: the failure of several large savings banks in 1878 and the failure of the California Safe Deposit and Trust Company in 1907.[63] The latter was the largest California bank to fail in this period with almost 9 million dollars in deposits; some of its managers were charged with felonies when the full extent of their manipulations was revealed.

In the cases of these large failures and in many other failing banks, the extent of the failing bank's weakness was hidden in the overvaluation of the bank's assets. When these assets were found to be worthless, usually by the Bank Commissioners, the bank closed. Financial panics and the ensuing closing of banks' doors also exposed the underlying weakness of unsound banks. While strong banks reopened after a crisis passed, weak banks could not absorb the losses generated by either bad loans or forced liquidation of assets. For example, the Bank Commissioners reported that of the twenty-five banks that had to close their doors in 1893, all but seven reopened a few days later, and of these remaining seven, three "will open ere long."[64] The Commissioners held that the other four failed through inherent weakness, rather than in consequence of the then prevailing unfavorable financial conditions. Had a source of liquidity been available to all these banks, they might have been able to avoid liquidating sound loans or securities in an unfavorable market, thereby avoiding capital losses. In the 1907 panic, various clearinghouses did provide such liquidity, and almost certainly reduced the number of banks that closed their doors. Not all banks benefitted, however, from this new source of liquidity. Crumb (1935) attributes the discovery of the true condition of the California Safe Deposit and Trust Company to the San Francisco Clearing House Association's refusal to accept this bank's assets as collateral for the Association's certificates.[65]

National banks failed for the same reasons as state banks. In 1887, the U.S. Comptroller of the Currency reported the reasons for the failure of 91 out of the 120 national banks placed in the hands of a receiver since the creation of the National Banking System.[66] The primary causes of these 91 failures were distributed as follows: defalcation of officers (16); excessive loans to others (11); fraudulent management (24); injudicious banking (24); depreciation of securities, failure of large debtors and investments in real estate and mortgages (16). In most cases, more than one cause was mentioned. In their 1887 Report, California's Bank Commissioners cited this report of the Comptroller, and cautioned state bankers to take note of the causes of national bank failures so that they might avoid such errors. Another review of the causes of national bank failures, which appeared in 1920, gave the following distribution of 594 such failures: 38.4 percent involved criminal actions (defalcation and fraudulent management); 19.2 percent involved unlawful acts (excessive loans); 14.0 percent depreciation of assets; 23.4 percent involved injudicious banking; 2.0 percent involved the failure of large debtors; 1.5 percent were closed by a run or in anticipation of a run; 1.5 percent had no record.[67] The pattern does not appear to have changed much between 1887 and 1920.

One of the difficulties in charting the extent of bank failures is determining which banks actually failed. Some banks that failed promptly paid all depositors in full, an aspect that the Bank Commissioners delighted in reporting. It is questionable whether these should be considered as failures of the same order of magnitude as banks that did not ever pay depositors fully. At the same time, some banks that voluntarily went into liquidation did not always pay depositors in full. A solution to gauging the extent of bank failures would be to add up the total losses of depositors and stockholders. Unfortunately, the data are insufficient for an accurate account of these losses, though one rough estimate is available for the decades 1880-1910.[68] A simpler, more readily available statistic is the rate of bank failures. This ignores two problems: the closing of solvent banks that subsequently paid depositors in full, and the voluntary liquidation of actually solvent banks that were not reported as insolvent by the Bank Commissioners, but at least these errors partially offset each other.

One way of answering the question posed at the beginning of this section concerning the relationship between regulation and bank failures is to compare the rates of failure for banks of different types as banking regulation changed. There were three distinct periods of state regulation of banking between 1860 and 1910. The first period was one of virtually no regulation with no inspection of state banks, which is taken to be the years 1860-1879, for the purposes at hand. Although the Bank Commissioners were established in 1878, the bank failures in 1878 and 1879 are here attributed to the first period, being a product of the minimal regulation in the years preceding 1878 and 1879. The second period stretches from 1880 to 1899, encompassing the years when the Bank Commissioners were pursuing their duties diligently. The third period, from 1900 to 1909, constitutes the years when the Bank Commissioners were less effective than earlier, but the state's banking laws were somewhat more restrictive than earlier. Even though the Office of the Superintendent of Banks was created in 1909 by the 1909 Bank Act, the bank failures in 1909 are here attributed to the preceding period of lax supervision.

The virtual absence of banking regulation in the years 1860-1879 does appear to have produced a greater rate of bank failures than the more extensive regulation of subsequent years. The average annual rate of failure for state banks, both commercial and savings, fell from 1.3 percent in the first period to just above 0.3 percent in the second and third periods (see Table 2-6). Private banks had almost the same failure rate as state banks in the first period, indicating that the legislation governing state banks in this period did not reduce the failure rate for state banks below that for unregulated banks.

The failure rate for state banks in the second and third periods, however, is almost the same in both periods, which appears to confirm the conclusion drawn above that the increases in restrictions on bank behavior beginning in 1895 were offset by laxer supervision on the part of the Bank Commissioners. While the choice of a different year as the dividing line between the periods of diligent and less-than-diligent supervision does affect the failure rates in these two periods, it does not change the conclusion that failure rates were similar throughout the years 1880 to 1909.

Some evidence, however, suggests that the extent of bank failures may have indeed been higher during the period beginning in 1900. While state banks had a much lower rate of failure than national banks in California in the period 1880-1899, they had a higher rate in the period 1900-1909. Though small, this difference does suggest that the Bank Commissioners were relatively less successful in preventing bank failures in the final period. Confirmation of this conclusion is to be found in a different measure of the extent of bank failures: the rate at which depositors experienced losses per year in each period. Estimates of depositors' losses suggest that on average only 0.09 percent of deposits was lost due to failures in the period 1880-1899, but 0.23 percent was lost in the period 1900-1909 (see Table 2-7). If just the period of 1890-1899 is considered, the rate of losses per year rises to 0.14 percent, still below that for the third period. The reason for the high rate in the third period is the huge impact on total losses of the failure of the California Safe Deposit and Trust Company in 1907, when depositors lost around 6 million dollars.[69] Depositors' losses were so high because the bank's assets were fraudulently overvalued. The bank's management reported the bank's investments as being worth almost 6 million dollars in 1907, but the receiver valued these investments at barely 400,000 dollars in 1908. An alternative measure of the extent of bank failures is the average rate at which deposits were impounded by bank failures, which puts less weight on the recovery of depositors' funds. With this measure, the difference in the rate of failure between the two periods 1880-1899 and

1900-1909 declines; it is completely eliminated if the periods 1890-1899 and 1900-1909 are compared (see Table 2-7).

The net effect of the changing nature of banking regulation on bank failures thus remains undetermined. If the failure of the California Safe Deposit and Trust Company is given the weight with which it collapsed on its depositors, then the laxity of the Bank Commissioners can be considered to have produced a higher rate of bank failures in the 1900s, in spite of the increasing restrictions on bank behavior imposed by legislation. However, if the Bank Commissioners are absolved of responsibility for the losses depositors sustained from this failure and the failure is attributed instead to undetectable fraud perpetrated by the bank's management, then banking regulation can be considered to have been equally effective in both periods.

In the previous section of this chapter, it was suggested that the declining reputation of state banks relative to national banks was one factor contributing to the expansion of national banking after 1899. This decline in reputation is consistent with the higher rate of state bank failures as compared to national bank failures in the 1900s, a reversal of the situation in the period before 1900. While the safety of national banks was ascending relative to state banks, that of the private banks was declining. With an average failure rate of 1.5 percent, well above the 0.35 percent rate for state banks, private banks were riskier for both owners and depositors in the 1900s (see Table 2-6). This higher risk combined with added restrictions imposed by legislation probably explains the decline in the number of private banks in the 1900s. Unfortunately, the relative riskiness of savings versus commercial banks is not readily determined because a record of the failure of each type of bank has not been compiled. This issue will have to be left for future research.

California's regulation of its banks may also be judged by reference to the record of banking elsewhere. A comparison of the rate of bank failures in California with that for the U.S. as a whole suggests that California's regulation of its banks was successful in reducing bank failures. After having had a higher rate of failure for non-national banks (state commercial and savings, and private banks) during the period 1877-1891, California had a substantially lower failure rate in the years 1892-1897, and a somewhat lower rate for the years 1898-1910 (see Table 2-8). The above-average failure rate for the first period is largely attributable to the absence of regulation of California's non-national banks in the years preceding 1878 that resulted in the large number of failures in 1877 and 1878.

Exactly how much California's banking regulation contributed to the below-average failure rates after 1891 cannot be determined. The strength and diversity of California's economy was probably a more important factor than regulation. In Wisconsin, where state banks were regulated at least as closely as in California, the failure rate for state banks in the years 1892-1897 was four times that for California's non-national banks (see Table 2-8). The failure rate for California's state banks during these years was 0.8 percent, almost identical to the failure rate for its non-national banks. One explanation for the much higher failure rate of Wisconsin state banks may have been Wisconsin's agriculture, which was less diversified than California's.[70] In the other two periods, however, Wisconsin's state banks had much lower failure rates than California's non-national banks. While much more work needs to be done before the contribution of regulation to preventing bank failures can be determined with any precision, it does appear that California's regulation of its banking did affect the extent of bank failures. By reducing bank failures without extensively curtailing bank behavior, California's regulation of its banks made a positive contribution to economic growth in California.

Conclusions

A close look at California's banking regulation and the development of banking reveals a complex pattern of interaction between legislation, regulation, bank behavior, and the development of different types of banks during the period 1850 to 1910. From the beginning, a feature of California's regulation of its banks was the difference between the law de jure and *de facto*.

Though California moved quickly after achieving statehood to ban bank notes and incorporated banks, which were believed to be closely associated with the issuing of bank notes, private or unincorporated banking flourished uncontrolled. Moreover, despite the prohibition, a few incorporated savings banks were established through a loophole opened up by a liberal interpretation of another section of the statutes. Instead of closing this loophole, the state legitimized incorporated savings banks with the 1862 Savings Bank Act, thereby taking the first step in the regulation of bank behavior in California. The Act specified certain restrictions on savings banks' behavior such as limiting the size of their buildings and the maturity of their loans.

Though enacted to encourage thrift and regulate savings banks, this Act's impact went much further when it was amended in 1864 to allow savings banks to carry on a commercial banking business. With the legitimacy of incorporated commercial banking established, commercial banks began to incorporate under the same loophole that had allowed savings banks to be established before the 1862 Savings Bank Act. In effect, California had unrestricted entry into incorporated banking by the second half of the 1860s. No special charters and no legislative acts were required for new banks, unlike in many other states and other countries.[71] There was no vetting of the characters of the prospective owners of a bank and no restriction on the location of a new bank as there are for new banks in the U.S. today.[72] As yet, there were no minimum capital requirements, and almost no restrictions on commercial bank behavior.

This state of affairs did not last. Failures and financial difficulties in the 1870s finally produced the 1878 Bank Act that created the Board of Bank Commissioners to regulate California's state banks. Though the Act did not introduce many specific restrictions on bank behavior, its major contribution was to require regular inspections of state incorporated banks by the Bank Commissioners. These inspections kept state bankers honest, at least more honest than they had been when judicial action, usually after the fact, was the only enforcement of the state's laws. The closing of many banks by the Bank Commissioners, on the grounds that their assets were overvalued and their capital and surplus funds non-existent, testifies to the immediate impact of these inspections. These actions indicate that a bank's capital position had become an important factor affecting a bank's behavior. It would remain important for the rest of the period. The model of individual bank behavior developed and estimated in Chapters 4 and 5 of this study verifies this hypothesis.

Over the next 30 years up to 1908, various amendments to the 1878 Bank Act added more restrictions on banking, two important ones being minimum capital requirements and reserve requirements. In practice, however, banking was less restricted than the law implied, primarily because the enforcement of the law did not keep pace with the increase in its restrictiveness. Ways around the restrictions or the lack of appropriate penalties enabled banks to flout the law. More importantly, the inadequate resources of the Bank Commissioners prevented them from closely supervising all the banks. By the 1900s, the Bank Commissioners were pursuing their duties far less diligently than in the previous two decades. The growth in the number and size of banks to be examined had exceeded the minimal increases in the Board's resources and, in addition, the Bank Commissioners had become political appointees in 1903. The end results were numerous bank failures in 1907 and 1908, including the largest failure in the period 1860-1910, and the passage of a far more extensive Bank Act in 1909.

An analysis of the rate of bank failures during the period 1860-1910 suggests that California's regulation of its banks did affect the pattern of bank failures. The bank failure rate was higher during the years 1860-1879, when there were almost no restrictions on banks and no examinations of banks, than it was in the next twenty years from 1880 to 1899, when the Bank Commissioners pursued their responsibilities diligently. Over the next ten years from 1900-1909, the Bank Commissioners' inadequate resources and their less diligent pursuit of their responsibilities resulted in greater losses for depositors than in the preceding period; the rate of bank failures, however, remained about the same. California's record of bank failures for non-national banks indicates that the Bank Commissioners reduced the rate of bank failures below that in the U.S. as a whole. Banking regulation cannot be given all of the credit for changing the rate of bank failures. The strength of California's economy, both its growth and its diversity, were also as important. The next chapter discusses California's economic development. Much more work remains to be done before the contribution of regulation, as opposed to the economy, to reducing bank failures can be determined.

Besides affecting the extent of bank failures, California's regulation of its banks also played an important part in determining the types of bank that developed in the state. One noticeable feature of banking in the state was the importance of savings banks; these banks had the advantage of being the first form of incorporated banking permitted in California. Unlike in many other states, California's savings banks were either joint-stock or membership banks rather than mutual banks. Though they often reported no capital stock, membership banks were not mutuals, a distinction that confused even the Bank Commissioners. In estimating the money market in the nineteenth century, therefore, Fand (1956) is incorrect in assuming that all savings banks in California with no reported capital were mutuals. California's savings banks also differed from the typical savings bank by being able to make unsecured personal loans, and generally carry on a commercial banking business, a situation which persisted until the 1909 Bank Act. Including stock savings banks as commercial banks in the Federal Reserve System's estimates of banking data for the period 1893-1910 thus appears appropriate in the case of California's savings banks. While this study has elaborated the position of California's savings banks, it has not explored in any detail the reasons for their success, nor has it made any attempt to compare them to their counterparts elsewhere in the country, leaving these tasks for the future.

The development of private or unincorporated banking in California also raises more questions than this study answers. Private banking was initially very successful in California, but much of this success appears to have been due to the state's prohibition of incorporated banking. When incorporated banking was made legitimate, private banking waned. Before 1878, incorporated banking offered the advantages of limited liability and the transferability of bank shares with almost no burden of regulation. The declining importance of private banking, even after the Bank Commissioners were making regular examinations of state incorporated banks, suggests that banking regulation was not so constraining as to overcome the disadvantages of unlimited liability and indivisibility of ownership. Private banking in California did not die out naturally, however, despite being subject to an increasing number of regulations and experiencing a higher rate of failure than other types of banks in the 1900s. It took an amendment to the 1909 Bank Act to finally eliminate private banking in 1913.

While the laws governing state banks varied from state to state, the national banking system has often been assumed to provide one constant across the United States; California, however, appears to have been something of an exception. National banking in California was at a disadvantage from the start facing almost unregulated state banking and the virulent opposition of Californians to bank notes and the banks that issued notes. It took the influx of immigrants and tourists from the East with their favorable experiences of national banking to advance the national system in California in the 1880s. After almost no progress in the 1890s, national banking grew rapidly in the 1900s. What had changed? Two causes have been advanced to explain the nationwide growth of national banking after 1900: the increasing regulation of state banks and the reduction in the minimum capital requirements for national banks. In California, there were two additional factors: the relative advantage of national banks over state banks in the payment of state property taxes, and the worsening reputation of state banks. As in many other things, California's method of taxing its own banks and its national banks was unique. Curiously, this method largely worked to the advantage of the national banks. There was further irony in the tax laws in that they discriminated against the savings banks, in spite of the Savings Bank Act's aim of furthering thrift, and in contrast to the favorable treatment these vehicles for thrift received in most other states.

Without the declining reputation of state banking in California, it is unlikely that national banking would have advanced as quickly as it did. This conclusion emphasizes the importance of looking at all aspects of banking regulation, not just the laws governing banking. While the laws were adding restrictions on state banks, the state's supervision of its banks was becoming less and less restrictive. The process was not without limits. As the reputation of state banks declined, bankers and depositors increasingly turned to national banking. Other responses to this declining reputation were increased pressure for new state banking laws and the introduction of examinations of member banks by the clearinghouse associations in San Francisco and Los Angeles. In a sense, bankers, depositors and voters all played a part in choosing the amount of regulation of state banks relative to that of national banks.[73]

The dual banking system, which has been a key characteristic of banking regulation in the United States since 1863, provided for competition between state and national banking regulators that limited both regulators' laxity and their restrictiveness. If regulation was too restrictive, bankers would switch to the less restrictive charter; if regulation was too lax, depositors, and thus bankers, would switch charters. While some continue to praise the freedom available in the dual banking system today as compared to the single nationwide systems of other countries, the extent of competition among regulators is now largely limited to the federal regulatory agencies. What upset the balance of power was the introduction of federal deposit insurance. With federal insurance, state regulators could impose less restrictive requirements on state banks without making them riskier to depositors. To counter this incentive, federal regulators imposed federal restrictions on state banks that obtained federal deposit insurance.[74] Federal banking regulators now hold most of the power that determines what banks can do, a far cry from the more equal balance of the 1900s. This is not to say that state regulators were above eliminating what they saw as unsound banking that competed with the state banks they regulated. Though small in number and unimportant in size, private banks in California were eliminated in 1913. One wonders what the future holds for the dual banking system in the 1980s. Perhaps there is an opportunity to redress the balance by re-establishing state deposit insurance, which was established in the early twentieth century by several states.[75] Alternatively, technology, economies of scale, and competitive factors may shift more power to even fewer federal regulatory agencies overseeing nationwide financial institutions that encompass more than just banking activities.

Notes

1. Crumb (1935), pp. 13-21.
2. U.S. Department of Commerce, Bureau of the Census (1975), pp. 1025-1031.
3. The main sources for this section on the legislation governing state incorporated banks are the California State Board of Bank Commissioners Annual Report, 1878-1908, Cross (1927), Crumb (1935), and the 1878 Bank Act and subsequent amendments.
4. Crumb (1935), pp. 5-10.
5. Ibid. pp. 13-21.
6. One of the first complaints of California's Bank Commissioners was the confusion created by the lack of distinction between commercial and savings banks. The issue was not resolved, however, until the 1909 Bank Act.
7. The Bank Commissioners noted that the Savings and Loan Society (1857), the Hibernia Savings and Loan Society (1859), the French Savings and Loan Society (1860) and the Sacramento Savings Bank were organized on the "mutual" plan. See California Bank Commissioners, Annual Report, January 1880, p. 18 and June 1880, p. 4. However, Crumb argues that these banks were actually on a membership plan, with the members owning the bank. See Crumb (1935), pp. 16-18.
8. Cross (1927).
9. Crumb (1935), p. 9.
10. Statutes of California (1878), Chapter CCCCLXXXI--An Act creating a Board of Bank Commissioners, and prescribing their duties and powers.
11. A.P. Giannini was caught with just such a loan on his books in 1914; the Superintendent of Banks for California fined him $1,000, even though the Bank of Italy stock was only one of many stocks used to collateralize the loan. Dana (1947), p. 77.
12. California Bank Commissioners, Annual Report 1889, p. 13-15.
13. Crumb (1935), p. 72.
14. Cross (1927), p. 653; Crumb (1935), p. 61.
15. The amendment makes no mention of any provisions for enforcing the reserve requirements. Presumably, the Commissioners could have used their ultimate sanction and closed the errant bank, but

such strong action would have been unlikely. Unfortunately, the Commissioners do not mention reserves in their annual report for 1905.

16. Cross (1927), p. 676; Wright (1910), p. 137.
17. Statutes of California 1913--Bank Act of 1909. This Act is discussed extensively by Crumb (1935), pp. 87-147.
18. Cross (1927).
19. Branch banking in California is discussed in Crumb (1935) and Southworth (1928).
20. Blackford (1972; 1977); Cross (1927); Armstrong and Denny (1916).
21. California Bank Commissioners, Annual Report, 1889, p. 1.
22. Crumb (1935), p. 83.
23. California Bank Commissioners, Annual Report, 1886, p. 4.
24. Crumb (1935); Cross (1927).
25. Crumb (1935), p. 86; Willis (1937), p. 42.
26. Cross (1927); Fankhauser (1913).
27. In one respect, the absence of state bank notes was beneficial: there were no state bank difficulties or failures when the ten percent tax was imposed on bank notes issued by state-chartered banks.
28. After travelling the state in 1876 with an eye to forming a national bank, Jay Cooke's brother decided there was no "money in it." Cross (1927), p. 834. Another factor may have been the failure of the National Bank of Nevada after two years. On this issue, see Cross (1927), Crumb (1935), and Wright (1910). An additional disadvantage of national bank notes was the refusal of the U.S. Treasury to accept these notes. This did not help the spread of national banking in California, since there was a sub-Treasury in San Francisco to which gold coins could be readily transported.
29. Fankhauser (1913), pp. 216-222, Lester (1939), pp. 161-171, and Moses (1892).
30. Moses (1892) begins his article with this argument, and goes on to explain how a black list of merchants paying in greenbacks was drawn up. See also Lester (1939), pp. 161-171.
31. Cross (1927), pp. 834-836.
32. Wright (1910), p. 88.
33. California Bank Commissioners, Annual Report 1886, p. 15; Cross (1927), p. 841.
34. Cross (1927).

35. Crumb (1935), Exhibit II.
36. California Bank Commissioners, Annual Report 1889, p. 10.
37. National banks were not permitted to lend on real estate except "in good faith by way of security for debts previously contracted." California Bank Commissioners, Annual Report, 1889.
38. Although keeping some funds with out-of-state bankers was the rule rather than the exception for California banks, even for small rural banks, the major correspondent of most banks at this time was another California bank.
39. California Bank Commissioners, Annual report 1889, p. 12.
40. California Bank Commissioners, Annual Report 1891, pp. 4-5.
41. California Bank Commissioners, Annual Report 1892, p. 1.
42. California Bank Commissioners, Annual Report, 1889, p. 11. National bank notes were unprofitable in the 1880s.
43. Ibid., p. 14.
44. Knox (1903; 1969), p. 127. Conzen (1973) studies the flow of funds in Wisconsin using national bank shares and the location of shareholders.
45. California Bank Commissioners, Annual Report 1886, p. 15, Cross (1927), Wright (1910), p. 97.
46. Robertson (1968).
47. According to Robertson, deposits had become more important than bank notes by 1890, as borrowers kept funds on deposit subject to check rather than taking bank notes; notes were still good advertising. Robertson (1968), p. 64. Sylla (1969) argues that the lack of note issue became less of a hindrance to state banks as the use of checks spread to smaller towns after the 1880s.
     The U.S. Comptroller of the Currency in 1896 gives details for the form in which deposits were made at a sample of banks (those banks which responded to the Comptroller's questionnaire). The results for the banks of all types responding in California were as follows: 29 percent of all deposits were in the form of gold and silver, 69 percent in checks, and only 2 percent in currency. For the nation as a whole the distribution was: 1 percent in gold and silver, 6 percent in currency, and 92 percent in checks. See, U.S. Comptroller (1896), pp. 79. James (1978), Chapter 2, discusses the growth in the use of checks and drafts and the declining use of bank notes in this period. One reason for the lower proportion of checks and drafts in the Mountain-Pacific region may have been the

widespread use, and easier availability, of gold and silver coins, and the preferences of the region's inhabitants, particularly in California, which dominated the region in terms of financial resources. The implication is that the inability of state banks to issue bank notes was no hindrance to their expansion in this region, despite the smaller proportion of checks and drafts.

48. California Commission on Revenue and Taxation (1906), pp. 226-240; U.S. Comptroller of the Currency Annual Report 1880, pp. 36-45.

49. Ibid.

50. California Commission on Revenue and Taxation (1906), p. 226. Customs of this kind persist today in California: the cost of title insurance is paid by the buyer of residential real estate in some counties, and by the seller in other counties.

51. Olmstead (1976) finds that constraints on the Bank for Savings in New York generated a substantial subsidy for New York State, particularly in the financing of New York's canal construction. The Bank was initially limited to investing in New York state debt, U.S. government securities, and deposits in commercial banks. When these constraints were changed, the Bank reacted by expanding its portfolio into newly authorized investments, showing the constraints had been binding. Unfortunately banks in California did not report their securities portfolios, so that a similar exercise cannot be readily performed for California's banks when taxation of the banks was shifted from bank property to bank capital.

52. California Commission on Revenue and Taxation (1906).

53. Ibid, p. 222.

54. The savings banks pointed this out as early as 1866. They argued (correctly) that deposits were claims against them and belonged to their depositors, not to the savings banks. The State Board of Equalization did not agree. In 1879, the savings banks failed to change the Second Constitution so as to remove this unequal assessment. Cross (1927), p. 264; California Commission on Revenue and Taxation (1906); Fankhauser (1913); Plehn (1899).

55. U.S. Comptroller of the Currency, Annual Report 1880, p. 40.

56. California Commission on Revenue and Taxation (1906), p. 227.

57. Ibid, pp. 227-228.

58. Fankhauser (1913), p. 374. Real estate owned by any bank was to be taxed by the county in which it was located. This Act brought California into line with other states by treating all banks equally. The methods of valuing bank stock and so forth still varied widely among the states. U.S. Comptroller of the Currency, Annual Report 1904, pp. 14-15.
59. California Commission on Revenue and Taxation (1906), p. 251.
60. Ibid. p. 237..
61. Cross (1927); Crumb (1935); Willis (1937).
62. Crumb (1935), p. 86.
63. Ibid.
64. California Bank Commissioners, Annual Report 1893.
65. Crumb (1935), p. 89.
66. U.S. Comptroller of the Currency, Annual Report 1887.
67. U.S. Comptroller of the Currency, Annual Report 1920.
68. Crumb (1935), p. 242.
69. Crumb (1935); California Commission on Revenue and Taxation (1906); California Bank Commissioners (1908).
70. Keehn (1972).
71. See Barnett (1913), Cameron (1967; 1972).
72. See Scott (1977).
73. This conclusion places more weight on economic factors than Blackford (1972), who attributes more of the changes to political and social forces.
74. White (1981).
75. Cooke (1909) gives a contemporaneous account of these states' deposit insurance schemes; White (1981) discusses the operation of these schemes and the introduction of federal deposit insurance.

Table 2-1
Number of Savings Banks, State Commercial Banks
Foreign Banks and Branches, Private Banks, and National Banks
in California, 1849-1880 [a]

Year	(1) Savings Banks	(2) State Com- mercial Banks	(3) Foreign Banks and Branches	(4) Private Banks[b]	(5) National Banks	(6) Total
1849	-	-	-	3	-	3
1850	-	-	3	20	-	23
1851	-	-	5	29	-	34
1852	-	-	4	33	-	37
1853	-	-	4	35	-	39
1854	-	-	6	32	-	38
1855	1	-	6	31	-	38
1856	1	-	4	21	-	26
1857	1	-	4	18	-	23
1858	1	-	3	22	-	26
1859	1	-	3	25	-	29
1860	2	-	3	24	-	29
1861	3	-	3	28	-	34
1862	4	-	3	29	-	36
1863	5	-	3	29	-	37
1864	5	1	4	28	-	38
1865	5	2	8	28	-	43
1866	5	2	8	34	-	49
1867	6	4	5	33	-	48
1868	11	5	5	32	-	53
1869	13	9	5	33	-	60
1870	18	12	4	31	-	65
1871	22	18	4	30	1	73
1872	24	20	4	31	2	81
1873	23	23	4	30	4	84
1874	28	31	5	29	6	99
1875	29	41	6	27	7	110
1876	28	53	7	25	9	122
1877	28	59	7	27	9	130
1878	29	59	6	28	9	131
1879	21	58	5	27	9	120
1880	22	57	5	28	9	120

a Numbers are for the beginning of each year unlike in Table 2-2, which accounts for the minor differences between the two tables.

b Includes Express Companies, Bullion Dealers and Brokers, and Commission Merchants and Mercantile Establishments that engaged in banking as a side line, as well as institutions devoted exclusively to banking.

Source: Crumb (1935), Table 1, p. 216.

64

Table 2-2
Number of Savings Banks, Commercial Banks, Private Banks,
and National Banks in California, 1877-1910

Year*	(1) Savings Banks	(2) Commercial Banks	(3) Private Banks	(4) National Banks	(5) Total
1877	29	65	27	9	130
1878	28	56	28	9	121
1879	23	60	27	8	114
1880	20	58	28	10	116
1881	17 [a]	59 [a]	30	11	--
1882	17	61	32	11	121
1883	17	67	31	15	130
1884	18	74	33	15	140
1885	21	73	31	17	142
1886	22	74	31	24	151
1887	24	88	29	28	169
1888	23	110	30	38	201
1889	28	122	34	35	219
1890	37	131	27	37	232
1891	45	144	20	37	246
1892	54	161	17	36	268
1893	60	173	15	34	282
1894	60	166	17	35	278
1895	59	173	18	31	281
1896	57	174	20	31	282
1897	56	173	21	31	281
1898 [b]	55	176	23	34	288
1899	53	176	18	35	282
1900 [b]	53	178	19	37	287
1901 [b]	56	180	21	42	299
1902 [b]	61	191	20	49	321
1903 [c]	68	210	19	60	357
1904 [b]	87	245	18	73	423
1905 [b]	110	270	24	83	487
1906 [b]	122	293	33	115	563
1907	129	323	21	128	601
1908	130	329	15	139	613
1909	474		12	151	637
1910	446		9	185	640

*All figures refer to June or July unless otherwise noted.   a January   b August   c September.
Sources:
Columns (1) and (2) - California State Board of Bank Commissionsers, *Annual Report*, 1878-1908.
Column (3) - 1878-1886, Crumb (1935), Tables 1 and 2; 1887-1908, CBC Reports; 1909-1910, Superintendent of Banks Reports, Crumb (1935). Column (4) - 1878-1886 and 1907-1910, U.S. Comptroller of the Currency, *Annual Report*, various years.

Table 2-3
Deposits of Savings Banks, State Commercial Banks
Foreign Banks and Branches, Private Banks, and National Banks
in California, 1849-1880[a]   (thousands of dollars)

Year	(1) Savings Banks	(2) State Com- mercial Banks	(3) Foreign Banks and Branches	(4) Private Banks[b]	(5) National Banks	(6) Total
1849	-	-	50	200	-	250
1850	-	-	250	1,500	-	1,750
1851	-	-	500	3,500	-	4,000
1852	-	-	500	5,000	-	5,500
1853	-	-	500	5,500	-	6,000
1854	-	-	750	5,500	-	6,250
1855	-	-	500	4,750	-	5,250
1856	-	-	500	4,500	-	5,000
1857	-	-	600	5,150	-	5,750
1858	20	-	750	5,250	-	6,020
1859	96	-	750	5,500	-	6,346
1860	69	-	650	5,000	-	5,719
1861	1,135	-	650	5,500	-	7,285
1862	2,952	-	700	5,600	-	9,252
1863	2,944	25	700	5,700	-	9,369
1864	3,858	1,000	1,000	5,750	-	10,708
1865	5,163	2,500	2,000	6,000	-	15,663
1866	7,393	2,750	2,500	6,250	-	18,893
1867	10,359	3,750	3,100	6,500	-	23,709
1868	17,365	5,000	3,200	6,750	-	32,315
1869	23,818	8,000	3,250	7,000	-	42,068
1870	28,893	12,000	3,300	6,750	-	50,943
1871	36,556	16,000	3,400	6,500	199	62,655
1872	44,234	21,000	3,500	6,750	3,144	78,626
1873	51,431	28,000	3,750	6,500	3,193	92,874
1874	57,833	35,000	4,000	6,500	5,406	108,739
1875	69,893	40,000	4,250	6,500	3,654	124,297
1876	70,083	46,172	4,500	6,250	2,499	129,484
1877	72,543	52,911	4,250	5,500	2,983	148,187
1878	71,468	24,410	4,218	4,500	3,403	107,999
1879	53,226	19,736	3,766	4,000	2,870	83,598
1880	47,719	26,965	4,592	4,500	3,873	87,559

a Figures are for the beginning of each year unlike in Table 2-4, which accounts for the minor differences between the two tables.
b Includes Express Companies, Bullion Dealers and Brokers, and Commission Merchants and Mercantile Establishments that engaged in banking as a side line, as well as institutions devoted exclusively to banking.
Source: Crumb (1935), Table 3, p. 227.

Table 2-4
Deposits of Savings Banks, Commercial Banks, Private Banks,
and National Banks in California, 1878-1910
($ in millions)

Year*	(1) Savings Banks	(2) Commercial Banks	(3) Private Banks	(4) National Banks	(5) Total
1878	71.5	28.6	4.0	3.4	108.0
1879	53.2	23.5	4.5	2.9	83.6
1880	47.7	31.6	4.5	3.8	87.6
1881	52.0ᵃ	34.4ᵃ	6.0	6.2	98.0
1882	53.2	35.6	6.5	7.4	102.7
1883	56.5	35.8	6.3	8.1	106.7
1884	59.5	36.5	6.3	6.5	108.8
1885	58.9	33.3	6.2	6.7	105.1
1886	62.8	40.5	6.1	11.2	116.6
1887	70.1	52.5	6.1	18.0	146.7
1888	77.7	48.3	6.5	18.6	151.2
1889	87.1	50.6	5.2	17.5	160.5
1890	98.4	50.7	4.4	17.7	171.2
1891	114.2	51.6	2.6	18.1	186.5
1892	125.4	53.2	1.4	16.7	198.7
1893	138.0	46.9	1.1	13.3	199.4
1894	125.4	55.6	1.0	15.0	197.0
1895	126.8	56.6	0.9	15.8	200.1
1896	131.7	53.6	1.0	16.3	202.7
1897	127.9	60.3	1.1	17.2	206.5
1898ᵇ	136.1	67.2	1.5	27.8	232.7
1899	145.9	77.6	1.4	31.9	256.7
1900ᶜ	158.2	85.9	1.6	34.2	279.8
1901ᵇ	170.8	98.7	1.8	42.0	313.2
1902ᵇ	187.7	126.4	1.9	52.6	368.6
1903ᵇ	212.9	130.6	2.3	70.4	416.3
1904ᵇ	224.8	134.3	2.2	73.5	434.8
1905ᵇ	247.9	150.0	2.6	92.0	492.5
1906ᵇ	273.7	194.4	3.8	130.1	602.0
1907	279.0	199.9	4.2	129.2	612.3
1908	246.1	160.4	2.1	123.8	532.4
1909	437.1		1.6	146.0	584.7
1910	452.0		1.3	198.5	651.8

*All figures refer to June or July unless otherwise noted.
a January   b August   c September.
Sources: See Table 2-2

Table 2-5
Failures, Voluntary Retirements, Conversions, New Organizations,
and Total Numbers of State and National Banks, 1878-1909*

	Bank Failures		Voluntary Retirements		Conversions		New Banks	
	(1)	(2)	(3)	(4)	(5)	(6)	(7)	(8)
					State to National	National to State		
Year	State	National	State	National	National	to State	State	National
1878	10	-	-	-	-	-	-	-
1879	1	-	2	1	-	-	-	-
1880	-	-	3	-	1	-	3	-
1881	-	-	3	-	1	-	2	-
1882	-	-	2	-	1	-	9	-
1883	-	-	2	-	1	-	7	1
1884	-	-	-	-	1	-	4	1
1885	-	-	-	-	2	-	5	3
1886	-	-	1	-	1	-	13	5
1887	-	-	1	-	-	-	17	6
1888	1	1	-	1	-	-	21	2
1889	-	-	3	-	1	1	15	1
1890	-	-	1	-	1	-	17	-
1891	2	1	-	-	1	-	27	2
1892	2	-	-	-	-	1	15	1
1893	6	1	12	1	-	3	14	1
1894	1	1	2	-	-	1	7	-
1895	1	1	5	-	-	-	7	-
1896	-	-	2	-	-	-	4	-
1897	1	-	1	-	2	-	1	-
1898	-	-	3	-	-	-	6	-
1899	-	-	4	-	1	-	4	1
1900	-	-	1	-	1	-	4	1
1901	-	-	4	-	5	-	11	4
1902	-	-	1	-	2	-	18	3
1903	-	-	1	-	8	-	79	7
1904	-	1	2	-	4	-	24	7
1905	-	-	13	2	3	-	68	20
1906	-	-	9	-	5	-	43	18
1907	5	-	15	1	6	2	46	14
1908	4	-	7	1	5	-	10	7
1909	7	1	6	-	-	2	23	14
Total	41	7	106	7	63	8	524	119

*Data are annual.

Sources:

Columns (1)-(8) - See Crumb (1935) Exhibits I and II. Columns (9) and (10) - See Table 2-2.

Table 2-6
Average Annual Rate of Bank Failure by Bank Type in California
1860-1910

Period	State Banks	Private Banks	National Banks
1860-1879	1.30%	1.20%	0.00%
1880-1899	0.33%	0.52%	0.71%
1900-1909	0.35%	1.46%	0.20%

Source: Tables 2-1, 2-2, and 2-5; Crumb (1935)

Table 2-7

Rates of Losses Caused by Bank Failures in California, 1880-1909

($ millions)

Periods	(1) Depositors' Losses	(2) Deposits Impounded	(3) Shareholders' Losses	(4) Average Annual Deposits	(5) % Rate of Depositors' Losses	(6) % Rate of Impounded Deposits	(7) % Rate of All Losses
1880-1899	0.00	0.15	0.07	102.5	0.00	0.01	0.01
1890-1899	2.60	5.99	2.11	183.9	0.14	0.33	0.26
1900-1909	9.64	13.16	3.60	416.7	0.23	0.32	0.32
1880-1899	2.60	6.04	2.18	143.2	0.09	0.21	0.17

Sources: Columns (1), (2) and (3) -- Crumb (1935), Table 10, p. 242.
Column (4) -- Table 2-4.
Column (5) = (Column (1)/10)/Column (4)*.
Column (6) = (Column (2)/10)/Column (4)*.
Column (7) = (Column (3)/10)/Column (4)*.
*For the twenty year period, 1880-1899, the divisor is 20 instead of 10.

Table 2-8

Average Annual Rates of Bank Failure for the United States,
California, and Wisconsin, 1877-1910

Period	United States	California	Wisconsin
Non-National Banks			
1877-1891	0.73%	1.11%	0.27%
1892-1897	1.90%	0.81%	3.20%
1898-1910	0.38%	0.29%	0.12%
National Banks			
1877-1891	0.24%	0.36%	0.00%
1892-1897	0.89%	1.47%	0.41%
1898-1910	0.22%	0.16%	0.21%

Sources:
  United States: Cagan (1965), Table 2, p. 41.
  California: Tables 2-1, 2-2, and 2-5
  Wisconsin: Keehn (1972), Table 2-4, p. 31 (includes only state banks)

Chapter 3

Banking and the Development
of California's Economy
1860-1910

Introduction

California's economy grew very rapidly over the period 1860-1910. This growth, however, was uneven with years of fast growth being typically followed by a period of slow growth or even stagnation. With the development of new industries, the introduction of new crops, and the opening up of new areas for cultivation, growth was also unevenly distributed among California's regions and industries. In view of the freedom from restrictions of California's banks, the important question is how much banking contributed to this pattern of economic growth. At present, this question cannot be answered directly. As Goldsmith (1969) notes, neither the theoretical nor the empirical bases exist to make such an assessment for any economy. The alternative to a direct answer is to use analysis that answers the question indirectly. In this chapter, the comparative methods employed by Goldsmith (1969) and Cameron (1967; 1972) are applied to California's history with the objective of providing some indirect answers.

The focus of attention in this chapter is the whole economy and aggregate bank behavior. Subsequent chapters deal with individual bank behavior. The chapter begins with a discussion of the growth of banking and the economy over time that shows both experienced very similar patterns of growth. In the next section, the development of banking in

California is compared with that in other states at various points in time. In the subsequent two sections, the patterns of development are explored on a more disaggregated level, first with a descriptive account of change in banking and the economy, and then with an analysis of the expansion of banking in the individual counties of California.

Before delving into the comparative development of banking in California, a brief description of the similar patterns of growth of banking and the economy in California is in order. This description sets the stage for subsequent analysis. The similar patterns of growth also suggest that the economy was the major factor determining the growth of banking in California. At the start of the period in 1860, there were 29 banks with about $6 million in deposits; by the end of the period, there were 640 banks with around $650 million in deposits (see Table 3-1A). Over the same period, California's population increased from 380,000 to 2,378,000, while the assessed value of property, or wealth, in California increased from $148 million to $2,374 million (see Table 3-1B). During this period, both banking and the economy experienced three periods of expansion.

Banking expanded rapidly in the 1860s and 1870s with the number of banks increasing from 29 in 1860 to 130 in 1877, while bank deposits grew from around $6 million to almost $150 million. A financial panic, a depressed economy, drought, and the closing of several banks by the newly-created Board of Bank Commissioners halted this expansion; the number of banks and bank deposits fell in 1878 and 1879. While the early 1880s were years of slow recovery for banking, the pace increased markedly in the second half of the decade. Between 1885 and the financial panic of 1893, the number of banks almost doubled from 142 to 282, an average rate of increase of nearly 20 banks per year. Bank deposits also nearly doubled from $105 million to $199 million.

The panic, however, initiated a period of stagnation so that by 1897 there were only 281 banks with $206 million in deposits. Though bank deposits started to grow again in 1898, it was not until the 1900s that the number of banks was increasing at a rate of more than 10 banks per year. The pace quickened thereafter with the number of banks climbing from 357 in 1903 to 601 in 1907. By 1907, bank deposits were $612 million, triple their level in 1897. A financial panic in 1907 halted banking's expansion yet once more; banks failed, and deposits fell to $532 million in 1908. The upward trend resumed in 1909. Thus, between 1860 and 1910, the banking industry experienced three periods of expansion, each of which was halted by a financial crisis: 1860-1875; 1884-1893; and 1898-1907.

California's economy experienced a similar pattern of growth over this period. The aggregate value of property in California increased in every year from 1861 to 1870 (see Table 3-1B). In 1872, a new Civil Code made various changes in the methods and definitions that governed the assessment of property for taxation, resulting in a doubling of the assessed value of property in the state. Part of this increase was due to better assessment methods, but part was also due to a new interpretation of the law: now mortgages were defined to be personal property. Legal wranglings and legislative discussions over the issue of double taxation were finally resolved by the 1879 constitution that designated mortgages as personal property. In the 1870s, year-to-year movements in the assessed value of property were as much a product of uncertainty over this legal issue as they were a product of economic conditions. It is thus impossible to tell precisely when in the 1870s this period of expansion ended. Historians have generally dated the end of this expansion as coinciding with the collapse of mining stocks and the ensuing problems of the Bank of California in 1873 and 1874.

The assessed value of property shows that the economy began to grow again in the early 1880s, reaching a peak in 1892. After a period of stagnation, the economy started to expand again in the late 1890s. This growth continued into the 1900s. Since population statistics are only available for census years, they can say little about the turning points in the pace of economic activity. They do show that the 1890s was the decade with the lowest percentage growth of population in the period, emphasizing the severity of the depression in the 1890s (see Table 3-1B). In general, historians have identified similar periods of expansion for California's economy to those identified by the pattern of growth of the assessed value of property.[1]

The very similar pattern of growth for both banking and the economy suggests that banking was closely tied to the economy. A more refined analysis of the pattern of growth is unlikely to change this conclusion. (For example, some allowance should be made for the different rates of inflation in different periods.) There is no evidence at this aggregate level that banking expanded in advance of the economy. Nor is there evidence that banking lagged behind the economy. Given the freedom of entry into banking in California, this outcome is to be expected. In the next section, some quantitative analysis is used to further assess the development of banking relative to the economy.

Comparisons of Banking Development Over Time and Across States

Cameron (1967) has suggested two measures for use in comparing banking development both over time and across economies. To measure the position of the banking sector in relation to the economy, he looks at various banking development ratios that relate the level of banking to the size of the economy. Two examples are: the ratio of bank deposits to national income, and the ratio of bank offices to every 10,000 people. Goldsmith (1969) bases his measurement of financial development on a much more complex methodology, but the end result, his FIR, is a similar type of ratio. Variations on these types of ratios are used in this section to explore banking's development in California.

All the banking development ratios presented in Table 3-2 increased over the period 1860-1910. The number of banks per 100,000 inhabitants more than tripled from 8 to 27. Bank deposits per capita increased from $16 to $274, and bank deposits per $100 of wealth increased from $4 to $27. Estimates of California's personal income for 1880 and 1900 indicate that the ratio of bank deposits to personal income also increased, rising from 0.26 to 0.53 between these two years.

The pattern of improvement is less certain. The 1870s and 1890s are identified as periods of slow or non-existent development by the ratio of banks to population, but bank deposits per capita increased in both these periods. Bank deposits per $100 of wealth followed neither of these patterns. A good part of the movement in this ratio can be explained by non-economic factors. In 1870, the underassessment of property explains the high value of this ratio. The closing of various banks by the Bank Commissioners in 1878 sharply reduced bank deposits in 1879. If the 1878 deposits are used, the level of bank deposits per $100 of wealth in 1880 rises from $13 to $19. This figure, however, exaggerates banking development since many of the banks would have failed sooner or later. The subsequent increase in this ratio is affected by the underassessment of property, particularly personal property, that occurred between 1880 and 1910. The extent of this underassessment remains undetermined. While it increased on some types of property, such as personal property, this increase was offset by improved assessment of other types.

Fortunately, the increase in the ratio of deposits to personal income confirms the increase in deposits per $100 of wealth.

The extent of banking's development in California can also be compared with that of banking in other states. Two banking development ratios are used here: deposits per capita and deposits per $100 of personal income. Comparisons using the latter ratio can only be made for 1880 and 1900, since estimates of personal income by state are only available for these two years. One question complicating these comparisons is which banks to include in calculating the ratios. Mutual savings banks were very important in some states. Excluding them, as most analysts of the U.S. money supply have done, may not be appropriate when the objective is to determine the extent of financial development and financial intermediation. This choice affects the outcome of the comparisons. In the available data, all savings banks are separated from commercial banks in 1880, but only mutual savings banks, and not stock savings banks, are separated from commercial banks in 1900.[2]

From the beginning of the period, California's banking industry was well advanced relative to most other states. In 1860, California ranked 6th in money per capita, where money comprises bank deposits plus bank notes.[3] In 1880, California ranked 5th in commercial bank deposits per capita, and 6th in commercial and savings bank deposits per capita (see Table 3-3A). In 1900, California ranked 2nd in commercial bank and stock savings bank deposits per capita, but ranked only 5th if mutual savings bank deposits are included. California's position in 1908 was almost the same in terms of per capita bank deposits.[4]

California's position changes slightly when the states are ranked by the ratio of deposits to personal income. In 1880, California ranked 8th by the ratio of all bank deposits to personal income and 12th by the ratio of commercial bank deposits to personal income (see Table 3-3B). In 1900, California ranked 10th by the ratio of all bank deposits to personal income, but ranked 2nd when mutual savings bank deposits are excluded.

In general, banking was relatively well developed in California from the beginning of the period. Over time, California's position only improves if mutual savings banks are excluded. Thus, the only safe conclusion is that banking in California developed about as rapidly as it did in the most advanced states.

The Patterns of Banking and Economic Activity

From the early days of Spanish rule until the beginning of the 1860s, the major agricultural activity in California was raising cattle, for which the large land holdings and open grazing of the Spanish era of California's history were ideally suited. In the 1850s, however, changes began to occur. The division of the large Spanish land grants following California's entry into the Union placed some limits on the pasture available for grazing. Grain provided a profitable alternative, being easily shipped from the grain-growing regions of central California. A drought in 1864 decimated many herds, and gave added impetus to grain production.[5] The domination of the cultivators over the stockowners was confirmed in 1872 by a "no-fence" law that made stockowners responsible for damage done by their livestock. Even by the 1850s, California's grain production was significant; in 1859, California, with a crop of 4.4 million bushels, was the nation's largest producer of barley, a position it held through the end of the century.[6] The state's output of wheat rose from 5.9 million bushels in 1859 to 16.7 million bushels in 1869.[7] Though sheep- and cattle-raising remained profitable, especially in the less developed southern portion of the state, grain production continued to expand rapidly. Due to a shortage of labor and the large size of the major grain-producing farms, agriculture in California was more mechanized than in other states.[8] Furthermore, to export their grain, large farms moved it directly to shipping points in the delta of the Sacramento River. This type of farming required large scale financing that was available primarily from banks in San Francisco.

According to the 1880 census, San Francisco was the largest city in California with 234,000 of the state's 865,000 inhabitants (see Table 3-4). As the major port, it was the center for the exporting of gold and grain and the importing of all types of goods. It provided all the necessary services from finance and insurance to storage and transshipment. Virtually all manufacturing was also located in the city. San Francisco's dominance of the state is reflected in the distribution of all property assessed for taxation. San Francisco County had more than five times the total property of the next wealthiest county, Alameda, in 1878 (see Table 3-5).

The first report of the Board of Bank Commissioners in 1878 showed that the distribution of the state's banks reflected the nature and location of economic activity. San Francisco's 19 banks dominated the state with $112 million in assets almost three times the assets of the remaining banks in the state which had only $40 million in assets (see Tables 3-6 and 3-7). The majority of the latter banks were located in northern California. Some were located in the various cities and towns around the San Francisco Bay, that benefitted from San Francisco's economic activity. Others were located in the cities in the central valley that serviced the grain trade and supplied the gold mining. The rest of the banks in the north were typically located in the seat of each county. The large-scale nature of grain production precluded the development of numerous small rural towns with their need for local banking. The few towns in the south and along the coast were the product of earlier Spanish settlements; the number of banks in these towns was correspondingly small.

Some fundamental changes occurred in the expansion of California's economy that began in the early 1880s.[9] During this period, agriculture diversified from producing primarily beef and grain to cultivating a wide variety of crops. With a growing population and improvements in transportation, many different crops became profitable, though it was not until the advent of irrigation in each region that extensive cultivation was possible. The new commercial crops included: citrus fruits, apricots, cherries, strawberries, hops, nuts, olives, melons, sugar beets, tobacco, cotton and hemp. Production of grapes for wine and raisins expanded not only in its established locations in Los Angeles and the Napa and Sonoma Valleys, but also in new areas in the central valley. These new, intensively cultivated crops had different requirements from those needed for the production of grain. They required a more settled labor force, smaller farms, irrigation, and, most importantly, processing. Canning and drying of fruit rapidly became a major industry in the state. Though some seasonability of labor demand continued, settlement in towns increased.

The demand for credit to finance the transformation of agriculture stimulated the formation of banks in old and new towns alike.[10] The number of banks increased from 140 to 1884 to 282 in 1893. Out of the 106 incorporated banks reporting in 1884, only 19 were in San Francisco. By 1893, there were 265 incorporated banks, but just 29 of these were located in San Francisco, indicating the development of banking in the rest of the state. However, a glance at Table 3-7 shows that San Francisco's banks continued to dominate the state's banking industry through their size.

The new banks were not evenly distributed across the state, but instead followed the pattern of regional economic development. Table 3-9 gives the number of entering banks for each county in various three-year periods. A brief review of the periods covering the years 1884-1893 indicates new banks were located in the developing areas of the state: in Alameda and Santa Clara Counties with the expansion of manufacturing and urbanization in the San Francisco Bay area; in Fresno, Kings and Tulare Counties with the increase in the cultivation of fruit and other crops at the southern end of the central valley; in Humboldt and Mendocino Counties with the growth of the lumber industry on the north coast; and in the southern portion of the state.

Perhaps the most radical transformation of a region was wrought in the southern counties (Los Angeles, Orange, Riverside, San Bernardino, San Diego and Ventura) by immigration from the East and by the development of citrus cultivation. The completion of the southern railroad route to California in 1885 brought competition to passenger fares and a flood of immigrants. During that year, 20,000 people are estimated to have arrived in Los Angeles.[11] By 1887, Los Angeles had approximately 80,000 inhabitants compared to the 11,000 reported in the 1880 census. The wealth of Los Angeles County rose from $28.0 million in 1884 to $69.7 million in 1887 (see Table 3-5). While the first citrus fruit was produced in 1877, its sale was limited to local markets until the advent of shipment by rail in the late 1880s. The introduction of oil heaters to prevent frost damage and the development of the necessary irrigation paved the way for a boom.[12] By 1889, over 1,000,000 navel orange trees were set out. (Production of lemons began a few years later in the early 1890s.) The result was a real estate boom. The average level of monthly real estate transactions in Los Angeles County was around $2 million in 1886.[13] This figure increased in the following year, and reached a peak of $11.9 million in July 1888. By November 1888, however, the boom had broken.

Existing banks were insufficient to meet the demand for funds generated by the rapid development of the southern counties. Not only was financing required for real estate transactions, but working capital was also needed by merchants, growers, and manufacturers. Entrepreneurs responded by organizing numerous banks, including several national banks. In the six years between 1884 and 1890, 23 banks were formed in Los Angeles County. Bank assets in this county rose from $4.6 million in 1884 to $15.7 million in 1887 (see Table 3-7). The end of the real estate boom, however, took its toll; bank deposits fell from $12.7 million in 1887 to $10.1 million in 1890. In addition, three banks closed (see Tables 3-8 and 3-9). This pattern was repeated in the other southern counties: Orange, Riverside, San Bernardino, San Diego, and Ventura. Between 1884 and 1890, 28 banks were organized in these counties. After rapid growth in the period 1884-1887, bank assets stagnated and bank deposits declined over the next three years.

The crisis of 1893 was the first financial panic in the East to have an immediate impact on California's economy.[14] The ensuing depression halted the rapid growth of the state's economy, though changes in the structure of the economy continued to occur. In particular, during the 1890s the oil industry became firmly established and hydroelectricity became a significant source of power.[15] This period also saw the beginnings of cooperation among fruit growers as they attempted to cope with overproduction, middlemen, and railroad companies. The depth of the depression affected the banking industry. The number of banks remained unchanged between 1893 and 1899 as the formation of new banks was matched by the closings of existing banks.

In 1900, when economic growth had resumed, agriculture was still the cornerstone of California's economy. According to the census of 1900, California produced a total of $118 million in farm products "not fed to stock," approximately equal to the value of manufacturing products less materials.[16] However, three of the top four manufacturing industries in 1899 were processing agricultural products: slaughtering and meat packing, canning and preserving, and flour and grist mill products. Lumber and timber products was the fourth. The next two industries were printing and publishing, and foundry and machine shop products. The latter industry was concentrated for the most part in San Francisco. As a result of rapid growth in its manufacturing, California was ranked eleventh in the United States, though it produced only about a sixth of New York State's manufacturing output. California, however, was the major state in canning and preserving, and in the production of vinous liquors. Not surprisingly, California was also the top producer of "all orchard products, grapes, and subtropical fruits."

California's economy expanded rapidly in the ten years after 1900 with the spread of irrigation fueling the growth of agriculture.[17] One major project brought water from the Colorado River to open up the rich Imperial Valley for cultivation. While the composition of manufacturing remained largely the same, manufacturing grew much more rapidly outside San Francisco. A notable feature of this decade of expansion was the declining dominance of San Francisco. Los Angeles in particular began to rival San Francisco not only in wealth and population but also in manufacturing and commercial activity, including banking. In 1900, Los Angeles County's wealth was only $95 million, far less than San Francisco's $366 million. By 1908, Los Angeles County's wealth of $454 million almost equalled San Francisco's $474 million, while Los Angeles County's estimated population of 471,000 even exceeded San Francisco's 410,000.[18]

The advance of banking in Los Angeles County was also remarkable. In 1896, this county had 34 banks with $21 million in assets, a tenth of San Francisco's 28 banks' assets (see Tables 3-6 and 3-7). By 1905, there were 88 banks in Los Angeles County with $110 million in assets, nearly a third of the assets held by San Francisco's 56 banks. Thus, the rapid growth of the Los Angeles County economy was matched by the expansion of banking. A similar pattern is evident in the other southern counties as the number of banks in these counties rose from 35 in 1886 to 60 in 1905. By 1908, there were 126 banks in Los Angeles County, and 92 banks in the remaining southern counties.

The expansion of banking was not limited to southern California. The expanding lumber industry stimulated the formation of banks in Mendocino County and the growth of bank assets in Humboldt County. The growth of cities around the San Francisco Bay also generated demand for banking services. The number of banks in Alameda County increased from 16 in 1896 to 25 in 1905, their assets rising from $15 million to $38 million. Fresno County's banks grew from 6 in 1896 to 16 in 1905 in response to that county's development; the output of canning and preserving in Fresno increased fourfold between 1899 and 1904. In 1907, a clearinghouse opened in Fresno and by 1908 there were 20 banks in the county. Other clearinghouses were started in Oakland (1906), San Jose (1906), Sacramento (1907), and Stockton (1907).[19] These institutions were largely a product of the disruptions caused by the 1906 earthquake and fire in San Francisco and the desire to issue clearinghouse certificates during the 1907 panic. An additional reason may have been to reduce the competition generated by the rapid growth of banking through the imposition of such things as uniform hours of business and maximum rates of interest on deposits.

Distribution of Banking Across California's Counties

The previous section provided a descriptive account of how the pattern of banking growth matched the pattern of economic growth in

California. In this section, the expansion of banking across California's counties is examined. The quantitative approaches taken by Cameron and Goldsmith suggest one avenue to explore. Given the assumption that a county's wealth reflects a county's demand for bank deposits, it follows that the ratio of deposits at the county's banks to the wealth of the county provides a measure of banking development in the county. One would expect this ratio to have varied widely across California's counties at the beginning of the period, but that as banking developed with no restrictions on entry, differences in the ratio among counties would decline substantially. In fact, the development of banking in California's counties did follow this pattern.

Since certain counties in California were created during the period 1878-1908, the individual county numbers had to be estimated in some cases. Orange County was created out of Los Angeles County in 1887. Glenn County was created out of Colusa County in 1892. In 1893, Madera County was created out of Fresno County, Kings was created out of Tulare County, and Riverside County was created out of San Bernardino and San Diego Counties. In 1907, Imperial County was created out of San Diego County. With the exception of Imperial County, the solution chosen was to use modern county boundaries for the analysis. For the bank data, this choice only required locating banks according to modern boundaries. For wealth and population, however, data for years prior to the creation of the county were estimated by assuming the proportion of wealth or population of the created county to that of the existing county was the same in the years before creation. The errors created by this method appear to be less damaging than either maintaining the old boundaries or eliminating those counties involved in these changes.

The early development of banking in San Francisco and its subsequent domination of banking in California is confirmed. In 1878, San Francisco had the highest ratio of bank deposits to county wealth with $29.5 in deposits for every $100 in wealth; it had the highest ratio for the rest of the period 1878-1908 (see Table 3-10). Two other counties had deposit/wealth ratios above 10 in 1878: Sacramento and San Diego. At the other extreme, 24 counties had no bank deposits. Between these two extremes, there were 9 counties with ratios between 5 and 10. By 1890, the expansion of banking had increased the number of counties with ratios above 10 to 8, while 12 counties had ratios between 5 and 10. Even though banking experienced stagnation during part of the 1890s, banking continued to advance, as the number of counties with ratios above 10 increased to 14 by 1899. This progress accelerated over the remainder of the period so that by 1908 there were 34 counties with ratios above 10, including 13 counties with ratios above 20. The spread of banking is emphasized by the sharp decline in the number of counties with no banks, and hence no locally-supplied bank deposits. This number declined from 24 in 1878 to 11 in 1890, and to only 3 in 1908.

Insufficient economic activity may explain why some counties had no bank for much of the period. Generally, counties with no bank had less than $2 million in wealth. Of the nine counties with no bank in 1899, six counties had under $2 million, two had $2.1 million, and one had $4.9 million (see Table 3-6). After 1900, banks were formed in these counties when their wealth climbed above the $2 million threshold. Del Norte and Trinity Counties are two examples. There was no bank in Plumas County while wealth was barely above $2 million; after a doubling of this county's wealth, a bank was formed there in 1905. In two cases where counties lost their only bank, Mono and Sierra Counties, wealth was below $2 million and declining when the sole bank failed. By 1908, only three counties had no banks, and in two of these counties, wealth was less than $2 million.

While this analysis demonstrates that banking did spread throughout California's counties, it cannot determine whether this expansion was fast enough to further economic growth or slow enough to hinder it. This issue is explored further in Chapter 6 with a model of bank entry. In the absence of similar analyses for other states, no precise comparison can be made of the pace at which banking spread across California's counties. Data for the number of banks in Wisconsin's counties provided by Keehn (1972) indicate that California's experience was not exceptional. The number of Wisconsin counties with no bank was 39 in 1870, 19 in 1880, 5 in 1890, 2 in 1900, 0 in 1910, and 1 in 1960. There were 58 counties in Wisconsin in 1870, and 70 in 1910. This comparison ignores differences in the level of demand for banking services among individual counties. Further work on the spread of banking needs to be done on Wisconsin and other states to provide comparisons with California's experience.

Conclusions

The pattern of growth of banking in California between 1860 and 1910 closely paralleled that of the state's economy as banking and the economy expanded together. Both experienced three periods of growth: the 1860s and early 1870s, the 1880s and early 1890s, and the years between 1898 and 1907. A comparison of various measures of the development of banking show that banking developed over time in California. Both the number of banks and bank deposits grew by more than the state's population, income, or wealth. Even as early as 1860, California's banking was well developed relative to most states. Over subsequent years, California remained one of the top states as its banking developed as fast as banking in the most developed states on the East Coast.

California does not fit exactly the general pattern of financial development described by Goldsmith (1969). While California banking developed over the period during which its economy became developed, the pattern of this development was somewhat different. In the first place, almost from California's obtaining statehood, banking in California was well developed by comparison with other states with much more developed economies. This advantage may be attributed to the role that gold mining played in California's economy. Gold stimulated not only the rapid growth of the state's economy, but also the rapid development of the financial institutions to finance this growth. As Goldsmith notes, financial knowledge and techniques are much easier to transfer than other types of technology, making this rapid development possible. California's early prohibition on bank notes and incorporated banking were not binding constraints. Unincorporated banking flourished and incorporated banking operated via a loophole. With an abundant supply of gold, the demand for money was met with gold coins or checks.

Having developed so quickly relative to the economy, banking in California could not then experience the spurt of development that Goldsmith finds to be a common characteristic of other economies. The typical economy, according to Goldsmith, experiences a period of rapid expansion of financial intermediation, particularly in its banking industry, relative to the growth of its economy, which is maintained for a short period of ten to twenty years. At some point, the development of banking relative to the economy levels off. In California, banking experienced several periods of rapid expansion and was still developing relative to the economy in the 1900s. Too much cannot be made of the differences between California's experiences and that of other economies. For one thing, the analysis has ignored other financial intermediaries, such as insurance companies. More importantly, California's economic development was unique in many respects. Its gold, fertile land, the influx of immigrants, and its ties to a larger political entity all worked to enhance the pace of this development. Some of these factors also facilitated the development of its banking industry, making it difficult to determine the importance of California's minimal regulation of its banks.

To the extent that financial development is important for economic growth, banking in California appears to have had a positive contribution at the aggregate level. At a disaggregated level, there is also evidence that banking contributed to economic growth. As new regions and new industries were developed, banking appears to have expanded to meet the demand for financing this growth. In the future, more effort needs to be devoted to exploring the relationship between banking and the financing of the development of these new crops, new industries, and new regions. Specific evidence that banking expanded with the regional development of California's economy is provided by the spread of banking across California's counties. While California's banking developed early on an aggregate basis, this development was not evenly distributed across the state. Over time, differences in the level of banking development among California's counties declined, indicating that banking contributed to the regional growth of California's economy. In the next three chapters, these issues are further explored with a model of individual bank behavior and a model of bank entry.

Notes

1. The economic history of California is presented with varying degrees of detail in the following books: Bean (1968), Caughey (1970), Cleland (1929), Cross (1927), Hutchinson (1946), Nash (1964), and McWilliams (1971). Cross (1927) has five chapter headings: "The Uncertain Fifties," "The Prosperous Sixties," "The Speculative Seventies," "The Solid Eighties," and "Depression and Recovery, 1890-1900."

2. Fand (1954) discusses these distinctions in compiling his estimates of the U.S. money supply during the nineteenth century.

3. The following table gives the top ten states:

Money Per Capita*

Massachusetts	$ 40.03
New York	36.15
Rhode Island	32.98
Louisiana	31.28
Connecticut	27.60
Delaware	17.77
Maine	16.13
California	16.00 (includes only bank deposits)
Virginia	15.51
Pennsylvania	13.04

*Includes currency and bank deposits, except for mutual savings deposits.

Source: Rockoff (1975), Appendix Table III, p. 181.

4. In 1908, the ranking of states by assets per capita was as follows:

New York	$637
Massachusetts	486
California	478
Rhode Island	444
Connecticut	401
Nevada	384
Pennsylvania	301
New Hampshire	283

Illinois was still the highest ranked midwestern state with $244 of bank assets per capita. See U.S. Comptroller of the Currency, *Annual Report*, 1909.

5. Caughey (1970), p. 198; Cleland (1929), Chapter 1.
6. The next largest producers were Wisconsin, Iowa and Minnesota.
7. Some indication of the speed of the grain production expansion in California is given by the following data:

Production of Wheat and Barley in California, 1894-1899
(bushels in millions)

Crop	1849	1859	1869	1879	1889	1899
Wheat	.02	5.9	16.7	29.0	40.9	36.5
Barley	.01	4.4	8.8	12.5	17.5	25.1

Sources: U.S. Bureau of the Census, *Abstract of the 11th Census*, Table 7; and *Abstract of the 12th Census*, Table 130.

8. The large scale of operation that was possible in the Central Valley of California combined with the pressure of labor shortages to produce a very mechanized agriculture. A variety of machines was invented to suit this environment. The Stockton gang plow, and later, the tractor are two examples. Bean (1968), p. 271. California's farms were noted for their scale and the speed with which mechanization was adopted. See McWilliams (1971), Caughey (1970), p. 199, and Nash (1966), p. 139.
9. Descriptions of this period of development are to be found in Bean (1968), Caughey (1970), Cleland (1929), and Nash (1964).
10. Nash (1964), p. 139.
11. Cross (1927), pp. 562.
12. Nash (1964), p. 139; Caughey (1970), pp. 352-356; Cleland (1929), Chapter 4.
13. Cross (1927), pp. 562-563.
14. California was largely isolated from the financial crises of earlier years. It took four years for the 1873 panic to reach California. The state was unaffected by the depression of 1883-1884. However, in 1893, it was only a few months after the crisis in the East began that California felt its effects. Cross (1927), p. 588.
15. Oil production increased from 0.69 million barrels in 1888 to 4 million barrels in 1900. It reached 72 million barrels in 1910. Cleland (1929), Chapter 6. The first hydro-electric plant opened in 1891. Cross (1927), p. 590. California's hydro-electric power capacity reached 30,500 kilowatt hours in 1900. Cleland (1929), p. 218.
16. U.S. Bureau of the Census, (1913), Chapter 5.
17. Ibid.

18. Ibid.
19. Wright (1910), pp. 128-129. Clearing houses were organized in Pasadena (1909), San Diego (1913). Bakersfield, Long Beach, and Santa Rosa had clearing houses by 1916. The State Clearing House Association was formed in 1908. Armstrong and Denny (1916).

Table 3-1A
Number of Banks and Total Deposits in California, 1849-1910

	(1)	(2) Deposits		(3)	(4) Deposits
Year*	Number	($ millions)	Year**	Number	($ millions)
1849	3	0.3	1878	121	108.0
1850	23	1.8	1879	114	83.6
1851	34	4.0	1880	116	87.6
1852	37	5.5	1881ᵃ	-----	98.0
1853	39	6.0	1882	121	102.7
1854	38	6.3	1883	130	106.7
1855	38	5.3	1884	140	108.8
1856	26	5.0	1885	142	105.1
1857	23	5.8	1886	151	116.6
1858	26	6.0	1887	169	146.7
1859	29	6.3	1888	201	151.2
1860	29	5.7	1889	219	160.5
1861	34	7.3	1890	232	171.2
1862	36	9.3	1891	246	186.5
1863	37	9.4	1892	268	198.7
1864	38	10.7	1893	282	199.4
1865	43	15.7	1894	278	197.0
1866	49	18.9	1895	281	200.1
1867	48	23.7	1896	282	202.7
1868	53	32.3	1897	281	206.5
1869	60	42.1	1898ᵇ	288	232.7
1870	65	50.9	1899	282	256.7
1871	73	62.7	1900ᵇ	287	279.8
1872	81	78.6	1901ᵇ	299	313.2
1873	84	92.9	1902ᵇ	321	368.6
1874	99	108.7	1903ᶜ	357	416.3
1875	110	124.3	1904ᵇ	423	434.8
1876	122	129.5	1905ᵇ	487	492.5
1877	130	148.2	1906ᵇ	563	602.0
			1907	601	612.3
			1908	613	536.2
			1909	637	584.7
			1910	640	651.8

* January.
** June or July unless otherwise noted: a - January   b - August   c - September
Sources: Columns (1) and (2) - Crumb (1935), Tables 1 and 2
           Columns (3) and (4) - Tables 2-1 and 2-2

Table 3-1B
Total Assessed Value of Property and
Population in California, 1860-1910

Year	(1) Assessed Value* ($ millions)	(2) Population (thousands)	Year	(3) Assessed Value* ($ millions)	(4) Population (thousands)
1860	148	380	1886	817	
1861	148		1887	957	
1862	160		1888	1108	
1863	174		1889	1112	
1864	179		1890	1101	1213
1865	184		1891	1242	
1866	200		1892	1276	
1867	212		1893	1216	
1868	237		1894	1204	
1869	261		1895	1133	
1870	277	560	1896	1265	
1871	267		1897	1089	
1872	637		1898	1132	
1873	529		1899	1194	
1874	611		1900	1218	1485
1875	618		1901	1241	
1876	595		1902	1290	
1877	587		1903	1598	
1878	585		1904	1546	
1879	549		1905	1624	
1880	666	865	1906	1596	
1881	660		1907	1879	
1882	609		1908	1990	
1883	766		1909	2439	
1884	821		1910	2374	2378
1885	860		1910		

* Some of the shifts in this series are due to changes in the methods of valuing and assessing property (see Chapter 3).

Sources: Column (1) - California State Board of Equalization, *Annual Report*, 1911.

Column (2) - U.S. Bureau of the Census, *Historical Statistics of the United States Colonial Times to 1970*, Bicentennial Edition, Series A 195-209, Washington, DC, 1975.

Table 3-2
Economic Growth, Bank Expansion, and Banking Development Ratios, 1860-1910

Year	Economic Growth and Bank Expansion*				
	(1) Population (thousands)	(2) Wealth ($ millions)	(3) Income ($ millions)	(4) Bank Deposits ($ millions)	(5) Number of Banks
1860	380	148		6	29
1870	560	278		51	65
1880	865	666	339	88 (108)	116 (121)
1890	1213	1101		171	232
1900	1485	1218	543	280	287
1910	2378	2374		652	649

Year	Banking Development Ratios*			
	Bank Deposits per Capita (dollars)	Number of Banks Per 1,000,000 Inhabitants	Bank Deposits Per $100 of Wealth (dollars)	Deposits/ Income
1860	16	8	4	
1870	91	12	18	
1880	101 (125)	13	13 (19)	0.26
1890	141	19	16	
1900	189	19	23	0.53
1910	274	27	27	

*Figures in parentheses are for 1878; the closing of several banks by the California Bank Commissioners in 1878 explains the decline between 1878 and 1880.

Sources: Column (1) - U.S. Bureau of the Census (1975), Series A 195-209, p. 25.
Columns (2), (4) and (5) - See Table 3-1B and 3-1A.   Column (3) - Kuznets (1960).

Table 3-3A
Bank Deposits Per Capita for Various States
1880 and 1900

1880

State	All Bank Deposits		Commercial Bank Deposits	
	Rank	$	Rank	$
Rhode Island	1	188	3	45
Massachusetts	2	179	2	66
Connecticut	3	160	5	40
New York	4	153	1	82
California	5	100	6	39

1900

State	All Bank Deposits		Stock Bank Deposits	
	Rank	$	Rank	$
New York	1	409	1	282
Massachusetts	2	338	2	148
Rhode Island	3	319	4	152
Connecticut	4	270	20	68
California	5	194	2	194

Sources:
  Deposits - U.S. Comptroller of the Currency
  Population - U.S. Bureau of the Census (1975).

Table 3-3B
Bank Deposits Per $100 of Personal Income
Various States, 1880 and 1900

1880

State	All Bank Deposits		Commercial Bank Deposits	
	Rank	$	Rank	$
Rhode Island	1	68	4	17
Massachusetts	2	61	2	23
Connecticut	3	60	6	15
New York	4	54	1	29
California	8	25	12	10

1900

State	All Bank Deposits		Stock Bank Deposits	
	Rank	$	Rank	$
New York	1	126	1	87
Massachusetts	2	111	4	49
Rhode Island	3	109	3	52
Connecticut	4	97	27	25
California	10	53	2	53

Sources:
   Deposits - U.S. Comptroller of the Currency
   Personal Income - Kuznets (1960)

Table 3-4
Population by County, Census Years 1860-1910
(tens)

County	1860	1870	1880	1890	1900	1910
Alameda	893	2,424	6,298	9,386	13,020	24,613
Alpine	-	69	54	67	51	31
Amador	1,093	958	1,138	1,032	1,111	909
Butte	1,211	1,140	1,872	1,794	1,711	2,730
Calaveras	1,630	890	909	888	1,120	917
Colusa	227	617	1,312	1,464	736	773
Contra Costa	533	846	1,253	1,351	1,805	3,167
Del Norte	199	202	258	259	241	242
El Dorado	2,056	1,031	1,068	923	899	749
Fresno	461	634	948	3,203	3,786	7,566
Glenn	-	-	-	-	515	717
Humbolt	269	614	1,551	2,347	2,710	3,386
Inyo	-	196	293	354	437	697
Kern	-	293	560	981	1,648	3,772
Kings	-	-	-	-	987	1,623
Lake	-	297	660	710	602	553
Lassen	-	133	334	424	451	480
Los Angeles*	1,133	1,531	3,338	10,145	17,030	50,413
Madera	-	-	-	-	636	837
Marin	333	690	1,132	1,307	1,570	2,511
Mariposa	624	457	434	379	472	396
Mendocino	397	755	1,280	1,761	2,047	2,393
Merced	114	281	566	809	922	151
Modoc	-	-	440	499	508	619
Mono	-	43	750	200	217	204
Monterey	474	988	1,130	1,864	1,938	2,415
Napa	552	716	1,324	1,641	1,645	1,980
Nevada	1,645	1,913	2,082	1,737	1,779	1,496
Orange*	-	-	-	1,359	1,970	3,444
Placer	1,327	1,136	1,423	1,510	1,579	1,824

Table 3-4 (continued)
Population by County, Census Years 1860-1910
(tens)

County	1860	1870	1880	1890	1900	1910
Plumas	436	449	618	493	466	526
Riverside[s]	-	-	-	-	1,790	3,470
Sacramento	2,414	2,683	3,439	4,034	4,592	6,781
San Benito	-	-	558	641	663	804
San Bernardino[s]	556	399	779	2,550	2,793	5,671
San Diego[s]	432	495	862	3,499	3,509	7,526
San Francisco	5,680	14,947	23,396	29,900	34,278	41,691
San Joaquin	944	2,105	2,435	2,863	3,545	5,073
San Luis Obispo	178	477	914	1,607	1,664	1,983
San Mateo	321	664	867	1,009	1,209	2,659
Santa Barbara	354	778	951	1,575	1,893	2,774
Santa Clara	1,191	2,625	3,504	4,801	6,022	8,354
Santa Cruz	494	875	1,280	1,927	2,151	2,614
Shasta	436	417	949	1,213	1,732	1,892
Sierra	1,139	562	662	505	402	410
Siskiyou	763	685	861	1,216	1,696	1,880
Solano	717	1,687	1,848	2,095	2,414	2,756
Sonoma	1,187	1,982	2,593	3,272	3,848	4,839
Stanislaus	225	650	875	1,004	955	2,252
Sutter	339	503	516	547	589	633
Tehema	404	359	930	992	1,100	1,140
Trinity	513	321	500	372	438	330
Tulare	464	453	1,128	2,457	1,838	3,544
Tuolome	1,623	815	785	608	1,117	998
Ventura[s]	-	-	507	1,007	1,437	1,835
Yolo	472	990	1,177	1,268	1,362	1,393
Yuba	1,367	1,085	1,128	964	862	1,004

s County in southern portion of the state.
Source: U.S. Bureau of the Census

Table 3-5
Wealth by County*
($ millions)

County**	1878	1884	1887	1890	1893	1896	1899	1905	1908
Alameda	42.8	56.4	59.5	76.5	90.3	90.7	84.4	114.7	188.3
Alpine	0.5	0.3	0.3	0.3	0.3	0.3	0.3	0.5	0.5
Amador	2.6	3.5	4.1	4.1	4.1	4.0	4.3	5.1	5.5
Butte	10.5	14.9	16.8	18.4	16.5	12.9	13.0	15.9	18.8
Calaveras	1.9	2.9	3.7	4.2	4.4	4.8	4.9	6.0	6.1
Colusa	6.6	10.5	12.1	12.9	13.3	11.0	11.4	11.7	12.2
Contra Costa	7.3	12.5	14.7	15.1	15.3	14.1	14.8	20.2	26.5
Del Norte	0.7	1.1	1.5	1.9	2.1	1.9	1.8	3.2	3.8
El Dorado	2.3	2.9	3.3	3.3	3.6	3.7	3.7	4.4	5.0
Fresno	5.2	10.4	18.1	30.7	32.4	24.7	26.0	34.8	47.6
Glenn	5.5	8.7	10.0	10.7	11.6	9.1	9.6	10.0	10.9
Humbolt	5.3	9.2	14.2	17.8	17.8	15.6	16.0	24.7	28.6
Inyo	1.4	1.1	1.2	1.4	1.4	1.4	1.6	2.5	3.6
Kern	5.1	5.3	7.2	10.6	12.0	14.0	13.1	21.9	29.7
Kings	1.4	2.7	4.6	6.5	6.9	5.8	6.3	7.7	9.2
Lake	2.2	3.0	3.3	3.9	3.7	3.1	2.9	3.4	3.6
Lassen	1.2	1.8	2.3	2.5	2.6	2.3	2.8	5.2	5.7
Los Angeles*	14.6	28.0	69.7	76.3	77.5	89.9	94.7	240.5	453.9
Madera	1.0	1.9	3.3	5.6	6.5	5.3	5.1	6.3	7.2
Marin	8.1	9.6	10.1	10.9	12.0	10.8	11.1	13.4	16.7
Mariposa	1.3	1.6	1.7	1.8	1.8	2.0	2.1	2.2	5.2
Mendocino	5.9	8.3	10.1	11.4	11.6	10.6	10.2	11.9	13.9
Merced	5.3	9.5	11.9	13.6	13.9	11.6	12.0	13.4	15.1
Modoc	1.2	2.3	2.8	3.1	3.2	2.5	2.8	4.3	5.2
Mono	1.1	1.9	1.0	0.9	0.8	0.8	1.0	1.1	1.2
Monterey	7.2	10.0	12.3	15.0	17.1	15.4	16.0	17.4	21.8
Napa	8.0	11.0	12.6	13.9	13.5	11.5	11.1	13.1	14.4
Nevada	6.9	6.0	5.4	5.4	5.2	5.8	6.3	6.6	6.8
Orange*	1.5	3.4	8.5	9.3	9.4	9.3	10.5	13.8	20.9
Placer	5.7	6.1	6.8	8.0	8.2	7.4	7.1	7.4	8.1
Plumas	2.0	2.0	2.2	2.3	2.2	2.4	2.1	4.0	5.0
Riverside*	1.4	3.0	9.0	11.6	12.1	10.7	10.6	13.5	20.0

Table 3-5 (continued)
Wealth by County*
($ millions)

County**	1878	1884	1887	1890	1893	1896	1899	1905	1908
Sacramento	18.3	26.1	28.7	32.7	32.9	32.3	32.1	35.8	54.5
San Benito	3.8	5.0	5.5	6.1	6.4	6.1	5.7	6.3	6.7
S.Bernardino*	3.1	4.5	9.1	12.8	15.5	14.3	13.4	16.3	23.8
San Diego*	1.5	5.0	19.6	24.0	22.8	19.5	18.4	20.8	34.4
San Francisco	238.9	241.6	251.7	331.5	375.4	365.9	389.2	467.7	474.3
San Joaquin	17.8	35.8	33.4	36.9	36.7	31.0	29.5	34.7	41.4
S.LuisObispo	4.3	8.3	11.8	13.7	14.3	12.1	11.0	13.4	15.0
San Mateo	6.4	9.7	11.4	14.1	16.1	15.1	13.8	18.0	25.0
Santa Barbara	4.4	7.9	14.4	15.5	15.6	13.2	12.4	17.6	24.3
Santa Clara	26.8	33.7	43.8	52.0	54.6	54.3	50.4	56.1	63.3
Santa Cruz	6.1	7.3	8.7	10.7	11.9	10.7	10.1	12.5	16.3
Shasta	2.0	3.2	4.0	5.4	5.8	5.3	6.7	10.7	12.6
Sierra	1.5	1.6	1.7	1.5	1.4	1.3	1.4	1.9	2.0
Siskiyou	2.7	3.9	4.4	5.8	6.9	7.5	7.1	10.8	14.4
Solano	8.8	15.9	17.7	18.5	18.6	15.0	16.0	18.0	19.4
Sonoma	15.4	22.8	26.9	29.0	28.9	24.8	23.7	29.2	32.2
Stanislaus	5.9	16.0	14.7	15.4	15.7	12.3	10.7	12.7	15.6
Sutter	4.0	7.0	8.3	9.3	9.0	6.1	5.9	6.0	6.3
Tehama	4.1	7.8	9.4	10.8	10.2	8.8	9.7	11.0	11.7
Trinity	0.8	1.1	1.1	1.2	1.3	1.3	1.4	2.2	2.8
Tulare	3.5	6.6	11.4	16.0	16.1	13.7	13.2	15.8	25.7
Tuolome	1.7	2.3	2.5	2.8	3.2	3.8	5.4	7.2	7.3
Ventura*	3.1	4.4	6.5	7.4	7.7	6.8	7.1	8.9	14.1
Yolo	10.0	16.1	18.2	19.7	19.6	15.3	15.1	15.4	17.0
Yuba	4.3	5.2	6.1	6.7	6.6	5.1	4.8	5.5	6.3

* Three-year moving average.
**Data for counties created after 1878 were estimated for the years prior to their creation; Imperial (1907) was included in San Diego.
s County in southern portion of the state.
Source: California State Board of Equalization, *Biennial Report*, various years.

Table 3-6
Number of Banks by County

County*	1878**	1884**	1887	1890	1893	1896	1899	1905	1908
Alameda	4	6	6	8	17	16	16	25	43
Alpine	-	-	-	-	-	-	-	-	-
Amador	-	-	-	-	-	1	2	3	2
Butte	2	2	3	4	6	5	5	7	10
Calaveras	-	-	-	-	-	-	-	1	1
Colusa	1	1	1	1	2	2	2	4	5
Contra Costa	1	1	1	1	2	2	2	5	8
Del Norte	-	-	-	-	-	-	-	1	1
El Dorado	-	-	1	1	1	2	2	2	2
Fresno	1	3	5	6	9	6	6	16	20
Glenn	-	1	2	2	2	2	2	2	2
Humbolt	1	1	3	6	7	7	6	8	9
Inyo	-	-	-	-	-	-	-	1	1
Kern	1	1	1	1	4	4	4	6	7
Kings	-	-	-	-	2	2	2	5	7
Lake	2	2	2	2	2	2	2	2	2
Lassen	-	-	-	-	1	1	1	1	1
Los Angeles*	3	5	17	27	31	34	33	88	126
Madera	-	-	-	1	2	1	1	2	2
Marin	1	1	2	2	2	2	3	3	5
Mariposa	-	-	-	-	-	-	-	-	-
Mendocino	3	3	4	4	5	4	2	6	8
Merced	2	2	2	3	3	2	2	3	3
Modoc	-	-	1	1	1	1	1	3	4
Mono	-	1	1	1	-	-	-	-	-
Monterey	1	1	1	2	4	4	5	10	11
Napa	2	2	5	5	6	8	7	7	7
Nevada	1	1	3	3	3	2	2	2	2
Orange*	1	2	4	6	6	8	8	10	19
Placer	-	-	2	3	2	3	2	5	7
Plumas	1	1	1	1	-	-	-	1	1
Riverside*	-	-	3	6	9	6	7	10	15

100

Table 3-6 (continued)
Number of Banks by County

County*	1878**	1884**	1887	1890	1893	1896	1899	1905	1908
Sacramento	4	4	5	5	6	6	7	12	12
San Benito	1	1	1	1	4	4	4	4	4
S.Bernardino*	-	2	5	9	10	9	10	15	23
San Diego*	2	1	5	12	10	9	9	16	22
San Francisco	19	19	26	29	29	28	31	56	53
San Joaquin	5	6	4	6	6	6	6	7	11
S.LuisObispo	1	1	2	6	8	8	5	8	8
San Mateo	-	-	-	-	1	2	2	6	8
Santa Barbara	2	2	4	5	7	7	7	14	14
Santa Clara	6	6	7	10	13	14	15	16	21
Santa Cruz	3	3	4	7	9	9	9	9	9
Shasta	-	1	1	2	2	2	2	3	3
Sierra	-	-	1	1	1	1	-	1	1
Siskiyou	-	1	2	2	2	2	2	5	7
Solano	4	5	5	5	5	5	5	9	10
Sonoma	8	9	11	12	13	14	14	20	20
Stanislaus	-	1	2	4	4	4	4	10	11
Sutter	-	-	-	1	1	1	1	1	1
Tehama	1	1	2	2	2	2	2	3	3
Trinity	-	-	-	-	-	-	-	2	2
Tulare	1	1	3	6	10	10	8	12	17
Tuolome	-	-	-	-	-	-	2	2	2
Ventura*	1	1	1	3	3	3	3	9	13
Yolo	1	2	3	3	4	5	5	5	7
Yuba	1	2	3	4	4	4	4	4	4

* Modern county boundaries were used for counties created after 1878; Imperial (1908) was included in San Diego.
** Does not include private banks.
s County in southern portion of the state.
Source: California State Board of Bank Commissioners, *Annual Report*, 1878-1908.

Table 3-7
Bank Assets by County
($ millions)

County*	1878**	1884**	1887	1890	1893	1896	1899	1905	1908
Alameda	4.52	6.23	7.40	10.52	15.54	15.26	21.35	37.59	57.95
Alpine	-	-	-	-	-	-	-	-	-
Amador	-	-	-	-	-	0.08	0.18	0.59	0.77
Butte	1.25	1.09	1.19	1.65	2.04	1.69	1.85	3.21	4.93
Calaveras	-	-	-	-	-	-	-	0.37	0.57
Colusa	0.85	1.04	1.19	1.48	1.60	1.54	1.44	2.29	2.80
Contra Costa	0.26	0.33	0.38	0.51	0.66	0.68	0.59	1.37	2.50
Del Norte	-	-	-	-	-	-	-	0.13	0.17
El Dorado	-	-	0.10	0.15	0.15	0.18	0.26	0.57	0.54
Fresno	0.08	0.43	1.57	2.52	3.22	2.35	3.06	7.30	11.79
Glenn	-	0.37	0.47	0.68	0.99	0.75	0.81	1.19	1.26
Humbolt	0.23	0.36	0.72	1.25	1.98	1.90	2.45	5.45	6.99
Inyo	-	-	-	-	-	-	-	0.24	0.45
Kern	0.17	0.17	0.23	0.31	0.94	1.03	1.27	3.05	4.07
Kings	-	-	-	-	0.11	0.10	0.15	0.72	1.76
Lake	0.31	0.25	0.29	0.36	0.34	0.32	0.31	0.37	0.50
Lassen	-	-	-	-	0.09	0.03	0.17	0.26	0.38
Los Angeles	1.96	4.59	15.74	15.73	19.23	20.96	29.61	110.53	139.49
Madera	-	-	-	0.05	0.26	0.20	0.22	0.44	0.56
Marin	0.14	0.23	0.52	0.59	0.71	0.73	0.85	1.39	2.20
Mariposa	-	-	-	-	-	-	-	-	-
Mendocino	0.57	0.81	1.04	1.17	1.38	0.78	0.54	1.31	1.78
Merced	0.28	0.58	0.61	1.21	1.40	1.09	1.11	2.06	3.41
Modoc	-	-	0.16	0.16	0.16	0.15	0.17	0.42	0.62
Mono	-	0.06	0.06	0.02	-	-	-	-	-
Monterey	0.34	0.53	0.64	0.71	1.02	1.24	1.45	3.33	4.91
Napa	1.14	0.57	1.44	1.64	1.75	1.91	1.88	2.46	3.98
Nevada	0.10	0.15	0.34	0.35	0.42	0.44	0.70	1.45	1.77
Orange	0.07	0.27	0.91	1.11	1.24	1.32	1.68	3.40	5.45
Placer	-	-	0.13	0.25	0.24	0.36	0.44	0.72	1.14
Plumas	0.07	0.05	0.07	0.04	-	-	-	0.08	0.26
Riverside	-	-	1.23	1.59	1.43	1.23	1.52	4.63	7.98

Table 3-7 (continued)
Banks Assets by County
($ millions)

County*	1878**	1884**	1887	1890	1893	1896	1899	1905	1908
Sacramento	8.20	6.56	6.07	7.86	9.23	9.03	10.60	16.39	26.68
San Benito	0.30	0.52	0.55	0.62	0.97	1.04	1.13	2.12	2.67
San Bernardino	-	0.29	1.70	2.15	2.23	2.06	2.58	5.58	9.19
San Diego	0.38	0.23	3.28	5.02	2.56	2.25	2.36	5.60	9.31
San Francisco	112.38	113.60	140.38	167.56	197.04	193.32	228.82	388.08	378.07
San Joaquin	3.47	4.79	4.46	5.84	6.52	5.68	6.23	11.05	13.57
San LuisObispo	0.38	0.55	1.00	1.92	3.08	3.23	1.53	3.13	3.63
San Mateo	-	-	-	-	0.23	0.32	0.42	1.25	2.73
Santa Barbara	0.32	0.68	1.44	1.48	1.81	2.07	2.40	6.08	8.20
Santa Clara	4.66	3.91	4.98	6.55	8.32	8.80	7.90	14.39	18.44
Santa Cruz	0.72	0.85	1.28	1.62	2.27	2.48	2.98	4.88	5.94
Shasta	-	0.06	0.12	0.38	0.36	0.34	0.54	0.94	1.55
Sierra	-	-	0.11	0.06	0.04	0.02	-	0.02	0.07
Siskiyou	-	0.25	0.38	0.41	0.39	0.40	0.59	1.21	1.77
Solano	0.93	1.34	1.34	1.59	1.82	1.60	1.73	3.36	4.59
Sonoma	2.39	3.43	3.68	4.46	4.82	4.82	5.90	10.69	12.95
Stanilaus	-	0.58	0.73	1.12	1.47	1.18	1.28	2.84	4.21
Sutter	-	-	-	0.25	0.28	0.22	0.26	0.39	0.38
Tehama	0.33	0.72	1.63	1.44	1.62	1.10	1.22	1.78	2.31
Trinity	-	-	-	-	-	-	-	0.21	0.28
Tulare	0.32	0.40	0.89	1.41	2.27	2.06	2.42	5.11	6.79
Tuolome	-	-	-	-	-	-	0.26	0.56	1.10
Ventura	0.18	0.24	0.45	0.73	0.89	0.94	1.20	3.05	4.04
Yolo	0.68	2.03	2.28	2.63	3.12	2.76	3.10	4.10	4.76
Yuba	1.20	0.17	1.60	1.84	1.98	1.73	2.09	3.36	4.02

* Modern county boundaries were used for counties created after 1878; Imperial (1907) was included in San Diego.
** Does not include private banks.
Source: California State Board of Bank Commissioners, *Annual Report*, 1878-1908.

Table 3-8
Bank Deposits by County
($ millions)

County*	1878**	1884**	1887	1890	1893	1896	1899	1905	1908
Alameda	3.14	4.49	5.66	8.50	12.37	11.80	14.79	30.94	46.93
Alpine	-	-	-	-	-	-	-	-	-
Amador	-	-	-	-	-	0.05	0.11	0.41	0.54
Butte	0.41	0.36	0.37	0.64	0.62	0.51	0.74	2.04	3.43
Calaveras	-	-	-	-	-	-	-	0.30	0.48
Colusa	0.25	0.31	0.50	0.53	0.46	0.57	0.66	1.21	1.50
Contra Costa	0.13	0.16	0.19	0.29	0.34	0.38	0.31	1.02	1.96
Del Norte	-	-	-	-	-	-	-	0.09	0.12
El Dorado	-	-	0.02	0.04	0.03	0.06	0.12	0.43	0.37
Fresno	0.03	0.24	0.90	1.19	1.47	1.27	2.05	5.06	8.35
Glenn	-	0.17	0.16	0.17	0.22	0.24	0.25	0.54	0.64
Humbolt	0.06	0.28	0.52	1.17	1.21	1.12	1.64	4.09	4.96
Inyo	-	-	-	-	-	-	-	0.20	0.35
Kern	0.06	0.10	0.14	0.18	0.51	0.49	0.74	2.12	3.14
Kings	-	-	-	-	0.03	0.03	0.07	0.44	1.15
Lake	0.12	0.11	0.14	0.13	0.12	0.07	0.11	0.17	0.27
Lassen	-	-	-	-	0.04	0.03	0.16	0.20	0.28
Los Angeles	0.86	3.30	12.74	10.12	12.48	14.26	22.33	81.51	94.10
Madera	-	-	-	0.04	0.04	0.07	0.16	0.30	0.42
Marin	0.06	0.08	0.17	0.22	0.22	0.24	0.37	0.80	1.59
Mariposa	-	-	-	-	-	-	-	-	-
Mendocino	0.32	0.46	0.50	0.59	0.71	0.22	0.23	0.84	1.16
Merced	0.17	0.45	0.54	0.72	0.84	0.63	0.91	1.59	2.76
Modoc	-	-	0.04	0.02	0.04	0.04	0.07	0.19	0.36
Mono	-	0.03	0.01	0.01	-	-	-	-	-
Monterey	0.12	0.25	0.28	0.28	0.45	0.51	0.56	2.06	3.38
Napa	0.77	0.21	0.66	0.82	0.72	0.74	0.85	1.27	2.46
Nevada	0.05	0.10	0.18	0.22	0.27	0.30	0.54	1.23	1.28
Orange	0.03	0.19	0.71	0.65	0.75	0.81	1.19	2.37	3.66
Placer	-	-	0.04	0.16	0.12	0.23	0.33	0.53	0.83
Plumas	0.04	0.01	0.05	0.01	-	-	-	0.06	0.22
Riverside	-	-	0.83	1.09	0.83	0.88	1.21	3.64	5.41

Table 3-8 (continued)
Banks Assets by County
($ millions)

County*	1878**	1884**	1887	1890	1893	1896	1899	1905	1908
Sacramento	6.57	5.25	4.50	6.01	6.63	6.44	8.06	11.39	17.60
San Benito	0.13	0.18	0.23	0.26	0.41	0.44	0.51	1.25	1.68
S.Bernardino	-	0.18	1.22	1.30	1.22	1.15	1.68	4.11	6.62
San Diego	0.23	0.13	2.66	3.23	1.65	1.52	1.65	4.21	6.86
San Francisco	70.74	75.36	97.39	115.41	133.18	136.65	170.28	272.57	246.26
San Joaquin	1.62	2.54	2.63	3.42	3.91	3.38	3.74	7.58	9.63
SanLuisObispo	0.08	0.29	0.69	1.10	1.90	1.84	0.87	2.27	2.56
San Mateo	-	-	-	-	0.13	0.14	0.22	0.82	2.08
Santa Barbara	0.15	0.43	1.12	0.90	1.20	1.37	1.75	4.54	6.10
Santa Clara	2.57	2.11	2.63	3.75	4.74	5.00	5.18	10.76	13.75
Santa Cruz	0.46	0.51	0.89	1.16	1.58	1.73	2.14	3.84	4.65
Shasta	-	0.05	0.07	0.18	0.13	0.15	0.35	0.68	1.20
Sierra	-	-	0.06	0.04	0.03	-	-	0.02	0.03
Siskiyou	-	0.15	0.23	0.19	0.18	0.19	0.39	0.81	1.15
Solano	0.35	0.54	0.47	0.61	0.66	0.63	0.86	2.08	3.04
Sonoma	0.98	1.66	1.48	1.66	1.95	2.12	3.29	7.12	8.68
Stanislaus	-	0.17	0.29	0.54	0.82	0.63	0.71	1.64	2.87
Sutter	-	-	-	0.15	0.20	0.12	0.18	0.19	0.23
Tehama	0.13	0.34	0.41	0.45	0.53	0.42	0.56	0.95	1.41
Trinity	-	-	-	-	-	-	-	0.17	0.23
Tulare	0.09	0.11	0.52	0.71	1.05	0.91	1.31	3.51	4.55
Tuolome	-	-	-	-	-	-	0.15	0.45	0.89
Ventura	0.06	0.14	0.33	0.38	0.22	0.40	0.63	1.77	2.46
Yolo	0.18	0.58	0.91	0.77	1.03	0.73	0.99	1.80	2.32
Yuba	1.12	0.07	0.86	0.90	0.96	0.83	1.41	2.53	2.81

* Modern county boundaries were used for counties created after 1878; Imperial (1907) was included in San Diego.
** Does not include private banks.
Source: California State Board of Bank Commissioners, *Annual Report*, 1878-1908.

Table 3-9
Number of New Banks and of Exit Banks by County*

County**	1878-1884[a]	1884-1887[b]	1887-1890	1890-1893	1893-1896	1896-1899	1902-1905[c]	1905-1908
Alameda	2	1 (1)	2	9	2 (3)	1 (1)	7	20 (2)
Alpine	-	-	-	-	-	-	-	-
Amador	-	-	-	-	1	1	-	- (1)
Butte	-	1	1	2	- (1)	-	2	3
Calaveras	-	-	-	-	-	-	-	-
Colusa	-	-	-	1	-	-	-	1
Contra Costa	-	-	-	1	-	-	1	3
Del Norte	-	-	-	-	-	-	-	-
El Dorado	-	-	-	-	1	-	-	-
Fresno	3 (1)	3 (1)	1	3	- (3)	-	10	4
Glenn	1	1	-	-	-	- (1)	-	-
Humbolt	-	2	3	1	-	-	1	1
Inyo	-	-	-	-	-	-	-	-
Kern	-	-	-	3	-	-	-	1
Kings	-	-	-	2	-	-	3	2
Lake	-	-	-	-	-	-	-	-
Lassen	-	-	-	1	-	-	-	-
LosAngeles[a]	2	10	13 (3)	6 (2)	6 (3)	1 (2)	47 (6)	57 (19)
Madera	-	-	1	1	- (1)	-	1	-
Marin	-	-	-	-	-	1	-	2
Mariposa	-	-	-	-	-	-	-	-
Mendocino	-	1	-	1	- (1)	- (2)	4	2
Merced	-	-	1	-	- (1)	-	1	-
Modoc	-	-	-	-	-	-	1 (1)	1
Mono	1	1 (1)	-	- (1)	-	-	-	-
Monterey	-	-	1	2	1 (1)	1	3	1
Napa	1 (1)	1	-	1	2	- (1)	-	2 (2)
Nevada	-	1	-	-	- (1)	-	- (1)	-
Orange[a]	1	2	2	-	3 (1)	-	4 (2)	9
Placer	-	-	1	- (1)	1	- (1)	2	3 (1)
Plumas	- (2)	-	-	- (1)	-	-	1	-
Riverside[a]	-	2	3	5 (2)	- (3)	2 (1)	2 (1)	6 (1)
Sacramento	2	-	-	1	-	1	5	1 (1)
San Benito	-	-	-	3	-	-	-	-
SBernardino[a]	2	2	4	2 (1)	1 (2)	1	4 (1)	9 (1)

County**	1878-1884[a]	1884-1887[b]	1887-1890	1890-1893	1893-1896	1896-1899	1902-1905[c]	1905-1908
San Diego	- (1)	3	8 (1)	2 (4)	1 (2)	1 (1)	6	10 (4)
San Francisco	2 (2)	1	5 (2)	4 (4)	2 (3)	6 (3)	26 (3)	16 (19)
San Joaquin	1 (1)	- (2)	2	-	-	-	1	4
SanLuisObispo	-	1	4	2	1 (1)	- (3)	2	1 (1)
San Mateo	-	-	-	1	1	-	4	2
Santa Barbara	-	2	1	2	-	-	6	-
Santa Clara	1 (1)	1	3	4 (1)	1	2 (1)	1 (2)	5
Santa Cruz	-	1	3	2	-	-	-	-
Shasta	1	-	1	-	-	-	1	-
Sierra	-	-	-	-	1 (1)	- (1)	1	1 (1)
Siskiyou	1	-	-	-	-	-	3	2
Solano	2 (1)	-	-	-	1 (1)	-	4 (1)	1
Sonoma	1	2	1	1	1	-	6	1 (1)
Stanislaus	1	-	2	-	-	-	6	2 (1)
Sutter	-	-	1	-	-	-	-	-
Tehama	-	-	-	-	-	-	1	-
Trinity	-	-	-	-	-	-	1	-
Tulare	-	2	3	4	-	- (2)	2 (1)	5
Tuolome	-	-	-	-	-	2	1 (1)	-
Ventura[s]	-	-	2	-	-	-	4	5
Yolo	1	1	-	1	1	-	-	2
Yuba	2 (1)	1 (1)	1	-	-	-	-	-
California	29 (11)	43 (6)	70 (6)	68 (17)	28 (29)	20 (20)	175 (20)	185 (55)

* Exit banks in parentheses.
** Modern county boundaries were used for counties created after 1878; Imperial (1907) was included in San Diego.
a Does not include private banks.
b Includes those private banks less than three years old in 1887. Does not include private banks exiting between 1884 and 1887.
c Entry banks are those banks less than three years old in 1905.
s County in southern portion of the state.
Source: California State Board of Bank Commissioners, *Annual Report*, 1878-1908.

Table 3-10
Bank Deposits per $100 of County Wealth
(dollars)

County	1878	1884	1887	1890	1893	1896	1899	1905	1908
Alameda	7.3	8.0	9.5	11.1	13.7	13.0	17.5	27.0	24.9
Alpine	-	-	-	-	-	-	-	-	-
Amador	-	-	-	-	-	1.2	2.6	8.0	9.8
Butte	3.9	2.4	2.2	3.5	3.7	4.0	5.7	12.8	18.3
Calaveras	-	-	-	-	-	-	-	5.0	7.9
Colusa	3.8	2.9	4.1	4.1	3.4	5.1	5.8	10.3	12.3
Contra Costa	1.7	1.3	1.3	1.9	2.2	2.7	2.1	5.1	7.4
Del Norte	-	-	-	-	-	-	-	2.8	3.1
El Dorado	-	-	0.5	1.1	0.8	1.6	3.2	9.7	7.5
Fresno	0.5	2.3	5.0	3.9	4.5	5.1	7.9	14.5	17.5
Glenn	-	1.9	1.6	1.6	1.9	2.6	2.6	5.4	5.8
Humbolt	1.2	3.0	3.7	6.6	6.8	7.2	10.2	16.6	17.3
Inyo	-	-	-	-	-	-	-	8.0	9.6
Kern	1.2	1.8	1.9	1.7	4.3	3.5	5.6	9.7	10.6
Kings	-	-	-	-	0.4	0.6	1.1	5.7	12.5
Lake	5.4	3.7	4.3	3.4	3.1	2.4	3.9	4.9	7.6
Lassen	-	-	-	-	1.4	1.3	5.6	3.8	5.0
Los Angeles	5.8	11.8	18.3	13.3	16.1	15.9	23.6	33.9	20.7
Madera	-	-	-	0.7	0.6	1.3	3.1	4.8	5.9
Marin	0.8	0.8	1.7	2.0	1.8	2.3	3.3	6.0	9.5
Mariposa	-	-	-	-	-	-	-	-	-
Mendocino	5.5	5.5	5.0	5.1	6.1	2.0	2.3	7.0	8.4
Merced	3.2	4.7	4.5	5.3	6.0	5.4	7.6	11.8	18.3
Modoc	-	-	1.4	0.8	1.2	1.5	2.5	4.5	6.9
Mono	-	1.3	0.9	0.7	-	-	-	-	-
Monterey	1.7	2.5	2.3	1.9	2.6	3.3	3.5	11.8	15.5
Napa	9.6	1.9	5.3	5.9	5.3	6.5	7.7	9.7	17.1
Nevada	0.7	1.7	3.3	4.1	5.2	5.2	8.6	18.6	18.9
Orange	2.2	5.5	8.3	7.0	8.0	8.7	11.3	17.2	17.5
Placer	-	-	0.5	2.0	1.5	3.1	4.7	7.1	10.3
Plumas	2.2	0.6	2.2	0.6	-	-	-	1.6	4.5
Riverside	-	-	9.2	9.4	6.9	8.2	11.4	27.0	27.1

Table 3-10 (continued)
Banks Deposits per $100 of County Wealth
(dollars)

County	1878	1884	1887	1890	1893	1896	1899	1905	1908
Sacramento	35.8	20.1	15.7	18.4	20.1	19.9	25.1	31.8	32.3
San Benito	3.3	3.7	4.1	4.2	6.5	7.3	9.0	19.8	25.1
S.Bernardino	-	4.0	13.4	10.2	7.9	8.0	12.6	25.2	27.8
San Diego	14.9	2.5	13.6	13.5	7.2	7.8	9.0	20.3	19.9
San Francisco	29.5	31.2	38.7	34.8	35.5	37.3	43.8	58.3	51.9
San Joaquin	9.1	7.1	7.9	9.3	10.6	10.9	12.7	21.8	23.3
S.LuisObispo	1.8	3.5	5.9	8.1	13.3	15.2	7.9	16.9	17.1
San Mateo	-	-	-	-	0.8	1.0	1.6	4.6	8.3
Santa Barbara	3.5	5.4	7.8	5.8	7.7	10.4	14.1	25.8	25.1
Santa Clara	9.6	6.3	6.0	7.2	8.7	9.2	10.3	19.2	21.7
Santa Cruz	7.5	7.0	10.2	10.9	13.3	16.1	21.2	30.7	28.5
Shasta	-	1.4	1.8	3.4	2.3	2.8	5.2	6.3	9.5
Sierra	-	-	3.4	2.6	2.4	0.2	-	0.9	1.6
Siskiyou	-	3.7	5.3	3.2	2.6	2.5	5.5	7.5	8.0
Solano	4.0	3.4	2.7	3.3	3.6	4.2	5.4	11.6	15.7
Sonoma	6.3	7.3	5.5	5.7	6.8	8.5	13.9	24.4	27.0
Stanilaus	-	1.1	2.0	3.5	5.2	5.1	6.6	12.9	18.4
Sutter	-	-	-	1.6	2.2	2.0	3.1	3.2	3.7
Tehama	3.2	4.4	4.3	4.1	5.2	4.8	5.7	8.6	12.1
Trinity	-	-	-	-	-	-	-	8.0	8.1
Tulare	2.6	1.6	4.5	4.5	6.5	6.6	9.9	22.2	17.7
Tuolome	-	-	-	-	-	-	2.9	6.3	12.2
Ventura	1.9	3.1	5.1	5.1	2.8	5.9	8.8	19.9	17.5
Yolo	1.8	3.6	5.0	3.9	5.3	4.8	6.6	11.7	13.6
Yuba	26.1	1.3	14.0	13.4	14.5	16.3	29.3	46.0	44.5

Source: Tables 3-5 and 3-8

Chapter 4

A Model of the Banking Firm

Introduction

In this chapter, a model of the individual banking firm is developed that predicts bank behavior under the assumption of profit maximization. The objective in developing this model is to be able to analyze bank behavior, and so answer questions that were raised in the preceding chapters. One important question, for example, is whether a bank's behavior was affected by the bank's capital position. Another issue is to see how the demand for loans affected a bank's behavior. The impact of banking regulation can also be explored with the model. The estimations of the model using data for California's banks between 1878 and 1908 are presented in Chapter 5 below.

The role of market concentration in determining banking behavior continues to be an important issue both for the current analysis of bank behavior, and for the importance of banking in the development of U.S. capital markets. The assumption underlying the model developed here is that an individual bank is an imperfect competitor in the market for loans; that is, a bank does not lose all its borrowers when it raises the rate it charges on loans. In the market for securities, however, the bank is a price taker; changes in the amount of securities the bank holds do not affect the rate the bank earns on securities. This view of the banking firm, which is discussed in more detail below, was first presented by Chandler (1938), who argued that banks fit the description of monopolistic competitors. The model presented in this chapter has its origins in a paper by Shull (1963) where Shull applies the theory of a price discriminating, multi-product firm to banks. Shull's approach is more elaborately modeled in Broaddus (1972; 1974), Klein (1970; 1971), and Miller (1975).[1] Wood (1975) extends the model to include more than one time period. John Scott (1977) amplifies the multi-product nature of the banking firm. Graddy and Kyle (1979) explore the implications of market imperfections in both asset and liability markets. In research in economic history, Shull's approach is used by Keehn (1971) to evaluate bank performance in Wisconsin in the nineteenth century. Sylla (1968) also employs the price-discriminating, multi-product firm in his analysis of national banking in the nineteenth century.

The development of the model in this chapter is carried out in two stages. First, the banking firm is analyzed as a firm that possesses market power in supplying bank loans and bank deposits. The bank is thus a monopolist in both goods. Economic theory is well equipped to analyze such a firm, and the model yields unambiguous predictions about individual bank behavior. The analysis in this section follows that of Broaddus, Klein, and Miller, but it differs in one important respect from the model used by Klein and Miller. In the second stage, the implications of the presence of other banks is explored. The individual bank's actions no longer take place in isolation. Reflecting the state of economic theory in the field of imperfect competition, the predictions derived in this stage are less clear-cut.

The Model

Underlying Assumptions. The model developed below predicts the bank's choices of the level of deposits, loans, reserves, and securities under the assumption that the bank maximizes the rate of return on its given level of capital. The model is a short-run model in which the bank makes decisions for one period only. The one-period time horizon implies that there are no interactions between the bank's choices about its decision variables in this period and its set of choices in the next period. This assumption appears reasonable in the context of the cross-section analysis carried out in this study.[2] While the bank's owners can increase the bank's funds by adding to its capital, the level of a bank's capital generally reflects long-term considerations, including expectations about future earnings, the composition of the liability portfolio, and the risk of failure.[3] For the short-run model developed here, the bank's capital is assumed to be fixed.

Demand for the Bank's Funds. The demand for loans from the bank is given by

$$r = l(L), \tag{1}$$

where r is the rate of return on loans. The only variable dimension of loans is assumed to be r. Other terms such as maturity, collateral, penalties for late payments, etc., are assumed to move with r. The bank is the only seller of its own loans. By assumption, any increase in the rate charged reduces the amount of loans the bank can make. That is,

$$\frac{\delta l}{\delta r} < 0. \tag{2}$$

For the moment, it is assumed that the probability of default is zero so that the rate charged by the bank equals the rate it expects to earn.

The bank is assumed to be a price taker in the market for securities. The bank must accept the going rate of interest on funds placed in securities. Thus,

$$s = \bar{s} \tag{3}$$

where s is the interest rate paid on securities, and $\bar{s}$ is the going market rate.[4] Provided banks face the same probability distribution of security prices, s can be formally adjusted for changes in the prices of securities by calling it the expected return on securities without affecting the results of the model.

Reserves Against Net Disbursement of Cash. If the bank holds no cash reserves, it must borrow or sell securities to meet any excess of withdrawals over receipts during the period. It is assumed that, in meeting net disbursements, the bank must either pay a penalty for borrowed funds, or accept some loss due to the hurried sale of securities. Banks cannot control the flow of funds, the withdrawal of deposits, payment on loans, or funds and drafts drawn on other banks. Thus, net disbursements are a random variable, albeit one whose distribution is approximately known by the bank. As was discussed in Chapter 2 above, there were no reserve requirements for state incorporated banks for most of the period 1878-1908. When such requirements were imposed in 1905, there were no provisions for enforcing them.

Assume that net disbursement, w, has a density function $F(w)$. In meeting net disbursements, the bank must either pay a penalty for borrowed funds or accept some loss on the hurried sale of securities that is assumed to be n per dollar of cash shortage. With no reserves, the bank would have an expected cost of covering the net disbursement of

$$n\int_0^c wF(w)dw \tag{4}$$

where c is the maximum possible net disbursement.

If the bank holds reserves of R, it has to pay a penalty only if the net disbursement exceeds reserves. That is, only if $w - R > 0$.

The cost of the net disbursement then falls to

$$n\int_R^c (w-R)F(w)dw. \tag{5}$$

For simplicity, assume $F(w)$ has a rectangular distribution equal to $1/(c-b)$, where b is the lowest possible net disbursement. The cost of net disbursements becomes

$$n\int_R^c (w-r)F(w)dw = n[(c-R)^2/2(c-b)]. \tag{6}$$

Cost of Deposits. The supply of deposits to the bank is given by

$$i = d(D), \tag{7}$$

where i is the cost of deposits for the bank. This cost combines both explicit payments of interest and any implicit services on deposits. It is assumed that the supply of deposits to the bank is less than perfectly elastic. That is,

$$\frac{\delta d}{\delta D} > 0. \tag{8}$$

Maximizing the Rate of Profit. The bank's profits are equal to the revenue it earns on its assets minus the cost of obtaining funds. Thus,

$$P = rL + sS - n[(c-R)^2/2(c-b) - iD, \tag{9}$$

where S represents the bank's holdings of securities. The rate of profit is

$$p = \frac{P}{K} = \frac{1}{K}\{rL + sS - n(c-R)^2/2(c-b) - iD\}, \tag{10}$$

where K is the bank's capital. The bank's optimal choices for its decision variables are determined by maximizing the rate of profit, P, subject to the balance sheet constraint, that is, maximize

$$p=\frac{1}{K}\{rL+sS-n[(c-R)^2/2(c-b)]-iD\},$$

subject to $L + S + R - D - K = 0$. The following first order conditions are generated, where λ is the Lagrangean multiplier.

$$\frac{\delta p}{\delta L}=\frac{1}{K}\{l(L)+l'(L)L\}-\lambda=0, \tag{11}$$

$$\frac{\delta p}{\delta S}=\frac{1}{K}S-\lambda=0, \tag{12}$$

$$\frac{\delta p}{\delta R}=\frac{1}{K}\{n(c-R)/(c-b)\}-\lambda=0, \tag{13}$$

$$\frac{\delta p}{\delta D}=-d(D)=d'(D)D+\lambda=0, \tag{14}$$

$$\frac{\delta p}{\delta \lambda}=L+S+R-D-K=0. \tag{15}$$

The first order conditions indicate certain optimal choices for the bank. From equations (12) and (14), the optimal level of deposits occurs when the marginal cost of obtaining deposits equals the rate of return on securities, i.e., when

$$d(D) + D\, d'\, (D) = s.$$

Since the level of the bank's capital is predetermined, the deposit decision also determines the level of deposit liabilities plus capital and, hence, the level of assets. From equations (11) and (12) the optimal level of loans occurs when the marginal return on loans equals the return on securities, i.e., when

$$l\, (L) + l'\, (L) = S.$$

Combining equations (12) and (13) shows that the optimal level of reserves occurs when the marginal return on reserves equals the rate of return on securities, i.e., when

$$n(c - R)/(c-b)=s.$$

Thus, reserves are increased until the reduction in the cost of borrowing to meet net disbursements from an additional dollar of reserves equals the opportunity cost of an additional dollar of reserves. This result establishes an important feature of the bank's behavior: the optimal amount of the bank's reserves is independent of the marginal return on loans, and hence, independent of the amount of loans the bank makes.

Unfortunately, the available data do not permit the estimation of this model because only balance sheet data are consistently available for California's banks for the period 1878-1908. Very few figures are available for the rates charged on loans, the rates paid on deposits, or the pattern of disbursements. However, the bank's choice of the composition of its asset portfolio is amenable to analysis with balance sheet data. The next three sub-sections show how the bank's optimal portfolio choice is determined.

The Optimal Asset Portfolio. Given that the bank has chosen the level of funds it desires by equating the marginal cost of funds to the rate of return on securities, the bank must now choose what proportion of these assets to place in loans (X_L), securities (X_S), and reserves (X_R). Because the bank's loan demand is assumed to be less than perfectly elastic, an increase in the proportion of loans in the portfolio can only be obtained if the bank lowers the rate charged on loans. The bank's loan demand is given by

$$r = f(X_L), \text{ where } f'(X_L) < 0.$$

Expected rates on loans are still assumed to equal actual rates.

Since the securities market is perfectly competitive, variations in the proportion of securities, X_S, do not affect the rate of return on securities.

Assume that net disbursement per dollar of assets, y, has a density function $F(y)$. With no cash reserves, the penalty per dollar of net disbursement is

$$n\int_o^c yF(y)dy,$$

where c is the maximum possible net disbursement per dollar of funds, and n is the cost of borrowing per dollar of funds. When the bank holds a proportion of its assets in reserves (X_R), the cost of net disbursement per dollar of assets becomes

$$n\int_X^c (y-X_R)F(y)d.$$

For simplicity, assume $F(y)$ has a uniform distribution equal to $1/(c-b)$, where b is the lowest possible net disbursement per dollar of assets. The cost of net disbursement is now

$$n\int_X^c (y-X_R)F(y)dz = n[(c-X_R)^2/2(c-b)].$$

The bank's optimization problem is to choose its asset portfolio so as to maximize the return on its assets, p, that is, maximize

$$p = f(X_L)X_L + sX_s - n[(c-X_R)/2(c-b)],$$

subject to the constraint,

$$X_L + X_s + X_R = 1.$$

Solving this problem generates the following first order conditions, where λ is the Lagrangean multiplier:

$$\frac{\delta p}{\delta X_L} = f(X_L) + f'(X_L) - \lambda = 0, \tag{i}$$

$$\frac{\delta p}{\delta X_s} = S - \lambda = 0, \tag{ii}$$

$$\frac{\delta p}{\delta X_R} = n(c-X_R)/(c-b) - \lambda = 0. \tag{iii}$$

Equations (i) and (ii) imply that the optimal proportion of loans occurs when the marginal return to X_L equals the return on securities, i.e.,

$$f(X_L) + f'(X_L)X_L = s.$$

From equations (ii) and (iii), the optimal proportion of reserves occurs when the marginal reduction in the cost of net disbursements equals the rate of return on securities. With X_L and X_R determined, X_s is a residual. These optimal portfolio choices are similar to those obtained above for the levels of loans, reserves, etc., in that the marginal returns to X_L and to X_R are equated with the given return on securities, which is the opportunity cost of funds. As a result, the decision about loans is again independent of the decision about reserves.

These results are similar to those obtained by Klein (1971) for his loan/asset model with one important difference. Klein finds that the optimal level of deposits occurs when the marginal cost of deposits equals the average return on the bank's assets, not the marginal return, here equated with s. The difference in the results hinges on the nature of the loan demand function and the decision-making process. The optimal asset portfolio choice portion of the model presented in this section assumes that the level of total funds is determined by the bank increasing deposits until the marginal cost of deposits equals the marginal return on securities, s. Klein, however, includes the rate paid on deposits among his decision variables to be determined simultaneously with the loan/asset ratio. But, to solve for the optimal conditions, Klein implicitly assumes that

$$\delta f(X_L)/\delta i = 0,$$

that is, he is assuming that any increase in funds obtained by increasing i, the rate paid on deposits, is allocated in the same proportions to loans, securities, and reserves as the funds already in the bank.[5] Thus, under this assumption, new funds earn the same average rate as existing funds. Yet, Klein also assumes that the loan/asset ratio varies with the rate charged on loans, implying a downward sloping demand curve for loans; any increase in the volume of loans due to an increase in deposits would reduce the rate charged on all loans. Thus, Klein's simultaneous approach appears to contain a contradiction that is avoided in the approach taken here, in which the level of assets and the allocation of assets are determined sequentially.

Adjusting Loan Demand for Risk. Assume the probability of loan default is no longer zero, but other aspects of the loan remain the same. The return the bank's management expects to earn on a loan is now less than the contracted rate, that is

$$e = \int rG(r)dr,$$

where e is the expected rate of return on loans, and $G(r)$ is the density function for r, which is assumed to be a random variable.[6] As long as the probability of default exceeds zero, e will be less than r. Hence, the return the bank can expect to earn is given by

$$e = g(XL), \quad \text{where} \quad \frac{\delta g}{\delta X_L} < 0.$$

If the management is risk neutral, it need only consider the expected return on loans to maximize expected profits. A risk averse management, however, requires some payment for incurring risk. Instead of an analysis employing a utility function, a simpler approach to risk aversion, proposed by Pratt (1964), is taken here. Suppose an individual is offered a choice between a proposition with an uncertain payoff and cash. Assume that the individual is indifferent between the proposition and a certain amount of cash, I. Then a measure of the individual's risk aversion, V, is the difference between the expected payoff of the proposition, E, and I, that is,

$$V = E - I,$$

where $V > 0$ implies risk aversion.

If the management is risk averse, then it is not indifferent between the expected return on a loan, e, and some certain return, i. A measure of the management's risk aversion, v, is the difference between the two rates, i.e.,

$$e - i = v, \text{ where } v > 0.$$

Thus, risk aversion can be directly introduced into the management's view of the loan demand function the bank faces. The contracted rate r must be adjusted for the probability of default and for the management's risk aversion.

The bank's management must also take into account the risk of the bank's failure when making loans. If the value of the bank's assets falls below its liabilities, the bank fails. The difference between the bank's total assets and its liabilities equals the bank's net worth. The smaller is the bank's net worth relative to its liabilities, the more the bank is exposed to the risk of failure.[7] Thus, a bank with a given ratio of net worth to liabilities can have the same probability of failure, *ceteris paribus*, as a bank with a lower ratio of net worth to liabilities.

Combining these two aspects of risk, risk aversion and the bank's net worth position gives the following premium

$$q = Q(v,k),$$

where v is the management's risk aversion, and k is a measure of the structure of the bank's liabilities.

The loan demand function can now be adjusted for all aspects of risk to give the following function:

$$e = g(X_L) - Q(v,k),$$

or, $e = h(X_L, v, k)$, where

$$\frac{\delta h}{\delta X_L} > 0, \quad \frac{\delta h}{\delta v} < 0, \text{ and } \quad \frac{\delta h}{\delta k} > 0.$$

The Effect of Differences in Market Power. The next section contains a discussion of the nature of the bank's market power. The concern here is for the effect of differences in a bank's market power on its loan decision. As a first step, the optimization condition can be restated as follows:

$$MR_{X_L} = h(X_L, v, k) + h'(X_L, v, k) = s.$$

But, the marginal revenue from increasing the proportion of loans in the bank's portfolio, with a given level of assets, can be rewritten as:

$$MR_{X_L} = e\left(1 - \frac{1}{E}\right),$$

where E is the elasticity of X_L with respect to e. Thus, when the bank is maximizing its profits, it is charging a loan rate, e, such that

$$e = \frac{s}{(1 - 1/E)}$$

Since the profit-maximizing firms facing a downward sloping demand curve never produce where the demand curve is inelastic, i.e., where marginal revenue is negative, E will always be greater than one. Hence, e will always be larger than s.

As the elasticity of the loan demand function increases, e tends towards s. The loan rate the bank charges to maximize profits moves closer to the rate earned on securities. The bank's mark-up falls. Under the assumption that the elasticity of a bank's loan demand function varies with the bank's market power, this model predicts that banks with less market power will charge lower rates than banks with more market power, and have higher loan/asset ratios. The next section discusses the sources of banks' market power.

Competition with Other Banks

Market Power of Individual Banks. The major assumption underlying this model is that individual banks possess market power, that is, a bank can raise the rate it charges on loans without losing all its borrowers. Chandler (1938) suggests several sources for this market power. One source is product differentiation among banks. Each bank has certain characteristics that make it unique, and on which customers base their choice of what bank to patronize. Chandler suggests the following characteristics are important: the age of the bank; its record for honesty, fair dealing and safety; the location, size, and architecture of its building; the social and financial standing of its officers and directors; and the quality of its services. Of these, he considers location to be especially important.[8]

A second source of market power is customer inertia. Bank customers establish a "habitual or continuing relationship not likely to be terminated by the buyer without deliberation, delay, and a prospect of obtaining significantly more attractive terms elsewhere."[9] One benefit that might be lost is a line-of-credit. Longtime customers may have better access to credit during times of credit restriction than new customers. Customer inertia is due in part to the convenience of established relationships. But, Chandler stresses, it is also due to a lack of knowledge. "Lack of knowledge diminishes in two ways the elasticity of a customer's demand for loans at his own bank. The customer's ignorance of borrowing opportunities elsewhere reduces his available alternatives. The ignorance of banks, other than his own, concerning his credit worthiness has the same effect."[10] Chandler believes this ignorance explains much of the monopolistic element in banking.

To the extent that information is costly to collect, Chandler's stress on inadequate information is well placed. It suggests an interesting application of Akerlof's "lemons" principle. If a borrower requests a loan from a bank other than his current bank, the former bank has good reason to suspect that the borrower is a poor credit risk, i.e., a "lemon." Accordingly, all such borrowers are classed as lemons to economize on information costs. This raises the interest rate the bank-switching borrower must pay on his loan, regardless of his characteristics. Thus, the market operates to tie borrowers to their present banks.[11]

The cost to banks of gathering information about out-of-town borrowers also serves to tie borrowers to their local banks. Edwards (1964) suggests that, in lending to out-of-town borrowers, banks must incur not only "transportation costs," but also additional risk and expense as compared to lending to local borrowers. The credit rating of out-of-town borrowers is more likely to be unknown than that of local borrowers, increasing the risk attached to the loan. Alternatively, the bank must gather sufficient information to establish the borrower's credit rating. Another factor for the bank to consider in making an out-of-town business loan is the amount of funds the borrower will keep on deposit at the bank.[12] Local loans are likely to be more attractive, if borrowers keep balances at the bank and if the funds spent by the borrowers remain in the local market, particularly if the lending bank can expect to gain from this redepositing. On this basis, the more isolated a market, the more attractive local loans are likely to be.[13]

A borrower's location also affects the borrower's costs of gathering information. If the borrower wishes to change banks, he must gather information about other banks, including their rates, other charges, services, past record, etc. While these costs may not be substantial for nearby banks, they clearly increase with the distance between the borrower and the alternative bank. Thus, borrowers tend to be tied to local banks by the costs of gathering information about out-of-town banks.[14]

The extent to which a borrower is tied to his local bank depends also on the size of the borrower's business and the size of his loan.[15] Large concerns are more likely to have established reputations than small businesses. They are also less risky. As loan size increases, the cost of obtaining information about alternatives falls for both lender and borrower. The market for large loans is more competitive than the market for small loans, because there are more alternatives available to large borrowers.

While distance and the associated information costs restrict competition from out-of-town banks, local banks nevertheless face the threat of competition from new banks. This threat limits the extent of their market power. Even if high rates and poor service do not attract funds from outside the local market, they are very likely to result in the formation of another bank. If bank regulations exist that reduce bank entry, then banks are able to enjoy market power for longer, or exploit it more fully, than they would without regulations. Regulations of this type are therefore considered an important, for some writers the most important,[16] source of banks' market power.[17]

Although bank entry was not restricted during 1878-1908, the cost of gathering information was probably higher than it is today. In the nineteenth century, credit markets were much more informal than today. For example, the credit rating of borrowers was only beginning. Instead, bankers prided themselves on their ability to discern the credit-worthiness of a borrower from personal contact.[18] Distance therefore substantially increased the cost of establishing a borrower's credit rating. At that time, many of the loans at California commercial banks were on personal security, i.e., unsecured. Information-gathering also raised the cost to the nineteenth century borrower of finding an alternative source of funds. The severity of financial panics during the nineteenth century made established customer relationships with their informal lines-of-credit even more important than today. Thus, borrowers were tied to their local banks by the cost of information-gathering as well as any "transportation" costs.

In combination, these factors provide a basis for banks to possess market power, where market power is taken to mean that a bank can raise its loan rate without losing all its borrowers. With more market power, a bank can raise its rates further while losing the same amount of business as a bank with less market power. This implies the elasticity of the loan demand function a bank faces varies inversely with the bank's market power. Thus, according to the model, banks with more market power, facing less elastic demand for their loans, will have lower loan/asset ratios than banks with less market power. (See section above.) The extent of banks' market power is not unlimited. The major factor restricting this power is the presence of other banks.

Market Concentration, Competition and Bank Behavior. Economists have taken a variety of avenues in analyzing the behavior of firms under imperfect competition. In general, studies of bank behavior have relied on the structure-conduct-performance approach as a basis for their analysis.[19] This approach, first elaborated in Bain (1951), argues that the structure of the firms in a market influences the conduct of these firms. A market's structure depends upon the degree of seller concentration, the degree of buyer concentration, the degree of product differentiation among the sellers, and the condition of entry into the market.[20] Market structure influences the type of pricing policies followed by firms in the market, and the interaction among competing firms.[21] In markets where sellers are few and entry is difficult, this approach suggests that firms collude, or at least coordinate their actions. As a result, prices are above the level that would obtain in a highly competitive market, and/or the quality of service is below that of a highly competitive market. Thus, a highly structured market has poor market performance, where market performance is the "composite of end results in the dimensions of price, output, production cost, selling cost, product design, and so forth, which enterprises arrive at in any market."[22] In practice, it has proved difficult to evaluate market conduct. Instead, most research on banking and on other industries investigates the relationship between market structure and market performance, leaving out the market conduct link.

Studies of banking have usually focused on the relationship between market concentration and the performance of individual banks in a market. Banks in markets where banking resources are concentrated in the hands of a few banks are expected to be able to coordinate their policies, resulting in higher prices to the consumer of banking services and higher profits to the banks than would occur in unconcentrated markets. Most studies test for an association between market concentration and bank profits, prices, or some other measure of performance such as the loan/asset ratio, the ratio of time deposits to total deposits, the types of loan offered, etc. Market concentration is typically measured by the market share of the three largest banks, the Herfindahl index (the sum of the squared market share of each bank in the market), or the number of banks.[23]

A key problem with the structure-conduct-performance approach to bank behavior under imperfect competition is defining the market. One facet of this problem is determining which firms should be included as competitors in providing banking services; this is called the line-of-commerce question. Another aspect of this problem is defining the appropriate geographic boundaries of the market. This is a long-standing problem in both the economic analysis of monopolies and the enforcement of anti-trust laws.[24] It is often very difficult to determine the substitutes for any particular product or define the limits of a firm's market. At some price, there is usually a substitute for almost any good, and if the price is low enough, customers will usually be willing to travel farther than they normally do to buy a good.

In the analysis of bank behavior, competition from non-financial institutions has generally been ignored. Competition from non-bank financial intermediaries has occasionally been incorporated into empirical work, with savings and loan associations being the type of intermediary most commonly included. While economic research has been willing to look at banking as having various lines of competition, the judicial system has determined that banking is a single line of commerce. Until recently, banks were the only supplier of demand deposits and were the major supplier of business loans. Because of the links among financial services, banks were viewed as providing a package of services that could not be matched by any other financial institutions.[25]

The importance of convenience in the provision of banking services has played a key role in the defining of banking markets. Retail customers are viewed as placing a high value on convenience in deciding which bank to patronize. The implication is that few customers would travel to another town, or even across town, to patronize a bank with lower prices, unless the prices were substantially lower. Substantially is taken to mean low enough to compensate for the added inconvenience of out-of-town banking. This view also applies to the provision of bank services to businesses. Credit for small businesses is limited by banks' knowledge of their local economy and the health of local businesses. The farther away is the credit applicant, the more expensive is the cost of evaluating the applicant's credit worthiness. Thus, there are reasonable grounds for viewing banks as having local markets for their services.[26]

What is difficult is defining these local markets. A common approach, and one that is taken in this study, is to adopt political boundaries on the grounds of expediency; in this study, counties are used to approximate local markets. Data are readily available for such entities, particularly for standard metropolitan statistical areas (SMSAs), which comprise those counties containing metropolitan areas of a certain size, and thus SMSAs have commonly been used as definitions of local banking markets. A more refined approach is to consider commuter patterns and various other factors to determine retail markets, as in the case of the Rand-McNally Metropolitan Areas (RMAs). Even more detailed work has been undertaken at various Federal Reserve Banks to identify the relevant banking markets for the analysis of the anti-competitive effects of bank holding company acquisitions. While these more refined definitions are probably closer to the actual markets, they require considerable work.[27]

Moreover, they are still open to the criticism that the level of prices determines the market. As Osborne and Wendell (1978) observe, if the banks in a geographically defined market lower their prices, customers from outside the market may buy services from the banks. Thus, the market's boundaries are determined in part by the current pricing policies of the banks in the market. Taken to its extreme, this criticism implies that all banks compete with each other, and the relevant market is national or even international in scope. The importance of convenience in banking, however, suggests that local banking markets may serve as a first approximation for the area over which banks could exert market power.[28]

Beside the difficulties with the definition of the banking market, there is also the question of the relationship between concentration of banks in a market, the level of competition among banks, and the extent of banks' market power.[29] Economic theory demonstrates that a profit maximizing monopolist charges a higher price than would obtain in a perfectly competitive industry. What is not clear is how additional firms affect the level of competition in a once-monopolized market. It is likely that more firms will increase competition, but the extent of this increase is not known.

Information costs provide one justification for the concentration-performance approach to bank behavior. Stigler (1964) argues that in markets where there are few firms the problem for the firms is policing a collusive agreement.[30] Any individual firm can improve its position by undercutting the collusively agreed upon price. The harder it is to detect such price cutting, the more likely price cutting will destroy any collusive agreement. Because the probability of detecting a price cut falls as both the number of sellers and the number of buyers rises, increasing the number of firms in the market strengthens competition. Price-cutting is inferred from the shifting of customers between firms. As the number of firms increases, the incentive to cut prices rises; a price cutter has more firms to gain customers from, yet the probability of detection falls.

If the firms are unequal in size, Stigler suggests that this inequality reduces the incentive to cut prices because changes in the distribution of customers due to price cutting are more rapidly detected than when the firms are all equal in size.[31] To determine whether price cutting is occurring, firms observe their market share. But there is some random variation in market shares as firms attract new customers and lose existing customers. Stigler shows that the variance of market shares depends, in part, upon the sum of the squared market shares of the firms in the market, i.e., the Herfindahl Index. Hence, the greater the concentration of the firms in the market, measured by the Herfindahl index, the lower the probability that any change in market share is due to chance. Thus, price cutting is more readily detectable in markets where concentration is high rather than low.

Price cutting is a competitive action, which brings some gain in profits to the price cutter if the market's price is above the competitive price. The extent and duration of this gain depend upon information costs, according to Nutter and Moore (1976). If both buyers and sellers must search for information on prices, then price cuts cannot be instantly matched by other firms. Nutter and Moore conclude that increasing the number of firms makes future prices more uncertain, thereby making price cutting more attractive to each firm.[32] Hence, the probability that some firm will opt for the immediate gain of a price cut also rises. Having more firms in the market leads to more competitive behavior (price cutting) and better market performance (lower prices) than having fewer firms. Thus, the concentration of banks in a market or the number of banks in the market affects the competitive behavior of the banks in the market.

The formation of a new bank in the market will also affect the competitive behavior of the existing banks. By increasing the number of banks and upsetting any established market shares, the entry of a new bank makes it more difficult for the existing banks to discover price cutting. Thus, a market's structure depends not only on the concentration of resources among the banks in the market, but also on the rate of entry of new banks into the market. Both factors help to determine the level of competition in the market.

This kind of bank behavior suggests that banks in highly concentrated markets where the rate of bank entry is low would have a greater ability to sustain prices that are above competitive prices than banks in markets with the opposite characteristics.[33] Again, this condition is equivalent to saying that banks are likely to face less elastic loan demand functions the more concentrated their banking market, and the lower the rate of entry into the market. Accordingly, these banks will have higher loan/asset ratios under the assumptions of the model presented above.

Applying the Model to California's Banks

In the preceding three sections, a general model of the profit maximizing individual bank was developed. The model generates predictions about how various factors affect the bank's optimal allocation of its asset portfolio, in particular its loan/asset ratio. More specifically, a bank's optimal loan/asset ratio is determined by the following equation:

$$X_L = F\{s, \ G(r), \ v, \ k, \ BC, \ MkD, \ MkC, \ MkE\},$$

where *BC* are the bank characteristics that give individual banks market power, *MkD* is the strength of local loan demand, *MkC* is the concentration of banks in the bank's local market, and *MkE* is the rate of entry into the local market. These latter four factors determined the elasticity of the bank's loan demand. Thus, the bank's optimal loan/asset ratio depends upon the rate it can earn on securities (the opportunity cost of loans), the default risk on its loans, its management's risk aversion, the bank's capital position, and various factors that determined the elasticity of the demand for the bank's loans. In the next chapter, a linear version of this model is estimated with regression analysis to determine how banks in California did behave. The data, the variables, and the market definitions used in this estimation are discussed in the next chapter.

The object of this estimation is to answer a variety of questions about bank behavior at a time when banking regulation was less restrictive and banking technology more rudimentary than today. In the absence of controls in bank capital, how did bank behavior reflect a bank's capital position? Did risk aversion affect bank behavior, and did this change over time? Did banks lend more in markets where loan demand was greater? How did concentration of banking resources in local banking markets affect bank behavior at a time when restrictions on entry were minimal and the cost of forming a new bank were small? And, finally, did banks with different types of charters behave differently?

Differences in behavior among the different types of banks in the United States have not been an important topic for recent research on bank behavior. Discovering if national banks, state-chartered banks, or members of the Federal Reserve System behave differently is a much less important issue than finding out whether banks affiliated with bank holding companies behave differently from unaffiliated banks, or whether acquisition by a bank holding company affects bank behavior. Legislative changes in 1980 and 1982 mandating universal reserve requirements and the uniformity of deposit rate ceilings across depository institutions have eliminated most of the remaining important differences in banking regulation across states. In the nineteenth century, however, there were important differences among states in their regulation of banking. Texas, for example, prohibited all state-incorporated banking between 1875 and 1905.[34]

Determining differences in bank behavior among different types of banks is important because it helps to identify the effects of regulation on bank behavior. Moreover, since research on U.S. financial development between 1860 and 1910 frequently employs data for national banks, such differences may be important. Conclusions obtained with national bank data may have to be qualified for states or regions where state banking was more important than national banking, such as California. As was noted in Chapter 2 above, there were few national banks in California until well into the 1880s. The results of the model presented in the next chapter show that national banks did in fact behave differently from state banks.

Notes

1. Other versions of this approach are presented in Galbraith (1963) and Moore (1968).
2. Wood (1975) demonstrates that bank behavior is different in a multi-period framework. However, his purpose is to explain bank behavior over time. In other respects his model is more restrictive than the one presented in this study.
3. Pringle (1974) analyzes the optimal level of capital.
4. Different securities are subject to varying risk premiums. For example, in the nineteenth century, risks attached to local utility bonds exceeded those associated with banks or major railroad corporations, which in turn were higher than the risk of default attached to U.S. government securities. It is reasonable to assume that all banks face some real rate of return on securities after adjustment for risk, a rate which no individual bank can affect. Broaddus (1974) discusses the role of secondary reserves and shows how they can be incorporated in the model of the individual bank.
5. Klein (1971), pp. 212-213.
6. If banks have different abilities to gather information about the probability of losses, then bank behavior will reflect this ability. For example, older banks may have more information about existing borrowers than newer banks. It is assumed here that all banks have the same ability to gather information.
7. California's Bank Commissioners were bound to fail a bank if they found its borrowed liabilities to be less than the value of its assets. See Chapter 2 above for a discussion of the Commissioners' examinations.
8. Chandler (1938), p. 3. See also Hodgman (1963), Phillips (1920), Riefler (1930), pp. 103-108, and Rodkey (1928) for the importance of compensating balances and close customer relationships.
9. Chandler (1938), p. 3.
10. Ibid, p. 4.
11. Akerlof (1970). The workings of the market for "lemons" may also act to restrict competition both among existing banks and from new banks. For example, if a bank lowers its interest on loans to increase its market share, it will probably attract a larger percentage of borrowers who are "lemons" than the average bank. The "lemons" can take advantage of the expanding bank's ignorance and

obtain loans at lower interest rates than they would obtain if full information was available to the expanding bank. In this case, the expanding bank will find more of its loans going sour, forcing it either to spend more resources on credit information, which may be passed on to the borrowers, or to raise its interest rate on loans. The expansionary policy is thus curtailed. New banks may also lack sufficient information and thus face higher costs than existing banks. Even if a new bank is started by local individuals, they may still be at a disadvantage in knowing less about their borrowers than existing banks, though the gap will be smaller. This suggests that areas where risk is high and personal contacts are important for determining credit worthiness will also be areas where banks are less competitive and face a lower threat of entry. It must be remembered that this argument rests on the assertion that the percentage of "lemons" will be higher for the expanding bank.

12. Edwards (1964), p. 297.
13. These redeposited funds also give an advantage to large banks in isolated markets. Alhadeff (1954) discusses this factor for statewide branch banks in California in the 1940s and 1950s.
14. Edwards (1964), p. 297.
15. Chandler (1938); Alhadeff (1954, 1967), who stresses this factor; Edwards (1964).
16. Benston (1973).
17. Regulations that restrict the type of activity that banks, or for that matter any financial intermediary, may engage in also limit the salutary effect of competition.
18. For example, see various speeches in California Bankers Association (1894).
19. Rhoades (1977).
20. Bain (1959), p. 8.
21. Ibid, p. 10.
22. Ibid, p. 11.
23. Benston (1973); Rhoades (1977).
24. For a recent discussion of the legal issues, see Hawke (1981) and Kareken (1982).
25. Evidence supporting this opinion is contained in Federal Reserve Bank of Atlanta (1982).
26. Ibid.

27. Examples of this type of work are Glassman (1973), Federal Reserve Bank of Boston (1980) and Stolz (1975).
28. Mote (1979); Stolz (1975; 1976)
29. Benston (1973).
30. Stigler (1964).
31. Ibid, p. 55.
32. Nutter and Moore (1976), p. 59.
33. Chandler (1938), p. 6, also suggests this effect of entry.
34. Grant and Crumb (1978).

Chapter 5

Individual Bank Behavior in California
1878-1908

Discussion of Data and Definition of the Variables

The model developed in the preceding chapter is used in this chapter to analyze bank behavior in California over the period 1878-1908. The first part of the chapter is devoted to the estimation of the equation presented in the last section of the previous chapter, with data that are available for California's banks and its economy in these years. The first section discusses the nature of the data and the definition of local banking markets, and explains the definitions of the variables used in the estimation of the model. The second section of the chapter reports the results obtained when a linear version of the model is estimated with multiple regression analysis. These results are then compared with those reported by other researchers. In the final section, some conclusions are drawn about bank behavior in California during this period, and some answers are given to the questions posed at the end of Chapter 4.

Bank Data. Balance sheets are available for state banks from the annual reports of the California State Board of Bank Commissioners for all the state banks in California for the years 1878 to 1896, 1899, 1900, and 1905 to 1908. In the missing years between 1896 and 1905 (1897, 1898, 1901-1904), the California Legislature did not provide the funds to publish the Bank Commissioners' reports, as an economy measure. (The 1890 aggregate balance sheets for California's state-chartered commercial banks and savings banks are given in Table 5-1.) Unfortunately, the actual bank balance sheets sent in by the banks were not retained in the State of California's archives. Between 1887 and 1907, the Bank Commissioners' reports include the national bank balance sheets, which were sent to the Bank Commissioners as a matter of courtesy. While national bank balance sheets are available for the years prior to 1887 from the annual reports of the U.S. Comptroller of the Currency, these balance sheets are usually for October of each year rather than the end of June, the typical date on which the state banks reported their balance sheets. Seasonal variations in loan demand mean that the national bank balance sheets in the years prior to 1887 reflect somewhat different circumstances to those of state incorporated banks. National banks were excluded therefore from the regressions for any year before 1887.

Private banks did not start to report their balance sheets until 1887. These banks, however, were not subject to inspection by the Bank Commissioners. In addition, they were often operated as an adjunct to other business interests of their owners. Thus, the accuracy of their balance sheets is questionable. Accordingly, private banks were excluded from all the regressions, though they were included in calculations of measures of market concentration and bank entry. In view of the small number and size of private banks, this exclusion eliminates only a small portion of the state's banking industry. While these banks constituted an unregulated portion of the banking industry, the restrictions on state banks were not so onerous as to have produced major differences in behavior between state and private banks. In any case, testing for any differences would be of dubious value in view of the deficiencies of the private bank data.

The state bank balance sheets are much more reliable. These banks were required to send their balance sheets for a particular day, usually at the end of June, to the Bank Commissioners. (In the early years, they also did this in January.) Although the banks undoubtedly window-dressed the reported balance sheets, they had to swear that their balance sheets were true. More importantly, the annual examinations by the Commissioners did much to keep the reported balance sheets close to the true state of each bank's affairs. As part of their examination, the Commissioners adjusted the values of any assets they believed were overvalued, reducing the bank's net worth in the process (see Chapter 2 above). The Bank Commissioners' reports also contain an annual examination balance sheet for each bank, but the dates of these reports differ among the banks depending upon when they were examined. While these balance sheets may be closer to the true state of affairs of each bank than the balance sheets reported by the bank at mid-year, seasonal factors and the timing of financial pressures preclude the use of these examination reports. In any case, a random review of the mid-year balance sheets and the examination reports indicated similar values for most banks for such items as capital and surplus.[1]

Because of the volume of data to be processed in each year, the model was only estimated for certain years: 1878, 1884, 1887, 1890, 1893, 1896, 1899, 1900, 1905, and 1908. The choice of these years was dictated by the data requirements for estimating the entry model that is presented in Chapter 6 below. That model is estimated for seven three-year periods between 1884 and 1908. Data for the year 1900 were processed to enable the entry model to be estimated for the period 1902-1905. The year 1878 was included because this was the first year for which the bank balance sheets are available. Only a sample of banks was included in 1905 and 1908 due to the large number of banks in each of these years. In 1905, every third bank was included, making the selection of banks random. In 1908, only every third state incorporated commercial bank was included, as there were over six hundred banks by 1908.

Market Definitions and Data. Local bank markets are defined to be the counties of California. The principal reasons for this definition is the availability of data for counties and the impossibility of constructing any more appropriately defined markets. The annual values of the property assessed for taxation provide several ways of measuring the demand for loans in each market. In addition, population data are available for counties from the decennial U.S. census. Population estimates were interpolated for the years between census years based on the assumption that population growth was constant in any decade. Though population data are available for smaller areas such as cities and towns, this is not the case for the property tax assessments for most of the period so these smaller entities could not be used for market definitions.

Defining local bank markets as counties is defensible on other grounds. On the whole, the major city in each county was located in the middle of the county, or at least the populated area of the county. Moreover, most residents of each county had direct contact with the major city through its performance of various functions as the commercial, judicial and social center. The rudimentary state of transportation during the period also made convenience an especially important attribute of banking services.

Dependent Variable: The Loan/Asset Ratio. The model developed above in Chapter 4 is a short-run model. Thus, the optimal loan/asset ratio must be one that the bank controls in the short-run. The ratio used here is the ratio of loans to available assets (L/AA). A bank's available assets are defined as its total assets less its buildings and equipment, and less its real estate taken for debt. In general, a bank's ownership of its buildings is a long-term decision that is not adjusted at the margin in the short run. Similarly, its holdings of real estate taken for debt reflect past problems and plans for the future liquidation of these holdings.

Because recently formed banks often reported few loans on their balance sheets (occasionally none), banks with loan-to-available assets ratios of less than 0.2 were excluded from the regression analysis.

Independent Variables: Bank Characteristics. The assumption that banks possessed market power in California in this period appears reasonable in view of the more rudimentary level of credit information and limited transportation and communications at that time. In practice, it is difficult to find variables that reflect an individual bank's market power. Of the factors listed by Chandler (1938), only a bank's age is readily measurable. This factor is captured by the variable AGE, which is the natural logarithm of the bank's age plus one year, meaning that AGE equals zero for a new bank. California's banks' balance sheets include the value of a bank's building, if it owned one, but there are no income statements that give the rent paid by banks that did not own their own building. Nor are there data for the other factors such as the quality of services, advertising, or the financial standing of a bank's officers. One variable that may reflect some of these features is a bank's size; accordingly, the total assets of each bank are included as a variable, called ASSETS.

The bank's capital position, k, is relatively straightforward. The ratio of a bank's net worth (assets less liabilities) to its deposits is an accepted measure of this risk factor, which can be obtained from the bank balance sheets.[2] This variable is denoted NW/D.

There is no such direct measure of the risk aversion of a bank's management. This aversion, however, can be inferred from other management decisions. One indicator is a bank's ratio of cash reserves to deposits. In the nineteenth century, insufficient cash-on-hand to meet deposit withdrawals could place a banker in a very difficult position. With more rudimentary transportation and communications than today, additional cash was not readily available. The importance of establishing the independence of the loan decision and the reserves decision in Chapter 4 now becomes apparent. Without this independence, the cash/deposit ratio could not be used to measure the risk aversion of a bank's management in a model determining the bank's optimal loan/asset ratio. Because there were no reserve requirements for state-incorporated banks in California before 1905, and no effective requirements until the 1901 Bank Act, the cash positions of state banks reflected only the management's view of cash requirements. The bank management's risk aversion is thus measured by the ratio of cash to deposits, denoted M/D. Banks that had cash-to-deposit ratios of more than unity were excluded because most were very new or very small. National banks did face reserve requirements but their behavior does not appear to have reflected these requirements directly, as is discussed below.

Besides cash, banks also held deposits at other banks as reserves. These deposits can be considered to be a secondary reserve as they were less liquid than cash. Banks earned a return on these deposits. Part of this return was in the form of an explicit yield, which was typically much lower than the rate on securities.[3] Banks also obtained implicit yields on these funds in the form of correspondent services such as the clearing of checks and access to lines of credit.[4] Individual banks are assumed to have held sufficient deposits at other banks to equalize the yield on these funds with the yield on securities. In effect, these deposits can be treated like a bank's holdings of securities.

The default risk on loans cannot be measured as simply. Very little data on loan defaults exist. While some idea of the statewide rate of default could be obtained from the loan losses of national banks, national banks were not a large enough proportion of California's banks to provide even a reliable measure of this rate.[5] There are no estimates of local market default risks. Some variation in loan default risk among markets is captured by variables that measure the strength of loan demand. These variables are discussed below.

Differences in behavior among the various types of banks are to be expected. National banks were more heavily regulated than state-chartered commercial banks, being subject to more restrictions and closer supervision. While the regulations governing savings banks were not very different from those governing state-chartered commercial banks, there were differences in the characteristics of these two types of banks. Generally, savings banks relied predominantly on time deposits and placed most of their funds in mortgages (see Table 5-1). To test for differences in behavior among the different types of banks, dummy variables are used for national banks and savings banks.

Independent Variables: Market Characteristics. The model incorporates two types of market characteristics into the individual bank's loan demand function. One type is the strength of the demand for loans in the market, and the other represents the market structure of banks in the local market.

The demand for loans in a market varies with the market's economic activity. More activity generates stronger demand for loans and rapid growth increases the demand for loans. Different types of activity also create demand for bank financing. In general, the more complex a market's economy, the greater is the use of credit and financial intermediation in the market. In practice, researchers have employed a variety of measures to capture the strength of local loan demand. The most commonly used measures are a per capita income measure and some measure of market growth, such as the rate of growth of income or population. Other variables used include the proportion of urban population in the market's population, the density of the market's population and the types of employment in the market.

In this study, two variables are used to measure the strength of market loan demand: county wealth per capita (WPC) and the rate of growth of county wealth in the previous three years (GRW3YR), where county wealth in any year is approximated by the three-year average of assessed value of all property in the county (see Chapter 3 above). Wealth per capita is a measure of the economic sophistication and complexity of each county's economy. Theoretically, higher wealth per capita is associated with more financial intermediation and greater use of credit.[6] A faster growing market generates more demand for loans to finance growth. There were insufficient data for such variables as the urban/rural population mix or the types of employment to be used. Some other loan demand variables were tried without success; these variables are discussed in the analysis of the empirical results. Insofar as strong market demand reduces the risk of loan default, these measures also allow for some variation among markets in the expected rate of loan default.

The concentration of the existing banks in each market is measured by the Herfindahl Index (H). This index is defined as the sum of the squared share of total county bank assets of each bank in the county.[7] It emphasizes the shares of the larger banks in the market, but also incorporates variations among markets in the size distribution of all the banks in the market. An alternative measure, often called the market concentration ratio, is inappropriate here. This ratio is usually defined as the share of the *n* largest banks in the market, where *n* is usually greater than two.[8] Because several markets had just one bank, only a one-bank concentration ratio would have been feasible without excluding those markets where market power should have been greatest. A one-bank concentration ratio, however, fails to incorporate any information about the size distribution of the remaining banks in the market. The same defect applies to the number of banks in the market as a measure of market concentration. The number of banks, however, is a measure of the number of competitors. Some estimations were made with this variable, although they are not reported here.

The entry of a new bank is expected to increase competition in a market. The measure used here is the rate of entry of new banks into the markets over the preceding three years (NEWBS). This variable is defined as the number of new banks formed in a county divided by the average number of banks in the county over the three preceding years. Bank entry is discussed in more detail in Chapter 6 below.

The Regression Model. The model is estimated in the following linear form:

$$L/AA_i = b_0 + b_1 AGE_i + b_2 ASSETS_i + b_3 NW/D_i + b_4 M/D_i + b_5 NB_i + b_6 SB_i + b_7 WPC_i + b_8 GRW3YR_i + b_9 HERFIN_i + b_{10} NEWBS_i + e_i,$$

where, for the *ith* bank,

L/AA	= ratio of loans to available assets,
(-) AGE	= natural logarithm of the bank's age plus one,
(-) ASSETS	= total assets of the bank,
(+) NW/D	= ratio of net worth to deposits,
(-) M/D	= ratio of cash-on-hand to deposits,
(-) NB	= 1 if the bank is a national bank, and 0 otherwise,
(+) SB	= 1 if the bank is a savings bank, and 0 otherwise,
(+) WPC	= county wealth per capita,
(+) GRW3YR	= growth of county wealth over preceding three years,
(-) HERFIN	= Herfindahl index for the banks in the county,

(+) NEWBS   = rate of formation of new banks in the county,

e   = error term, assumed to be normally distributed.

The signs in parentheses give the expected direction of the effect on the loan/asset ratio of an increase in each independent variable.

The Regression Results

The model is reasonably successful in explaining individual bank behavior in California in most of the years for which it was estimated. The results of the estimation of the model with ordinary least squares are presented in Table 5-2. Most of the variables have the predicted signs, though they are not all significant. The R^2's range from 0.57 to 0.10, with six out of the ten years generating R^2's of 0.40 or more. The standard errors of the regression are of the same order in all years. In general, the model is less successful in explaining individual bank behavior in the later years, especially 1905. One explanation for this decline in explanatory power may be the rapid entry of banks combined with the less diligent supervision of state banks after 1900.   Bank behavior varied widely among new banks, with some having very high loan/asset ratios, but low capital/deposit ratios. Rapid entry may also have disrupted established patterns of banking. The 1906 earthquake and the 1907 panic also created banking problems that persisted into 1908.

Of the two variables used to measure individual banks' market power, only bank size (ASSETS) has the predicted sign. The coefficient of ASSETS was negative in all years and statistically significant in many, suggesting that larger banks did lend less than smaller banks. There is no evidence of economies of scale in lending. Older banks, however, do not appear to have lent less than younger banks, suggesting that banks' market power did not vary with age. In fact, the coefficient of AGE is positive in almost every year, significantly so in some years. One explanation for this unexpected sign may be that young banks took time to establish their loan programs, while seasoned banks faced lower costs in making loans. This explanation is given some credence by the significantly positive coefficients for AGE in 1887, 1890, and 1893, when the number of new banks was relatively large.

Risk appears to have played an important role in determining bank behavior. Banks with high ratios of net worth to deposits (NW/D) had higher loan/asset ratios than banks with low capital ratios. The coefficient of NW/D is positive in all years, and significant in all years except 1908.

The standardized regression coefficients for this variable also indicate that a bank's capital ratio was important in determining its loan/asset ratio. The cash/deposit ratio (M/D), representing management's risk aversion, was also very important in explaining bank behavior. The regression coefficient of this variable is negative as expected, and is significant in all except two years, 1905 and 1908; its standardized regression coefficient is also relatively large in most years. Thus, as expected, the less risk averse the management and the better the bank's capital position, the more the bank lent.

Lending behavior varied among the different types of banks. On average, savings banks had higher loan/asset ratios, and national banks had lower loan/asset ratios, than state incorporated commercial banks. The coefficient of the dummy variable for the savings banks (SB) is positive in every year, and significant in most years; it shows that savings banks had loan/asset ratios that were from 0.014 to 0.103 above that of a state commercial bank with similar characteristics depending on the year considered. For the national banks, the coefficient of the dummy variable (NB) is always negative. Though it is not highly significant, its value remains fairly similar in the years in which national banks were included, with the exception of 1905. These results are to be expected given the greater regulation of national banks and the more stable deposits of savings banks. More complex versions of the model that incorporated interaction terms did not indicate any consistent differences in behavior among the different types of banks.[9]

One question raised earlier in this study was whether changes in banking regulation affected bank behavior in California. The empirical results indicate there were some changes in behavior over time, but it is not clear that these changes were induced by regulatory changes. The coefficient of the national bank dummy variable in 1905 is both small and insignificant. This apparent narrowing of differences between national and state banks is somewhat surprising, since national banks were still much more closely supervised and regulated than California's state banks in the 1900s. One contributing factor may have been the formation of new national banks and the conversion of state banks to national banks in the 1900s (see Chapter 2). At the same time, however, the supervision of state banks was becoming more relaxed which suggests that some difference between national and state bank behavior should have continued.

The decline in the coefficient of the net worth to deposit ratio in the 1900s appears to be evidence of this relaxation of banking regulation. A smaller coefficient indicates that bankers were less sensitive to their banks' capital position when determining the optimal level of loans. This decline in sensitivity in the 1900s was not due to generally stronger capital positions among banks, since the average net worth to deposit ratio was lower than it had been in the 1890s (see Table 5-3). Besides the less diligent supervision by the Bank Commissioners, bankers also may have expected a lower rate of bank failure as the memory of the 1893 panic receded. While this expectation was not fulfilled over the whole decade, bankers may have adjusted their behavior, at least until 1907 (see Tables 2-6, 2-7 and 2-8). The increase in the coefficient of the net worth/deposit ratio between 1878 and 1884 also may be attributable to regulatory change, but in this case an increase in supervision and regulation generally. The balance sheets for 1878 were the first collected by the Bank Commissioners, and thus were a product of an unsupervised environment, unlike the 1884 balance sheets, which reflected six years of supervision that included the closing of several banks by the Bank Commissioners.

Another coefficient that may have been affected by regulatory changes is the cash to deposit ratio. Reserve requirements were first imposed on state commercial banks in March 1905. The effects of this change should be apparent in the 1905 regression results, since the 1905 balance sheets are for August. In 1905, and also in 1908, the coefficient of the cash to deposit ratio is still negative, but is insignificant and much smaller in size than in earlier years. This result may be attributable to the imposition of reserve requirements, as banks began to keep more uniform reserves and differences in banks' cash to deposit ratio became less indicative of differences in bank management's risk aversion. Though bank managements may have become generally less risk averse, due for instance to more diversified ownership of banks, the lower risk aversion cannot be inferred from the smaller coefficient on its own. At any point in time, the payments system and financial arrangements are fixed. When these change, the relationship between the cash/deposit ratio and the risk aversion also changes. At least part, and possibly all, of the decline in the cash/deposit ratio's coefficient may have been due to improvements in the payments mechanism and the imposition of reserve requirements rather than a reduction in bank management's risk aversion. An indication of a general trend of improving financial arrangements is the decline in the average cash/deposit ratio of banks between 1878 and 1905 (see Table 5-4). The increase in this ratio for state commercial banks in 1905 suggests that reserve requirements may have had an effect, even though there were no provisions for the Bank Commissioners to enforce them, except by closing the bank. More work clearly needs to be done on these issues before any firm conclusions can be drawn; in particular, the sample of banks in 1905 and 1908 needs to be increased, and statistical tests need to be performed to establish any significant changes in behavior.

Of the two market demand variables, county wealth per capita (WPC) is much more successful than the rate of growth of county wealth in the preceding three years (GRW3YR). While the coefficient of the former is positive in all years except 1908 and significant in several years, the coefficient of the latter is significantly positive only in 1893. These results provide some support for the hypothesis that banks contributed to economic growth by meeting the demand for loans. They also raise questions about the appropriate variables that should be used to measure the demand for loans. In assessing market demand, county wealth per capita and the rate of growth of county wealth make no allowance either for differences in the economic structures of counties or for changes in these structures. If data were available, this deficiency could be remedied by including such variables as the type of employment, or the urban/rural population ratio.

The extent of market concentration among banks, measured by the Herfindahl index (H), did affect bank behavior, but not in a consistent fashion. The coefficient of this variable was significantly negative in 1899, 1900, and 1908, but was significantly positive in 1890 and 1893. This result is more interesting than it appears because Keehn (1972; 1980) reports a similar pattern for banks in Wisconsin in this period. An explanation of this similarity is provided below.

Bank entry had the unexpected effect of reducing banks' loan/asset ratios. The coefficient of the rate of entry of new banks (NEWBS) is negative in every year it was included, significantly so in 1890 and 1899. Thus, the results do not show that bank entry stimulated competition and led to higher loan/asset ratios. A possible explanation of the lower loan/asset ratios is that counties with high rates of entry were experiencing a more rapid growth in the supply of funds than in the demand for funds.[10] The high capital/deposit ratios of banks during this period makes this explanation more reasonable than it would be today (see Table 5-3). Other measures of bank entry, such as the growth of assets or deposits, were no more successful in explaining individual bank behavior; nor were variables that incorporated the difference between the market's growth and the growth of banking.

In sum, the model is successful in explaining individual bank behavior. In this explanation, the variables based on individual bank characteristics generally contribute more than those based on local market characteristics. The lack of success with the market characteristics is paralleled in other studies.

Comparisons With Other Studies of Bank Behavior

In this section, the results obtained for California's banks are compared with those reported in other studies of individual bank behavior.[11] Most studies of bank behavior include only one of the variables used here to characterize individual banks: bank size. The results obtained in these studies are mixed. In general, bank size, typically measured by total deposits, has no significant effect on bank behavior. One study that obtains a significant coefficient for bank size is John Scott (1977), which reports bank size reduced the rate of interest on small business loans.[12] In Keehn (1972), the natural logarithm of bank assets has a significantly positive effect on the loan/asset ratios of Wisconsin banks in 1880 and 1900, but a negative effect in 1870 and 1900; the results for absolute bank size are not reported. Keehn includes this variable to capture any economies of scale in lending. One reason for the mixed results obtained with this variable, however measured, may be the offsetting effects of market power and economies of scale.

Although several studies have considered the relationship between risk and bank behavior, only two have included a measure of individual banks' capital positions as part of models that are comparable to this study's model. Keehn (1972) finds that the net worth/deposit ratio had a negative effect on the loan/asset ratio of Wisconsin banks between 1870 and 1900. Keehn explains this unexpected result by suggesting that banks' capital positions reflected their management's risk aversion.[13] By introducing a separate variable for the risk aversion of a bank's management, this study demonstrates that bankers in nineteenth century California did consider their capital position when making loans. It is likely that the same results would obtain for Wisconsin bankers if the cash/deposit ratio were to be included in Keehn's model. Keehn reports a positive association between the net worth/deposit ratio and the cash/deposit ratio for Wisconsin banks, which, he argues, is evidence that management risk aversion varied with the net worth/deposit ratio.

Graddy and Kyle (1979) report that for their sample of 463 banks the capital/risk-asset ratio had a significantly positive effect on the ratio of U.S. Treasury securities to total assets, when ordinary least squares regression analysis was used, though the effect was not significant when a simultaneous model was estimated with three-stage least-squares analysis. This variable had the opposite effect when the ratio of business loans to total assets was used as a dependent variable. Again, these results, which are the reverse of what one would expect, suggest that bank management's risk aversion must be taken into account independently of the bank's capital position, something neither study does. Other studies of recent bank behavior that take different approaches have found evidence indicating that banks' capital positions do affect bank behavior, a result which is supported by this study.[14]

The evidence from California also demonstrates that regulation and type of charter affected a bank's behavior. Studies of modern banking have paid little attention to the effect on bank behavior of differences in regulations according to bank charter, preferring instead to focus on the effects of differences in size, bank holding company affiliation, or type of institution. The results are nevertheless important, particularly in view of the widespread use of national bank data in U.S. financial history.[15] This study finds that national banks generally had lower and savings banks higher loan/asset ratios than state-chartered commercial banks. Keehn (1972) also reports significantly lower loan/asset ratios for national banks in 1880 and 1900, but not in 1870 or 1890.[16] In 1900, the coefficient of the dummy variable for Wisconsin national banks is even similar in size (approximately 0.048) to that found for California banks in 1900 (0.047).[17]

While Keehn does not include savings banks in his analysis, he does provide evidence that concurs with the results of this study. In a regression equation estimated for 1900, he includes the ratio of time deposits to total deposits, and finds that this ratio had a positive effect on banks' loan/asset ratios.[18] Thus, banks that were more similar to savings banks tended to lend more than banks with less stable sources of deposits. Unfortunately, the balance sheets for California's banks do not separate deposits by type.

Keehn's findings for private banks, however, are surprising. As late as 1890, private banks in Wisconsin were more numerous than either national banks or state-chartered banks. Though they were also less regulated, private banks did not have higher loan/asset ratios. Keehn attributes this surprising result to private banks' small size, their unsophisticated managements, and their location in small towns that limited the possibilities for loan portfolio diversification.[19] This explanation, however, brings the model into question by suggesting that important variables have been omitted in the case of the private banks. An alternative, consistent explanation may be that private bankers were more risk averse because of their unlimited liability. Thus, *ceteris paribus*, a private bank would lend less than a state-incorporated bank.

In contrast to the lack of attention to the effects of regulatory differences on bank behavior, research on bank behavior have paid considerable attention to the effects of differences in local market characteristics on bank behavior. Success with these market variables has been limited, however. As in this study, the most successful market variable measuring the demand for loans is some measure of per capita income or wealth, with most studies finding significant coefficients with the right sign for this variable.[20] Measures of market demand that reflect the growth of the market are far less successful. In many studies, the coefficients of variables such as income or population growth are typically insignificant, and occasionally significant with the wrong sign.[21] That is, faster growth is associated with lower loan/asset ratios, or lower interest rates charged on loans. While such results are frequently reported with no comment, the association between growth and entry, which is found in this study, does not escape attention altogether. Yeats (1974), for example, suggests that the negative coefficients he finds for population growth and those found in Kaufman (1966) may be explained by bank entry, as the growth of banking outstrips the growth of the market.[22]

By including a specific measure of recent bank entry (NETBS), this study should have overcome the problem of growth in the supply of funds, but market growth (GRW3YR) still does not have a consistently positive coefficient, suggesting a weakness in this measure of market demand. When NETBS is omitted from the regression equation, the coefficient of GRW3YR becomes negative, in almost all years, and significantly negative in some. Since the entry model estimated in Chapter 6 below, reveals that bank entry was a function of market growth, this result is not surprising. Nevertheless, the argument that supply increased faster than demand appears suspect. Some studies of the impact of entry on bank behavior indicate that entry did increase loan/asset ratios. These studies, which are reviewed in the Appendix to Chapter 6 evaluate the short-run impact of a single new bank on banks in markets where there were only one, two, or three banks. In such markets, entry is likely to have a major impact on the level of competition as well as the supply of funds.[23] An alternative explanation is that rapidly growing markets tend to have younger banks, which have lower loan/asset ratios than other banks.

Many studies of bank behavior have focused on the effect of market concentration, but surprisingly few have reported significant coefficients with the correct sign for this variable.[24] Moreover, those studies that also report the relative importance of market concentration as measured by elasticities or standardized regression coefficients indicate that even when concentration has a significant effect on behavior, this effect is small. Thus, this study is not exceptional in reporting that market concentration has an inconsistent and small effect on bank behavior.

With the rudimentary state of transportation and communications during the period under investigation, one would have expected banks to have possessed and exerted some market power. An offsetting factor, at least in California, was the relative freedom of entry for new banks. In contrast, communications today are far more sophisticated, but bank entry is much more restricted. In Wisconsin, bank entry was also largely unrestricted during the period 1870-1900, and Keehn (1972; 1980) attributes his failure to find a consistent and significant effect of market concentration on bank behavior to the ease of bank formation.

Keehn's inconsistent results are more important than they appear because the pattern of inconsistency is similar to that reported here for California's banks. In 1890, market concentration had a significantly positive effect on Wisconsin bank behavior, while in 1900 it had a negative effect. For California's banks, the Herfindahl index (H) had a significantly positive coefficient in 1890 and 1893, but a significantly negative coefficient in 1899 and 1900. One factor that may explain this pattern is bank entry. An important difference between 1890 and 1983, and 1899 and 1900 is the pace of bank entry in the preceding years. In the three years before 1890, 70 banks were formed in California. During 1890-1893, 68 banks were formed. In the period 1893-1896 only 28 banks entered; and only 25 banks were formed in the three years before 1899 (see Table 2-5). While the regression results show that the rate of bank entry reduced loan/asset ratios, this variable may not capture all the effects of entry. Moreover, the results for the bank entry model indicate that bank entry was lower in more concentrated markets. Thus, a possible explanation of the positive effect of market concentration on banks' loan/asset ratios in 1890 and 1893 is lower entry in more concentrated markets. Bank failures, deflation, and the lower level of entry in the six years preceding 1899 probably enhanced banks' market power, which explains the significantly negative effect of market concentration on banks' loan/asset ratios in 1899 and 1900.

The pattern of bank formation appears to have been similar in Wisconsin. In the two periods 1887-1890 and 1890-1893, the number of banks increased by 44 and 40 respectively.[25] In the next two three-year periods, 1893-1896 and 1896-1899, the number of banks increased by only 14 and 19 respectively. However, between 1899 and 1900 the number of banks increased by 25. This surge in bank numbers may explain why Keehn does not find a significantly negative effect on Wisconsin bank behavior in 1900 for all his measures of market concentration and for both his market definitions (county and town-city). Thus, in both Wisconsin and California, the pace of bank entry can help to explain the changes in the effect of market concentration on bank behavior. Besides these changes, growing bank market power in the 1890s is also indicated by the coefficient of bank size (ASSETS) in both California and Wisconsin. What makes this finding of changing market power interesting is that it may explain the pattern of regional interest rate differentials, as these differentials widened in the 1890s. This issue is discussed further in Chapter 7 below.

Too much weight cannot be placed on this explanation of the changing effect of market concentration on bank behavior, since the importance of bank entry remains a matter of conjecture. Moreover, alternative explanations are plausible. It is possible that the Herfindahl index and other measures of market concentration are correlated with another set of factors that may explain the regression results. For example, markets with fewer banks tended to be more remote, and therefore slower to respond to changes in general economic activity. When the economy rebounded in the last years of the nineteenth century, more isolated markets may not have felt this increased activity immediately. As a result, banks in these markets may have had lower loan/asset ratios than banks in markets closer to financial centers. Similarly, the slower recovery from the 1907 panic of more remote markets may explain the significantly negative coefficient of the Herfindahl index in 1908.

The lack of success of the local market variables in explaining bank behavior suggests that the errors introduced through the use of counties for local markets may be significant. One error is that the political boundaries probably differed from the boundaries determined by the convenience of the banks to their customers. Another error is that banks outside each county probably supplied some loans to the local economy, while banks in each county probably also supplied some loans to other local economies. Pierson-Doti (1979) provides evidence showing that many California savings banks lent in more than one county between 1879 and 1905, based on the location of the real estate used for collateral.[26]

Still another error is the omission of sources of funds other than banks. Non-bank financial intermediaries such as insurance companies and building and loan societies also provided credit, particularly for mortgage borrowers. Fortunately, building and loan societies were not very important in California during this period, and in any case tended to be located in the larger cities.[27] Insurance companies were more important, but there are no data on their loans by county; in fact, there are no data on their loans even by state.[28] In addition to these non-bank financial intermediaries, there were other private lenders such as merchants and individuals, as well as financial markets that businesses could access through bonds and other forms of debt. For example, there is evidence that private individuals were an important source of credit in financing gold mining in California.[29] Through the late-payment of taxes, firms and individuals could also borrow from the government. These errors and omissions are not new in research on bank behavior, and have plagued those who have sought to identify the effects of local market conditions on bank behavior.

Conclusions

The model successfully explains bank behavior in California between 1878 and 1908, though it is somewhat less successful after 1900. In most years, the model explains a significant amount of the variation in individual banks' loan/asset ratios. The lack of success in later years may be attributable to the combination of a large number of new banks and less diligent supervision of state banks. The most important variables explaining bank behavior are individual bank characteristics rather than local market factors. Nevertheless, there are conclusions to be drawn from the effects of both groups of variables.

One important conclusion is that banks in this period of relatively minimal regulation did consider their capital position when determining their loan/asset ratios. While this finding concurs with the results obtained by some analysts of bank behavior, it differs from the findings reported by others who use models that are similar to the one used in this study. The reason for this different result is the use here of separate variables for the bank's capital position and the risk aversion of the bank's management. This separation overcomes the problem that more risk averse managements are likely to operate a bank with a higher capital/deposit ratio, ceteris paribus. This role of risk in determining bank decisions has implications both for the pattern of interest rate differentials, which is discussed in Chapter 7 below, and for the regulation of banking.

Bank behavior also varied according to a bank's charter. Savings banks generally had higher loan/asset ratios than state commercial banks, which probably reflected their more stable sources of deposits and their emphasis on mortgage loans. National banks, however, had lower loan/asset ratios than state commercial banks, reflecting their more extensive regulation and closer supervision by the U.S. Comptroller of the Currency. This generally lower loan/asset ratio, which is similar to that found for national banks in Wisconsin, suggests that there was a burden attached to the closer regulation of national banks.

If all the banks in California had been national banks, the annual volume of bank loans would have been about 5 percent less than it was, other things being unchanged. Of course, other things would have changed; there would have been more alternative sources of funds to banks and so forth. The lack of good substitutes for banks during this period, however, suggests that the regulation of national banks did impose a burden in states where state-chartered banking was restricted. On the other side, there is the cost of less regulation, particularly the increase in bank failures and financial crises. In California, however, the evidence presented in Chapter 2 suggests that the rate of state bank failures was not dramatically higher than that for national banks. A full assessment of the burden of regulation would require a complete model not only of the individual bank, but also of the role of the regulators in determining the rate of entry and the level of bank regulation. Still, the evidence for California, and Wisconsin, suggests that there was some cost to states prohibiting state incorporated banks. Moreover, Keehn's results suggest that private banking was not a good substitute in terms of the provision of loans.

Though it would be tempting to argue from the results presented here that banks can operate with less regulation than they bear today, removing restrictions on the level of bank capital now would almost certainly lead to even lower capital/deposit ratios than at present. As long as deposit insurance premiums are based on a flat rate, and not the riskiness of a bank's balance sheet, there is no incentive for banks to maintain capital/deposit or capital/asset ratios at the levels that reflect the full risk of failure. Moreover, even non-insured creditors appear to have gained some de facto protection, further reducing the pressures on banks to maintain adequate capital. The only recourse is for the bank regulators to regulate the level of bank capital.[30]

The model also provides information on the effect of loan demand and market power on bank behavior, but unlike the roles of risk and regulation, the information on these factors is less clear-cut. Banks in markets with higher levels of wealth per capita did lend a higher proportion of their portfolios, suggesting banks may have furthered economic growth. In faster growing markets, however, banks' loan/asset ratios were not consistently higher. Others have suggested that this result may reflect the growth in the supply of funds to the market as new banks are formed in rapidly growing markets. By including an explicit measure of the rate of bank entry, the model should take account of this factor, but it does not. An alternative explanation is that these markets have a higher proportion of new banks with generally lower loan/asset ratios. Both these arguments, however, are largely conjecture.

Considerable attention has been paid to the role that market power plays in determining bank behavior. Most of this research has focused on the relationship between local bank market concentration and bank behavior. In this study, two variables were introduced to capture the market power that individual banks might possess: a bank's age and its size. The regression results suggest that bank market power did vary with size, but not with age, as older banks lent more, not less, than younger banks. Market concentration, measured by the Herfindahl index, had a small and inconsistent effect on banks' loan/asset ratios. The coefficient of this variable is significantly negative, as expected, in some years, but is significantly positive in other years. In view of the similar pattern reported for Wisconsin's banks in this period by Keehn (1972; 1980), this inconsistency warranted further analysis. One possible explanation is that the positive effect of market concentration in the late 1880s and early 1890s is attributable to the rapid entry of banks during these years. The much lower rate of entry in the middle 1890s explains the negative effect on banks' loan/asset ratios of market concentration in 1899 and 1900. This change in banks' market power has been put forward as an explanation of the widening of regional interest rate differentials in the last decade of the nineteenth century, an issue which receives more attention in Chapter 7 below.

The entry of a new bank is generally predicted to be a pro-competitive factor. The results, however, do not fulfill this prediction. A higher rate of entry generally depressed banks' loan/asset ratios rather than increasing them. One explanation of this result may be that younger banks had lower loan/asset ratios, though this effect should have been picked up by the age variable. Another explanation is that new banks with their high capital/deposit ratios may have added more to the supply of funds than they absorbed by making loans, given the time needed to get a loan program going. While plausible, these explanations are not supported by any solid evidence, and remain suspect. One of the difficulties of incorporating bank entry into the model is that bank behavior may be influenced as much by the threat of entry as by actual entry. Keehn (1980) attributes his failure to find a consistent effect of market concentration on Wisconsin bank behavior to the pervasive threat of entry in a period when bank formation was almost unrestricted.

Incorporating the threat of entry adds another dimension to the problems of measurement in employing the local market approach to analyze bank behavior under imperfect competition. Undoubtedly, a major source of the problems with the market variables in the model is the use of inappropriate definitions for the local markets and the omission of competition from non-bank sources of credit. Moreover, the unexpected signs of the variables associated with change, market growth and bank entry, suggest that dynamics are confusing the statistics even in this short-run model. Nevertheless, the model as it stands does provide some useful results. It shows how individual banks reacted to risk, regulation, market demand, and proxies for market power. The next chapter explores how these factors affected the pace and pattern of bank entry into local markets in California.

Notes

1. Crumb (1935) also discusses the veracity of the bank data. According to Keehn (1972), national bank balance sheets were also window-dressed in that national banks reduced their interbank borrowings prior to reporting.
2. Orgler and Wolkowitz (1976); Vojta (1973).
3. James (1976a) shows that New York bankers' balances paid around two percent in the 1880s. Smiley (1976) estimates interest on reserve deposits was just above two percent for 1883-1913. See Smiley (1976), Table 5.
4. A bank received benefits from its deposits in the form of reduced domestic exchange costs and the establishment of lines of credit with other banks for its own borrowing needs. Banks' balances brought lower, and often no, charges for handling checks drawn by their customers. These implicit returns were high during the nineteenth century, as can be seen from bankers' discussions of costs of domestic exchange. Redlich (1968) provides general information on this topic. For a specific example, see American Bankers Association (1885), pp. 135-140. Banks' balances brought returns in the form of liquidity. The balance sheets presented in the Reports of the California Bank Commissioners show that California banks kept deposits in a wide range of Eastern, Midwestern, and foreign banks. The extent of interbank borrowing is discussed in James (1978) and Lockhart (1921).
5. For more discussion of national bank loan losses and loan loss rates, see section 2 of Chapter 7 below.
6. Goldsmith (1969); Cheng (1980).
7. Smith (1965); Scherer (1970).
8. Benston (1973); Rhoades (1977).
9. Interaction terms were introduced into the regression equation in the following form: (NW/D * NB) and (M/D * NB). Statistical tests did not show any consistent pattern of differences in behavior among banks of different types for these variables.
10. Broaddus (1972; 1974) models this effect of entry.
11. Studies on bank behavior are reviewed in Guttentag and Herman (1967), Mote (1979), Benston (1973), Rhoades (1977), Osborne and Wendell (1978); and Graddy and Kyle (1979).

12. Fraser and Rose (1976) report that bank assets had a negative effect on the return to assets, but no significant effect on the loan/asset ratio or on other dependent variables.

13. Keehn (1972) finds a positive association between the net worth/deposit ratio and the cash/deposit ratio for Wisconsin banks. This finding, he argues, is evidence that the risk aversion of the management of banks was associated with net worth/deposit ratios.

14. Orgler and Wolkowitz (1976); Fraser and McCormack (1978).

15. See Chapter 7 for a discussion of some of these studies.

16. The coefficient reported in Table 1 of Keehn (1980) for the national bank dummy variable in 1900, when S2 is the market concentration variable, appears to have the wrong sign, given the consistency of the other regression coefficients with the results reported in Keehn (1972).

17. Keehn (1972), p. 128.

18. Keehn (1980), p. 52.

19. See Keehn (1972), p. 130. A dummy variable for California's private banks also had a negative coefficient when it was included in regression equations for the years 1890 and 1900 in the preliminary analysis of this study.

20. For example, significantly positive coefficients are reported in Brucker (1970), Aspinwall (1970), and Kaufman (1966).

21. Negative and significant coefficients are reported in Kaufman (1966), Keehn (1972), and Yeats (1974). Significantly positive coefficients are found by Edwards (1964), Aspinwall (1970) and Kaufman (1966). Other studies find this variable to be insignificant.

22. Interestingly enough, directional signs for the population growth variable frequently run counter to expectations in Kaufman's study of the effect of structure on performance in Iowa markets. One possible explanation is that "banks are moving into these growth markets at a rate which exceeds that of population change, perhaps in anticipation of higher future profits. While banks jockey vigorously for position in these potentially lucrative markets, the net effect may be to create a highly competitive environment in which present profit levels are held below normal." Yeats (1974), p. 98, fn. 10.

23. See the discussion of Motter (1965), Chandross (1971), Fraser and Rose (1972) and McCall and Peterson (1976) contained in the Appendix to Chapter 6 below.

24. Even in his favorable review of the studies of market concentration's effect on behavior, Rhoades concludes that "on the one hand, there is little question that bank market structure affects bank performance. On the other hand, the measured effect is indeed small." Rhoades (1977), p. 30. Benston (1973) and Osborne and Wendell (1978) raise many questions about the methodology of these studies. The latter review, in particular, disagrees with the conclusions drawn by Rhoades (1977).

25. The number of banks in Wisconsin was as follows:

1887	199
1890	243
1893	304
1896	318
1899	337
1900	362

    See Keehn (1972), Table F-1, pp. 288-289.

26. Most savings banks lent predominantly on real estate located in their own county, but typically had some loans on property located in other counties. The large savings banks in San Francisco lent throughout the state. The data are for loans by location of collateral, not borrower. Moreover, commercial borrowers and borrowers on personal security may have been tied more closely to local banks by convenience and information costs than mortgage borrowers.

27. See California State Board of Commissioners of the Building and Loan Associations, Annual Report.

28. See Blackford (1977) and Nash (1964) for a discussion of insurance companies' activities in California; Davis (1975) and Silber (1975) discuss the contribution of insurance companies to the financial development of the United States.

29. In a study of California gold mining, Hallagan (1977) gives some examples of a non-institutional source of investable funds. The lack of buyers with sufficient capital to purchase gold mines led mine owners to finance the purchase of their mines at rates of one percent per month or ten percent a year. In some cases, this practice extended to the purchase of other assets apart from mines.

30. Buser, Chen and Kane (1981) show how deposit insurance reduces banks' capital/liability ratios.

Table 5-1
Aggregate Balance Sheets for State Chartered
Commercial and Savings Banks, 1890

Resources	Commercial Banks* ($ thousands)	Savings Banks** ($ thousands)
Bank Premises	2650	1468
Other real estate	1918	576
Invested in bonds and stocks	2572	17034
Lonas on real estate	14852	75998
Loans on bonds and stocks	5759	8403
Loans on other securities	3334	191
Loans on personal security	33074	376
Money on hand	10293	2596
Due from banks and bankers	9834	2166
Other assets	3606	283
Total Resources	**87922**	**109092**

Liabilities		
Capital paid-up	25449	6257
Reserve fund, etc.	14501	3518
Due depositors	42331	98442
Due banks and bankers	4881	61
Other liabilities	760	813
Total Liabilities	**87922**	**109092**

* 126 banks (does not include 5 foreign banks).
** 37 banks.
Source: California State, Board of Bank Commissioners, *Annual Report*, 1890.

Table 5-2

Regression Results for the Loan/Asset Ratio Model for Various Years, 1878-1910*

CONST.	AGE	ASSETS	NW/D	M/DD	NB	SB	WPC	GRW3YR	HERFIN	NEWBS
1878 (R^2 = .57, SE = .082, F = 12.8, N = 75)										
.800	.012	-.009	.190	-.494		.073	.035	.010	-.005	
(16.33)	(1.04)	(-3.15)a	(3.08)a	(-7.12)a		(2.56)b	(0.83)	(0.32)	(-0.15)	
	((.08))	((-.28))	((.34))	((-.70))		((.27))	((.07))	((.03))	((-.01))	
1884 (R^2 = .57, SE = .112, F = 15.0, N = 99)										
.688	.017	-.015	.359	-.619		.033	.095	-.078	-.014	
(8.98)	(1.04)	(-3.93)a	(4.17)a	(-7.90)a		(0.76)	(2.16)b	(-0.96)	(-0.34)	
	((.08))	((-.33))	((.39))	((-.66))		((.07))	((.17))	((-.08))	((-.03))	
1887 (R^2 = .41, SE = .137, F = 8.7, N = 137)										
.554	.051	-.010	.327	-.405	-.044	.062	.063	.025	-.023	-.086
(6.75)	(3.23)a	(-2.33)a	(3.71)a	(-3.91)a	(-1.37)	(1.50)	(1.26)	(0.36)	(-0.42)	(-0.92)
	((.28))	((-.19))	((.38))	((-.31))	((-.10))	((.13))	((.09))	((.05))	((-.03))	((-.12))
1890 (R^2 = .42, SE = .114, F = 13.6, N = 201)										
.648	0.18	-.005	.344	-.439	-.041	.069	.033	.114	.076	-.136
((11.57))	(1.75)c	(-1.77)c	(5.66)a	(-6.69)a	(-1.87)c	(2.28)b	(1.04)	(1.50)	(1.75)c	(-3.07)a
	((.12))	((-.12))	((.44))	((-.44))	((-.11))	((.18))	((.06))	((.09))	((.10))	((-.20))

157

Table 5-2 (continued)

Regression Results for the Loan/Asset Ratio Model for Various Years, 1878-1910*

CONST.	AGE	ASSETS	NW/D	M/DD	NB	SB	WPC	GRW3YR	HERFIN	NEWBS
1893 (R² = .53, SE = .093, F = 28.9, N = 262)										
.622	.019	-.005	.297	-.490	-.025	.080	.097	.225	.079	-.045
(18.76)	(2.73)a	(-2.62)a	(7.53)a	(-11.41)a	(-1.40)	(3.93)a	(4.09)a	(2.34)b	(1.96)c	(-1.33)
	((.14))	((-.13))	((.45))	((-.62))	((-.06))	((.25))	((.19))	((-.11))	((.10))	((-.07))
1896 (R² = .40, SE = .110, F = 16.4, N = 256)										
.640	.013	-.003	.335	-.485	-.044	.103	.020	-.074	.024	-.108
(16.32)	(1.34)	(-1.19)	(6.49)a	(-7.92)a	(-1.96)c	(4.45)a	(0.63)	(-1.10)	(0.52)	(-1.40)
	((.08))	((-.07))	((.47))	((-.47))	((-.10))	((.30))	((.03))	((-.06))	((.03))	((-.08))
1899 (R² = .28, SE = .144, F = 9.8, N = 261)										
.579	-.002	-.007	.298	-.359	-.053	.092	.139	-.207	-0.116	-.172
(12.44)	(-0.17)	(-2.64)a	(4.53)a	(-3.67)a	(-1.89)c	(3.02)a	(3.58)a	(-1.46)	(-2.11)b	(-1.72)c
	((-.01))	((-.17))	((.32))	((-.23))	((-.11))	((.22))	((.21))	((-.09))	((-.12))	((-.11))
1900 (R² = .21, SE = .143, F = 6.8, N = 268)										
.596	0.20	-.008	.180	-.503	-.047	.014	.107	.052	-.100	-.119
(13.22)	(1.56)	(-3.60)a	(2.77)a	(-4.82)a	(-1.76)c	(0.49)	(2.95)a	(0.15)	(-1.88)c	(-1.10)
	((.10))	((-.23))	((.19))	((-.32))	((-.10))	((.04))	((.18))	((.01))	((-.12))	((-.07))

158

Table 5-2 (continued)

Regression Results for the Loan/Asset Ratio Model for Various Years, 1878-1910*

CONST.	AGE	ASSETS	NW/D	M/DD	NB	SB	WPC	GRW3YR	HERFIN	NEWBS
1905 (R² = .10, SE = .174, F = 1.4, N = 140)										
.581	.011	-.007	.232	-.161	-.004	.078	.043	.093	.011	-.103
(6.59)	(0.79)	(-1.92)c	(1.87)c	(-0.70)	(-.10)	(1.86)c	(0.59)	(1.07)	(0.10)	(-1.07)
	((.08))	((.19))	((.19))	((-.08))	((-.01))	((.19))	((.06))	((.11))	((.01))	((-.11))
1908 (R² = .19, SE = .134, F = 2.8, N = 107)										
.729	.021	-.017	.040	-.248			-.046	-.037	-.223	-.000
(10.60)	(1.39)	(-1.50)	(0.41)	(-1.56)			(-2.32)b	(-0.38)	(-2.75)a	(-0.00)
	((.15))	((-.16))	((.04))	((-.12))			((-.22))	((-.05))	((-.28))	((-.00))

* "t" values for each regression coefficient are reported in parentheses; standardized regression coefficients (beta coefficients) are reported in double parentheses; N is the number of observations;; the F-statistic exceeds the critical value of F in all regressions except 1905; the variables used are described in Chapter 5.

a Significant at the 1-percent level, two-tailed test.
b Significant at the 5-percent level, two-tailed test.
c Significant at the 10-percent level, two-tailed test.

Table 5-3
Average Net Worth/Deposit Ratios by Bank Type
1878-1905

Year	National Banks	State Commercial Banks	State Savings Banks	Private Banks	All Banks
1878	0.53	0.58	0.24	-	0.47
1884	0.40	0.51	0.19	-	0.44
1887	0.32	0.46	0.23	0.51	0.39
1890	0.42	0.50	0.20	0.54	0.43
1893	0.46	0.53	0.20	0.60	0.44
1896	0.39	0.51	0.23	0.54	0.43
1899	0.32	0.40	0.15	0.37	0.34
1900	0.30	0.37	0.14	0.39	0.31
1905*	0.29	0.37	0.20	-	0.27

* Includes only a sample of banks.
Source: California State Board of Bank Commissioners, *Annual Report*, 1878-1905.
United States Comptroller of the Currency, *Annual Report*, 1878-1887, and 1905.

Table 5-4
Average Cash/Deposit Ratios by Bank Type
1878-1905

Year	National Banks	State Commercial Banks	State Savings Banks	Private Banks	All Banks
1878	0.33	0.29	0.09	-	0.21
1884	0.23	0.27	0.09	-	0.21
1887	0.20	0.22	0.22	0.35	0.18
1890	0.20	0.21	0.14	0.33	0.20
1893	0.28	0.26	0.07	0.33	0.14
1896	0.20	0.18	0.06	0.26	0.12
1899	0.18	0.14	0.03	0.18	0.11
1900	0.15	0.13	0.03	0.24	0.09
1905*	0.14	0.22	0.03	-	0.11

* Includes only a sample of banks.
Sources: See Table 5-3.

Chapter 6

Entry Into Local Banking Markets in California, 1884-1908

Introduction

Between 1884 and 1908, the restrictions on the formation of new banks in California were minimal in that neither California's Bank Commissioners nor the U.S. Comptrollers of the Currency denied bank charter applications because these regulators believed a local community did not need a new bank.[1] Given this freedom, the pattern of bank entry in California in this period provides information in two areas. First, it shows how largely unrestricted banking spreads through a rapidly developing economy. Second, it indicates the importance of various market factors in determining the attractiveness of local bank markets when regulators' preferences do not affect the location of new banks.

Economic theory argues that entry in a competitive economy is a response to differences in expected profit rates. In the absence of barriers to entry, such as economies of scale, entrepreneurs maximize the return to capital by forming firms in those industries or locations where they expect newly-invested capital to earn the highest rate of profit. While several studies have investigated entry into the banking industry as a whole during the decades 1920-1970, most of the research on bank entry has focused on the formation of banks in local banking markets.[2] Recent research on bank entry is discussed in the Appendix to this chapter. Two methods have predominated in the analysis of bank entry. One method looks for differences in the characteristics of banks and markets both before and after entry, including comparisons with the behavior and characteristics of control groups of banks or markets not experiencing entry.[3] The other method, which is the one used in this study, employs multiple regression analysis and other multivariate statistical techniques to estimate models of bank entry into local markets.[4]

The consensus that emerges from this research, which is reviewed in the Appendix to this chapter, is that bank entry is clearly a response to economic opportunity. Banks are more likely to be formed (or acquired) in larger, less concentrated, and faster growing markets where incumbent banks have higher rates of earnings and lower levels of performance than in markets with the converse attributes.[5] When it occurs, bank entry usually improves the performance of the existing banks, though both the nature and the duration of this improvement remain uncertain. Studies of entry into the banking industry as a whole show that bank capital and entry into banking are functions of the relative profitability of banking and the restrictiveness of bank chartering policies.

In the next section, a model of entry into local banking markets is developed, and the results from the estimation of this model with data on bank formations in California between 1884 and 1908 are presented. The subsequent section assesses the impact of entry on aggregate bank performance in local markets. In the final section, some conclusions are drawn from the results of the analysis of a period of unrestricted bank entry.

A Model of Bank Entry Into Local Banking Markets

According to economic theory, banks should be formed in locations where they are expected to be most profitable. Given the large number of alternative locations for a new bank, it would be very difficult to estimate the expected rate of return for each possible location. Instead, the analysis focuses on bankers' choices of which local banking market to enter. In striving to maximize their expected profits, bankers will form new banks in those local banking markets that offer the highest rate of profit to new banks. Though the concept of a local banking market is not without flaws, as discussed above, it is used here as a practical construction that permits analysis of bank entry.

The lack of data on bank earnings for this period means that the expected profit rate for a local market cannot be simply approximated by the past profit rates of the banks already in the market. In the absence of another feasible method of directly estimating expected profit rates, it is assumed that a new bank's expected rate of profit depends primarily on its expected deposit growth. Given that a bank's earnings depend on its asset size, and thus on its volume of deposits, this assumption appears reasonable. Moreover, this assumption is consistent with the behavior of many bankers today who presently pay close attention to a new bank's prospective deposit growth when determining the optimal location for a new bank. Hence, to establish which markets are attractive to a new bank, those factors which determine a new bank's prospective deposit growth must be explored.[6]

The key to deposit growth for a new bank is attracting customers, many of whom will come from existing banks already in the market. In attracting customers, the new bank faces competition from the existing banks. A growing market is attractive both because market growth supplies new customers, and because it provides replacements for the customers of existing banks who switch to the new bank. Thus, to the extent any lost business is replaced, the existing banks have less need to take competitive actions to retain their customers. A new bank benefits from market growth regardless of which bank obtains the new business.

More customers are likely to switch to a new bank when the existing banks are providing inadequate service. If the customers of existing banks are paying too high a rate on their loans and receiving too little interest on their deposits relative to competitive prices, then the market will have plenty of dissatisfied customers for a new bank to attract. In the aggregate, poor performance could be due to the existing banks' inefficiency, insufficient investment in banking relative to demand, or the exercising of market power by the existing banks. Regardless of the cause, however, a new bank will be able to capitalize on its novelty and attract dissatisfied customers by offering better terms and improved service.

A new bank may find it more difficult, however, to attract customers in a market where the incumbent banks possess market power. A bank possesses market power if it can raise the rates it charges its customers without losing all of them to its competitors. The bases for this market power are the established relationships between banks and their customers and the degree of competition among the banks in the market. The greater the degree of market power, the fewer customers the bank would lose if it raised its rates. Hence, the stronger the market power of the existing banks, the harder it will be for the new bank to attract customers with lower prices and better service.[7]

In the absence of a method for determining the degree of banks' market power in each market, a common assumption is made that it is directly related to the concentration of banking resources among the existing banks in the market. Some justification for this assumption is provided in Chapter 4 above. If this assumption is valid, then concentrated markets should be less attractive to new banks than unconcentrated markets. Concentrated markets may also be less attractive because concerted action by the existing banks to retain their customers and restrain the growth of the new bank is more likely.[8] However, if market power and the ability to act together are not directly related to market concentration, the opposite may be true. Concentrated markets may be more attractive to new banks because such markets typically have fewer banks than unconcentrated ones.

The attractiveness of a market to a new bank also depends on the market's size. When compared with small markets, large markets offer more alternative sites, greater opportunities for specialization, and less likelihood of eliciting concerted retaliatory action from the existing banks.

Besides predicting deposit growth, bankers must also consider the risk of bank failure, which varies across markets and over time. For example, markets whose economies depend on one crop or one major employer are likely to have a higher probability of bank failure than markets with diversified economies. Unfortunately, no feasible measure of inter-market differences in the risk of failure was available.[9] However, a measure of the statewide risk of failure was included to capture changes over time in this factor.

In summary, the market that offers a new bank the best prospects for deposit growth has the following characteristics: rapid expected growth, poor performance by the existing banks, large size, and low risk of failure. If market power and the ability to act together depend on concentration, an unconcentrated market is more attractive than a concentrated market. The more attractive a market appears to be, based on these factors, the greater the number of bankers who will form new banks in that market during the subsequent period, here assumed to be three years. Hence, entry into local banking markets can be analyzed with the following model:

> Bank Entry = f(Expected Market Growth, Current Bank Performance, Market Concentration, Market Size, Risk of Failure)

For the estimation of the model, local markets are defined as California counties.[10] Justification for this assumption was provided in Chapter 5 above. The time taken between recognition of the need for a new bank and the opening of a new bank is assumed to be three years.[11] All types of banks are included in the analysis: commercial banks (state-chartered and national banks), savings banks, and private, unincorporated banks.[12] The model was estimated in linear form using ordinary least squares regression analysis applied to pooled cross-section data for bank formations in California counties for seven consecutive three-year periods between 1884 and 1908. (The period 1899-1902 was omitted due to missing data.)[13]

The variables used in the estimation are defined as follows:

Bank Entry

NET BS = The net rate of formation of banks in the county between year t and year $t+3$, i.e., the number of new banks minus the number of banks going out of business divided by the average number of banks between year t and year $t+3$.

NET TA = The net rate of change in bank assets due to entering and existing banks in the county; i.e., the assets of new banks in year $t+3$ minus the assets of existing banks in year t divided by the average assets of all banks in the county between year t and year $t+3$.

Proportional measures of bank entry were employed because market size varied substantially among markets (between \$2 million and \$467 million). The proportional measures provide a correction for heteroscedasticity associated with market size.

Expected Market Growth

GRW3YR = The proportional change between year t-3 and year t in WEALTH, the value of county property assessed for taxation. Past county growth is assumed to be a good predictor of future county growth.

Current Bank Performance

TD/W =   The total deposits of all banks in the county in year t
           divided by WEALTH.

TA/W =   The total assets of all banks in the county in year t
           divided by WEALTH.

These two ratios indicate the extent to which banks in the county are meeting the demand for bank deposits and bank assets, where this demand is assumed to be primarily a function of county wealth.[14]

Market Concentration

HERFIN =   The Herfindahl index; i.e., the sum of the squared market
           shares of total assets of all the banks in the county in year
           t.

Market Size

WEALTH =   The three-year moving average in year t of the value of
           county property assessed for taxation. During this period,
           such property included not only real, but also personal
           property.[15]

Risk of Failure

FAILRT =   The number of bank failures in California between year
           t-2 and year t divided by the average number of banks in
           the state in the same period. FAILRT measures the
           general risk of failure for banks in California, which
           changed over the period covered.

The model is estimated in the following linear form:

$$(\text{NET BS or NET TA}) = b_0 + b_1 \text{ GRW3YR} + b_2(\text{TA/W or TD/W})$$
$$+ b_3 \text{ HERFIN} + b_4 \text{ WEALTH}$$
$$+ b_5 \text{ FAILRT} + e,$$

where e, the error term, is assumed to be normally distributed.[16]

The regression coefficients, reported in Table 6-1, have the predicted signs, and are statistically significant at the five-percent level or better, with the exception of the coefficient of WEALTH.[17] During this period, bank entry appears to have been higher in faster growing markets, lower in markets with better current performance, lower in more concentrated markets, higher in larger markets, and lower in periods when the risk of failure was higher. The R^2's range from 0.10 to 0.13, indicating that the linear model fails to explain much of the variation in entry rates among markets. The low R^2's, which are common in cross-section analysis, are discussed below. F-statistics for all the regression equations are statistically significant at the one-percent level.

The regression results are broadly similar for both measures of bank entry, with only some small differences in the relative importance of the independent variables. The standardized regression coefficients indicate that the expected rate of market growth (GRW3YR) is the most important variable explaining the net rate of bank formations (NET BS), while current bank performance (either TA/W or TD/W) is the most important factor explaining the net rate of growth of new bank assets (NET TA). Drawing any further implications would appear to be speculative in view of the small differences in the size of the standardized regression coefficients. There is little to choose between the two performance ratios. Given the use here of proportional measures of bank entry, it is not surprising that market size does not have a statistically significant coefficient. The results do not support the hypothesis that larger markets are more attractive *per se* than smaller markets.

The standardized regression coefficients appear to show that the effect of any one variable upon bank entry was small; the largest standardized regression coefficient is only 0.27. The large standard deviations of both measures of entry partly explain this result. In fact, an increase in GRW3YR of one standard deviation, 0.19, generates an increase in NET BS equal to 0.12, which is a large increase by comparison with the mean for NET BS of 0.19.[18] An increase in TD/W of one standard deviation reduced NET BS by 0.06; a one standard deviation increase in HERFIN reduces NET BS by 0.05. The independent variables have a similar effect on NET TA, with one standard deviation increases in GRW3YR, TD/W, and HERFIN generating changes in NET TA of 0.07, 0.09, and 0.07, respectively, as compared with a mean of NET TA of 0.10.

Despite the importance of the independent variables and their statistical significance, the independent variables explain only a small part of the variation among the counties in the rate of bank entry. Several factors may explain these low R^2's. The omission of some relevant market characteristics from the model is one possible cause of the low R^2's. For example, the model does not take account of variations among markets in the opportunity cost and availability of capital to prospective bankers. Errors in measuring the variables included in the theoretical model may also contribute to the low R2's. Expected market growth, for example, should incorporate expectations about changes in the economic structure of the market such as the development of a new town or industry. Discrepancies between the theoretical model and the estimated model may also arise from the use of counties for local banking markets. The validity of this assumption undoubtedly varies among counties. In addition, the extent of competition from banks in other counties, which is assumed to be negligible under the local banking market concept, differed among counties.[19] If the errors associated with individual counties are stable over time, a cross-section, time-series model might improve the regression results. This type of model could also allow for correlation between entry in the previous period and entry in the current period.[20] Unfortunately, the missing data for 1901-1904 create a stumbling block that needs to be surmounted if such a model is to be estimated.

Assessing the Impact of Entry on Performance

The positive response of bank entry to poor performance suggests that bank entry improved aggregate performance. The following model is used to assess the impact of bank entry on bank performance in local banking markets during each three-year period:

(Change in Performance = f(Bank Entry, Market Concentration, Market Growth).

While performance is expected to improve in entered markets, market concentration is likely to slow improvements in performance if market power is a function of market concentration. Current market growth is included to allow for errors in expectations of market growth on which the decision to enter was based.

The model was estimated in the following linear form using pooled cross-section data for the same seven three-year periods as in the estimation of the entry model:

(GR TD/W or GR TA/W = b_0 + b_1(NET BS or NET TA) + b_2 HERFIN + b_3 GRWTP3 + e,

where GR TD/W and GR TA/W are the proportional changes in the two performance ratios, TD/W and TA/W, between year t and year t+3, GRWTP3 is the proportional change in WEALTH between year t and year t+3, and e, the error term, is assumed to be normally distributed.

The regression results, reported in Table 6-2, indicate that bank entry was indeed a major factor leading to an improvement in performance. Both measures of entry have positive coefficients that are significant at the one percent level. Market concentration, however, does not appear to have constrained the improvement of performance; the coefficient of HERFIN, though negative, is not significant even at the ten percent level.

Conclusions

The analysis of the pattern of bank entry in California during 1884-1908 suggests four findings: first, bankers did respond to profitable opportunities offered by market growth and the deficient performance of existing banks; second, market concentration reduced bank entry; third, a higher probability of bank failure led to a lower rate of bank entry; and fourth, bank entry improved aggregate performance. These findings are generally consistent with those reported in other research on pattern of bank entry, the attractiveness of markets for de novo entry and foothold acquisitions, and the impact of bank entry on bank performance.[21]

In the analysis of banking's role in economic development, one of the important issues is whether the banking sector can initiate economic development.[22] The findings of this study indicate that banking was generally a response not only to economic growth, but also to the existing levels of banking relative to the economy. Bankers appear to have looked for growing areas that needed more banking, rather than first forming banks and then generating economic growth. In specific instances, a bank may have been formed that did play a key role in subsequently developing a local economy, but the broad mass of banks did not perform this role. Though some banks were undoubtedly organized that initiated development, bank organizations generally were a response to the demand for banking services. In this respect, banking contributed to economic growth. By responding to the demand for banking services, bank entry improved the provision of financial services to California's developing economy. Without this response, economic growth might not have been sustained, implying that banking contributed to economic growth. The amount of this contribution, however, and how it was influenced by the lack of significant regulatory barriers to entry remain unknown. In the next chapter, this latter question is explored in an indirect fashion. The effects of changes in minimum capital requirements are estimated to see if these changes affected entry, and so help to explain the pattern of regional interest rate differentials.

The results reported here are consistent with the hypothesis that banks possessed market power even at a time when restrictions on bank entry were minimal. This finding runs counter to the argument that banks' market power depends largely on entry restrictions arising from banking regulation.[23] The relationship between market concentration and market power, however, remains undetermined. Market concentration does not appear to have slowed the improvement in bank performance. Moreover, the analysis of individual bank behavior in California during this period in Chapter 5 above reveals that market concentration had only a small effect on individual bank behavior in some of the years sampled. The negative effect of market concentration on entry may thus have been due to the relationship between market concentration and the perceived threat of the existing banks acting together, rather than the relationship between market concentration and individual banks' market power.

Poor performance, whatever its cause, did not pass unobserved, as banks were formed in those markets with deficient bank performance.[24] At a time when communications and business techniques were less developed than they are today, bankers chose to start banks in markets that needed banking services. There is no reason to expect that modern bankers are less able to seize profitable opportunities for new banks. Certainly, modern bankers have access to far more information about prospective markets than their counterparts eighty years ago. Thus, if the objective of banking regulations is to satisfy the demands of bank customers, the chartering process should place greater emphasis on the judgment of prospective entrants about the need for a new bank than occurs at present.[25] To the extent that present regulatory restrictions inhibit bank entry, banking regulations delay an important remedy for deficient performance: the formation of a new bank.

Notes

1. For more details on the regulation of state and national banks, see Chapter 2 above.
2. Peltzman (1965) and Throop (1975) are two examples of studies of entry into the banking industry as a whole.
3. See Benston (1973) and Rose (1977).
4. The studies using this method are Boczar (1979), Hanweck (1971), and Rose (1977). Regulation affects the results Rose obtains, even though his sample of SMSAs is taken from a single state; Rose suggests that the failure of his model to explain the pattern of bank entry in 1961-1965 and 1966-1969 is due to the liberal chartering policies of the Saxon years, and the subsequent retrenchment.
5. In these studies, bank performance is measured by such variables as the rate charged on loans, the rate paid on deposits, the ratio of loans to assets, the ratio of time and savings deposits to total deposits, and so forth.
6. The emphasis in two widely known handbooks of bank location analysis, Bennett (1975) and Littlefield, Burney and White (1973), is placed on the estimation of a market's deposit potential for a new bank, though the bottom line of profitability is also stressed. While deposit growth does not ensure increased return to capital for an existing bank, a new bank's profit rate is likely to increase with deposit growth. A new bank is usually operating at less than optimal output in its early years. Under this condition, and provided marginal cost is below marginal revenue, deposit growth, and the asset growth it generates, will increase the rate of return to a given amount of capital.
7. Various reasons were offered in Chapter 4 above to explain why banks might possess market power. One fact that was explored is the cost to both customers and banks of gathering information. Such costs suggest an interesting application of the "market for lemons," a concept first presented by Akerlof (1970). The workings of this market may act to restrict competition among banks and inhibit the entry of new banks. For example, if an existing bank lowers its interest on loans to increase its market share, it will probably attract a larger percentage of borrowers who are "lemons" than the average bank. The "lemons" can take advantage of the expanding bank's ignorance and borrow at lower interest rates than they would obtain

if full information was available to the expanding bank. In this case, the expanding bank will find more of its loans going sour, forcing it to spend more resources on credit information, which may be passed on to the borrowers in the form of increased loan fees or higher loan rates. The expansionary policy is thus curtailed. New banks may also lack sufficient information and thus face higher costs than existing banks. Even if a new bank is started by local individuals, they may still be at a disadvantage in knowing less about their borrowers than existing banks, though the gap will be smaller than if the bank is started by outsiders. This suggests that areas where risk of loan defaults is high and personal contacts are important for determining creditworthiness will also be areas where banks are less competitive and face lower threat of entry. It must be remembered that this argument rests on the assertion that the percentage of "lemons" will be higher for the expanding bank. Only if the proportion of "lemons" among a new bank's customers varies directly with the existing banks' market power, will entry be correspondingly discouraged by the existing bank's market power.

8. The lack of any barriers to entry during this period, such as regulation or economies of scale, suggest that an alternative strategy of limit pricing would not be a profit-maximizing strategy. For a discussion of limit pricing, see Osborne (1966). Hannan (1979) presents evidence that banks presently follow limit pricing strategies. However, the current regulation of bank entry provides a barrier behind which such a strategy may be profitable.

9. Possible candidates are the proportion of the population living in urban areas and the percentage of workers employed in non-agricultural activities.

10. As in Chapter 5, modern county boundaries were used in the analysis, except for Imperial County, which was not created until 1907, leaving 57 counties to be included in the analysis. These definitions required some extrapolations for those counties created during this period, as noted in Chapter 3 above.

11. Other studies employ various periods: Rose (1977) uses three-year periods, while Boczar (1977) uses two-year periods. McCall and Peterson (1976) consider three years to be the dividing line between the short-run and the long-run effects of a single bank's entry.

12. Given the recent changes in the laws and regulations governing financial institutions, the inclusion of savings banks appears particularly appropriate.

13. The absence of bank balance sheets for 1902 necessitated the omission of 1899-1902 and the modification of the variables for 1902-1905. Each three-year period begins in mid-year.

14. These performance ratios are simple indicators of performance that incorporates a single measure of a market's supply of banking services and a single measure of the demand for banking services, while ignoring differences among markets in such characteristics as the quality of banking services, the cost of providing these services, and the structure of each market's economy. They are similar in nature to ratios such as bank offices/population that are presently employed by bankers and regulators in determining a market's attractiveness to a new bank. See Mayor and Fraser (1976).

15. Three-year moving averages were used because changes in the laws and methods governing the valuation of property occasionally affected year-to-year changes in property valuation.

16. Because of the definition of the dependent variables, which can take on two limiting values, the assumption of a normally distributed error term is open to question. While the use of ordinary least squares regression analysis still provides the best estimates of the regression coefficients, the tests of the hypotheses using the t-statistics may not be strictly valid. In practice, the limiting values of the dependent variable occur in few observations (each net entry rate has the value of +2 in 8 out of 354 observations, and -2 only once) suggesting that these tests are generally reliable. This problem is somewhat different from that faced by Boczar (1977) and Rose (1977) who use Tobit analysis because their dependent variables do not have negative values, but do take on the limiting value of zero in a significant number of observations.

17. For all the variables except HERFIN, one-tailed t-tests are used to determine the statistical significance of the regression coefficients because the theoretical model predicts the sign of each of these coefficients unambiguously. A two-tailed test is appropriate for the coefficient of HERFIN because the effect of market concentration on entry is ambiguous.

18. The means, standard deviations, and ranges of the regression variables for counties with more than $2 million in wealth are as follows:

Variable	Mean	Standard Deviation	Range	
TA/W	.12	.11	.00 -	.83
TD/W	.07	.08	.00 -	.58
GRW3YR	.13	.19	- .38 -	1.19
HERFIN	.43	.32	.00 -	1.00
WEALTH	22.22	52.98	2.10 -	467.70
NET BS	.19	.42	-2.00 -	2.00
NET TA	.10	.36	-2.00 -	2.00
FAILRT	1.06	1.62	0.00 -	4.80

19. The pattern of mortgage lending is analyzed by Pierson-Doti (1978), who reports that banks in California frequently made mortgage loans on property located outside their own county during this period. The location of the mortgage borrowers, however, is not known.

20. This correlation would be negative if the entry of a bank in the previous period forestalled entry in this period, despite the attractiveness of the market. However, if the entry of a new bank was a good indication of the attractiveness of a market, this correlation would be positive. Although both Boczar (1977) and Hanweck (1971) report that past bank formations or acquisitions increased subsequent bank formations or acquisitions, neither include another measure of market growth. Thus, past entry serves only as a proxy for the rate of market growth, leaving the issue undecided.

21. One apparent difference between the results reported here and those reported in Boczar (1977), Hanweck (1971), and Rose (1977) is the importance of market size in explaining entry. The explanation for this difference is the use in these studies of the number of new banks or acquisitions rather than the proportional rate of entry that is employed here. Typically, large markets will have a large number of new banks, but not necessarily a high proportional rate of entry.

22. See Cameron (1972).

23. See Benston (1973).

24. The success of the performance ratios in explaining entry suggests that similar ratios (such as deposits/personal income) may be useful today in establishing the attractiveness of local banking markets for *de novo* entry. It also suggests that regulators should include a measure of income or wealth when determining the need for a new bank. According to Mayor and Fraser (1976), no income measures are included in the information requested from national bank charter applicants by the Comptroller of the Currency. For an application of the deposits/personal income ratio to recent banking growth, see Lister (1979).

25. Scott (1975) discusses critically the federal banking agencies' licensing decisions. Preventing bank failures has also been one of the objectives of bank regulators, particularly since the 1930s. As Peltzman (1965) and Throop (1975) demonstrate, pursuit of this objective has led to a reduction in bank entry during the past four decades from preceding years. Many critics of current regulatory policies question whether the benefits to the public of fewer bank failures offset the costs of less bank entry. See, for example, Benston (1973) and Scott (1975). In California, bank failures during the period 1884-1908 appear to have had little to do with overbanking and free entry. Instead, the discussion in Chapter 2 suggests they resulted from poor management, malfeasance, inadequate communications, and the absence of a lender of last resort or some other means of increasing banks' liquidity during a financial crisis.

Appendix to Chapter 6:
Research on Bank Entry

Empirical studies of bank entry focus on three issues: the explanation and prediction of entry, the impact of entry on performance, and the effect of regulation on entry. The following classification of empirical studies is suggested by the method and type of data employed in each study: (1) studies that use multiple regression analysis to test models of entry into local markets, where entry includes the acquisition of existing banks by bank holding companies located outside the local market, (2) studies testing for differences in the characteristics of banks and markets before and after entry, where comparisons are made with the behavior and characteristics of control groups not experiencing entry; and (3) studies applying models of entry and bank capital formation to the U.S. banking industry over time, and to cross-sections of states. The discussion below considers each group in order, indicating in each case how their results contribute to the three basic issues.

Among the local market studies, Rose (1977) is the most similar in method and results to the present study. He reports that entry into 20 Texas secondary banking markets (he uses SMSAs as market definitions) over the period 1962-1973 was positively and significantly related to the three-year market average of the net income/total asset ratio for all the banks in the market, total market deposits, and the rate of growth of total deposits, where entry is measured by the number of new banks. The three-bank concentration ratio had a significantly negative, though weak, impact on entry. These results are confirmed by regressions for the shorter period 1970-1973, but not for the periods 1962-1965 and

1966-1969, when most of the variables' coefficients are not significant, even at the ten percent level of confidence. Rose suggests that the liberal entry policy under Comptroller Saxon and the retrenchment in the years after Saxon left, explain these results for the shorter periods. Market size is the only variable with the same sign in all regressions, though the coefficients of market profitability and market concentration have unanticipated signs only for the 1966-1969 regressions.

Using a sample of 220 SMSAs for 1968 and 1969, Hanweck (1971) also finds market size and bank concentration significantly affected bank formations, but does not include any measure of bank profitability. The market population/bank office ratio, one measure of current performance, is not significant. However, lagged entry did have a positive and significant impact on bank entry.

Another study in the same vein, Boczar (1977), is an analysis of multi-bank holding company (MBHC) acquisitions in a sample of 100 metropolitan markets for the period January 1971 through December 1973. He concludes:

> MBHCs are more active in markets characterized by: (1) relatively fast growth in terms of banking offices; (2) relatively favorable conditions as shown by total deposits per bank office; (3) relatively high rates of return; and (4) relatively low concentration. (Boczar (1977), p. 146)

Using similar methodology and econometric techniques, these three studies largely confirm the multiple regression results reported in Chapter 6. They report that banks were formed or acquired in large, growing markets with low three-bank concentration ratios where market conditions were favorable. Evidence on the latter factor is not clear cut. Rose finds bank formations responded to existing banks' profits, while Boczar finds they responded to the average deposits of existing banks. Hanweck does not find the population to bank office ratio to be significant, a failure which Rose attributes to Hanweck's omission of a variable to account for differences among markets in the ability to branch.

One apparent difference between these results and those reported in Chapter 6 above is the consistent importance of market size in all three studies. This difference may be explained by the use of the number of bank formations or acquisitions in these studies rather than the rate of entry used in this study. Typically, large markets will have a large number of new banks, but not necessarily a high rate of entry.

All three studies use the past growth of banking to project future market growth rather than some measure of the market's economic growth. Hanweck and Boczar report that past bank formations increase current bank formations or acquisitions. They do not allow for the possibility that past entry might reduce present entry. Rose finds past growth of deposits increases current bank formations. Again, deposits could be growing faster or slower than the market's demand for deposits. Although their projections of market growth appear to be no less successful than the past rate of growth of wealth used in the model in Chapter 6, their results may be explained by correlation between these variables. In this study, there is some correlation between past growth in wealth (GRW3YR), current growth in wealth (GRWTP3), and the rates of bank formation (NETBS & NETTA). The simple correlation coefficients are:

Variable	GRW3YR	GRWTP3	NET BS
GRW3YR	1.00		
GRWTP3	0.52	1.00	
NET BS	0.31	0.38	1.00
NET TA	0.23	0.25	0.87

The second group of studies uses a comparative approach to analyze bank entry. Four studies, Motter (1965), Chandross (1971), Fraser and Rose (1972), and McCall and Peterson (1976) evaluate the impact of bank entry on performance by comparing the behavior of banks in entered markets before and after entry. In each case, a selected group of control banks in unentered markets is used for comparison over time. In the latter three studies, banks in entered markets (sample banks) had lower loan/asset ratios, lower time deposit/total deposit ratios, and higher capital/asset ratios relative to the control banks. Entry improved performance as both the loan/asset and time deposit/total deposit ratios increased after entry, though McCall and Peterson report the increase in the loan/asset ratio only lasted one year. Motter finds the same pattern for the loan/deposit ratios of sample banks. Only Motter, and McCall and Peterson observe sample banks paying higher interest rates on deposits after entry. After entry occurred, sample banks in all studies, except Fraser and Rose, experienced a decline in their net earnings/asset ratios, relative to the control group, as the average cost of funds rose with the time deposit/total deposit ratio and/or the interest rate paid on deposits. Increased revenue from higher loan/asset ratios after entry was insufficient to offset the rising cost of funds.

The sample used by Chandross (1971) comprised 98 banks in one-bank towns that experienced entry during the period 1950-1961. The performance of these sample banks is compared with that of nonmember banks in the relevant state. As a check, Chandross also reports the comparisons with the averages for all banks in the relevant state; the results are similar in sign and significance. Motter (1965) studies the national banks chartered in 1962, and analyzes the impact of some of these bank formations on incumbent banks in one- and two-bank towns. All insured banks with $10-25 million deposits constitute the control group. Fraser and Rose (1972) compare the performance of 34 banks in one-, two-, and three-bank nonmetropolitan communities in the Eleventh Federal Reserve District experiencing entry during the years 1962-1964, with the performance of 56 banks in communities with similar economic and structural characteristics that did not experience entry. "Among these (economic characteristics) were the number and size of the banks in the community, the level of income, the agricultural-industrial mix of the area, and the rate of growth of population." (See Fraser and Rose (1972), p. 67.) For the period 1966-1969, McCall and Peterson (1976) find controls for 31 of the 57 banks entering similar markets with fewer than four banks in unit bank states and for 11 out of the 35 banks entering such markets in states permitting branching. The choice of control banks is based on certain similarities. "Each control bank is similar to its paired sample bank in terms of size, charter, organizational structure, competitive environment including number of banks in the market, their unit-branch mix, the presence of such thrift institutions as savings and loan associations, deposit market share, and rural nonmetropolitan markets growing at similar rates in the same state." (McCall and Peterson (1976), p. 5.)

The significance of differences in net profit rates appears to depend upon the similarities between the sample and the control banks. Both Motter (entry into one- and two-bank towns) and Chandross (entry into one-bank towns) report sample banks (i.e., banks in entered markets) had higher net profits/capital ratios than the control banks. For the control banks, Motter uses the averages for all insured banks with $10-25 million deposits and Chandross employs averages for all nonmember banks in the relevant state. Only Motter finds sample banks' net profit/capital ratios remained higher after entry. The other two studies choose banks in isolated rural one-, two-, and three-bank towns for both the sample and control banks. The control group comprises banks in markets that are similar in size, growth, employment pattern, and other characteristics to the markets containing the sample banks. Given this selection of very similar banks in the control group, it is not surprising that no differences are found in net profit/capital ratios between sample and control banks. However, both studies suggest that this failure reflects the higher capital/asset ratios of sample banks compared with the control banks. These higher ratios offset higher net profit/asset ratios in sample banks. In McCall and Peterson, dummy variables do not reveal consistently different patterns in one-, two-, or three-bank towns. Motter suggests that the impact of entry did differ between one-bank and two-bank towns, but admits that the sample is too small (five of each kind) and the period too limited for more than a suggestion.

A comparison of entered markets with unentered markets highlights the characteristics of entered markets. Using a sample from de novo bank formations in 1964, R. Alton Gilbert (1974) tests modifications of the Federal Reserve's predictors of de novo entry with these results: for markets with populations of similar size, the population per banking office in entered markets was significantly greater than in nonentered markets and deposits per banking office were greater (though not significantly) in entered markets. He uses the same ratios but changes the yardstick from the Federal Reserve's statewide average to the average for similar sized counties. Population growth in entered markets was significantly faster than the relevant state's population growth.

The choice of banks for acquisitions also provides information about the potential of the markets where the acquired bank is situated. From 55 merger cases decided between 1960 and 1967, Gary Gilbert (1974) constructs a ranking of fifteen market factors using a conditional deletion test. The top factors in this ranking are all banking market structure measures: the number of banks, the number of banking offices, average size of banks, and the total deposits of the three largest banks. The next factor is total disposable income, a measure of "market growth prospects for bank services," followed by five factors describing the expansion history and characteristics of the applicant bank. Two other market characteristics, relative industrialization (employment in manufacturing) and total retail sales appear in the eleventh and thirteenth positions. Gilbert argues that this ranking incorporates the interactions among the factors, which are important in this case, and is therefore to be preferred to a simple univariate, analysis of variance, F-test ranking. The latter test still ranks the number of banks first, but the market characteristics, relative industrialization, retail sales, and disposable income are the next in order.

David Motter and Deane Carson (1964) analyze the rapid expansion of banking in New York State's Nassau County after the legalization of branching in 1960. They find that this expansion improved performance in local markets. This conclusion is based on the following observation: new banks and offices gave added convenience, increased competition, lowered interest paid on installment loans, and raised interest paid on deposits, while rates of return to incumbent banks did not fall below normal levels. The distribution of offices was correlated with family income and population in local markets, suggesting the importance of the economic base for the decision to enter.

The third group of studies analyze entry into the U.S. banking industry during the decades 1920-1970: Edwards and Edwards (1974) Pakonen (1970), Peltzman (1965), and Throop (1975). All four explain entry as a response to the expected relative rate of return in manufacturing. Peltzman and Throop find that bank profits were an important determinant of bank entry, and that increases in the restrictiveness of entry regulations significantly reduced bank formations.

Although Edwards and Edwards (1974) argue that Peltzman's model of regulation is incorrectly specified, their model also finds regulation's impact on entry to have been substantial. Pakonen (1970) reports entry restrictions in the form of states' branching regulations had a significant impact on bank office formations over the same period (i.e., new banks plus new branches), with the lowest levels of bank office formations occurring in states prohibiting branching. The market characteristics of the individual states also influenced entry: income and population density had positive impacts, though income was not significant for unit banking states; the number of office closures had a negative impact, though it was not significant for statewide branching states.

Nosari (1975) develops a model to explain national bank charter applications between 1936 and 1968, and finds bank charter applications increased with the relative rate of profit in banking. He reports that the coefficient of the rate of profit in banking is positive and significant in three out of four regressions; charter applications also increased when the rate of return in manufacturing fell and when the standard deviation of this rate (a measure of its stability) rose. However, when the standard deviation of the banking profit rate rises, and presumably becomes less certain, the regression results show that charter applications increased rather than decreased. The real wealth of the United States has a positive and significant effect on charter applications. Nosari introduces dummy variables to evaluate the impact of each U.S. Comptroller of the Currency on charter applications; only some of these are found to be significant. Perhaps this reflects a misspecification of the model; it does not contain any variables reflecting the probability of successful application.

The conclusion suggested by the research reviewed in this appendix is that bank formation, or acquisition, is a response to economic opportunity. The larger, less concentrated, and faster growing a market is, the more likely is a new bank to be formed in that market. There is also evidence that high earnings and/or poor performance stimulate bank formations. The entry of a new bank appears to improve the performance of the existing banks, although the nature and the duration of this improvement remain uncertain. Restrictions on bank entry (or bank office formations) have had a major impact on the expansion of the number of banks (or bank office formations) both over time and among states.

Table 6-1
Entry Into Local Banking Markets: Regression Results[+]

Dependent Variable	GRW3YR	TA/W	TD/W	HERFIN	WEALTH	FAILRT	CONSTANT	R^2/S.E.
NET TA	.323[a] (3.23) [.17]	-.893[a] (3.90) [-.27]		-.212** (3.44) [-.19]	.00049 (1.05) [.07]	-.022[b] (1.83) [-.10]	.274 (5.41)	.11/.34
NET TA	.363[a] (3.66) [.19]		-1.110[a] (3.38) [-.25]	-.209** (3.36) [-.18]	.00038 (.80) [.06]	-.023[b] (1.89) [-.10]	.243 (5.04)	.10/.35
NET BS	.561[a] (4.87) [.26]	-.677[a] (2.56) [-.18]		-.171* (2.41) [-.13]	.00057 (1.06) [.07]	-.032[a] (2.35) [-.12]	.300 (5.13)	.13/.40
NET BS	.593[a] (5.19) [.27]		-.775[b] (2.07) [-.15]	-.166* (2.32) [-.13]	.00043 (.79) [.05]	0.033[a] (2.35) [-.13]	.271 (4.88)	.12/.40

+   Degrees of Freedom - 348; the F statistic exceeds F (0.01, 5, 348) in all regressions; "t" Values for each regression coefficient are reported in parentheses; standardized regression coefficients are reported in brackets.

*   Significant at the 5 per cent level, two-tailed test.

** Significant at the 1 percent level, two-tailed test.

a   Significant at the 1 percent leve, one-tailed test.

b   Significant at the 5 percent level, one-tailed test.

Table 6-2
Entry and Changes in Performance: Regression Results[+]

Dependent Variable	GRWTP3	HERFIN	NET BS	NET TA	CONSTANT	R^2/S.E.
GR TA/W	.115 (1.06) [-.05]	-.026 (0.46) [-.02]	.704* (14.76) [.66]		.129 (3.90)	.42/.34
GR TA/W	.042 (0.47) [.02]	.012 (0.23) [.01]		.911* (19.52) [.73]	.139 (4.82)	.55/.30
GR TD/W	-.128 (1.00) [-.05]	-.020 (0.29) [-.01]	.669* (11.75) [.57]		.167 (4.24)	.31/.41
GR TD/W	.014 (0.12) [.01]	.018 (0.28) [.01]		.879* (15.17) [.65]	.176 (4.89)	.42/.38

+   Degrees of Freedom - 348; the F statistic exceeds $F_{(0.01, 5, 348)}$ in all regressions; "t" Values for each regression coefficient are reported in parentheses; standardized regression coefficients are reported in brackets.

*   Significant at the 1 per cent level, one-tailed test.

Chapter 7

California Banking and the Evolution of a National Capital Market

Introduction

Economists generally agree that an important characteristic of an advanced economy's development is the evolution of a national capital market. One way of gauging the unity of capital markets in a geographically large country such as the United States is to see whether interest rates differed among the various regions of the country. In an original article on this question, Davis (1965) provides evidence that regional interest rate differentials in the United States narrowed between 1870 and 1914, and offers his explanation for the evolution of a national market for short-term capital. Subsequent research refines Davis' interest rate measures and explores a variety of alternative explanations.

In preceding chapters of this study, attention was focused on bank behavior and economic development in a single state. The purpose of this chapter is to explore the broader question of how a national market for short-term capital evolved in the United States over this period, in the light of this study's findings for California.

The review of the literature on this issue contained in the introduction to this study concluded that the explanations of the pattern of interest rate differentials fall into four hypotheses. The perfect market hypothesis argues that regional rate differentials were due to differences in risk and transaction costs among regions. The market power hypothesis asserts that regional differences in the market power of banks can explain regional rate differentials. The market demand or disequilibrium hypothesis argues that disequilibrium between demand and supply in the capital market explains these differentials. The fourth hypothesis is that financial innovations played a major role in bringing unity to the U.S. capital market. These four hypotheses, which are not mutually exclusive, are referred to here as the perfect market hypothesis, the market power hypothesis, the market demand hypothesis, and the financial innovation hypothesis.

In its analysis of banking in California, this study has provided specific evidence about the importance of certain factors in determining bank behavior. Risk, market power and market demand all helped to determine the pattern of bank entry. These same factors also affected individual bank behavior. Bank behavior was found to have varied among banks with different types of charters, indicating that banking regulation also played a part in banks' decisions. This study thus provides further evidence on at least three of the four hypotheses economic historians have offered to explain regional interest rate differentials.

The first issue, which is taken up in the second section of this chapter, is to clarify what has been written about the pattern of regional interest rate differentials. Part of this section shows how interest rates behaved in California. The next three sections of the chapter look at the first three of the four hypotheses: perfect market, market power, and market demand. In each case, the evidence supporting the hypothesis is considered in the light of this study's findings for California. The fourth hypothesis, although it is discussed, does not warrant a separate section because this study has no direct evidence on the role of financial innovation. The final section of the chapter draws some conclusions about what explains the evolution of a national capital market, and the role of financial institutions in economic development.

The Pattern of Interest Rates

In the first article to use national bank data to calculate proxies for regional interest rates, Davis (1965) presents two sets of rates: the net earnings rate on earning assets for the years 1870-1914 and the gross earnings rate on earning assets for the years 1888-1914. He aggregates over all national banks in each of six regions, using the regional definitions of the U.S. Comptroller of the Currency. Although the gross earnings rate is a better measure of the average rate charged on short-term capital, the Comptroller's reports provide only net earnings for national banks prior to 1888. Beginning in 1888, these reports contain gross earnings, as well as losses and operating costs. Davis argues, however, that the two series move together in the period 1888-1914, and thus the net earnings rate is a reasonable rate for identifying regional interest rate differentials in the years before 1888.[1]

Smiley (1973, 1975, 1976, 1977) criticizes Davis' use of the net earnings rate and the construction of Davis' gross earnings rate as a proxy for the short-term interest rate. Smiley argues that the net earnings rate moves very differently from the gross earnings rate; in some states and some reserve cities, net earnings were negative.

Thus, in calculating an annual rate for each state, Smiley (1973) restricts himself to the gross earnings data available for the period after 1888. In fact, Davis partially overcomes some of the problems Smiley raises by aggregating over regions and averaging over three years. If operating costs were the same in all regions, as Davis assumes, then regional differences in the net earnings series would reflect regional differences in the expected yield on banks' earning assets. Smiley, however, shows that these costs were not similar after 1888.[2]

In his most recent calculation, Smiley (1976) adjusts national banks' gross earnings by subtracting earnings on U.S. government bonds and earnings on bankers' deposits. Dividing these earnings by loans plus securities, he obtains the average yield on private earning assets, which he argues is a better proxy for short-term rates than Davis' yield on all earning assets that include U.S. government bonds.

James (1974) develops a semi-annual real rate rather than an annual nominal rate for each state, and goes further than Smiley in calculating a proxy for the average rate on short-term capital. Besides making the adjustments to national banks' gross earnings that Smiley makes, James also deducts banks' earnings on non-government securities from gross earnings.[3] Dividing these earnings on loans and discounts by total loans and discounts, he obtains an average yield on loans and discounts by state. Since the U.S. Comptroller reported income statements for national banks semi-annually, James is able to calculate a semi-annual series. He deflates this series using the Warren-Pearson wholesale index to obtain the average real yield on loans and discounts.

Whether James' rates are a better proxy for short-term loan rates than Smiley's is debatable. James estimates the earnings on "Other Stocks and Bonds" (non-U.S. government securities and not "Due from

Bankers") using Macaulay's index of yields on railroad bonds.[4] If private securities provided higher returns in regions with less developed capital markets, this procedure increases the regional differentials indicated by James' interest rate series. Loan rates will be overstated to the extent that regional security yields were higher than the New York rate. While a national market may have existed for railway bonds, many banks, at least in California, held considerable amounts of local securities such as those issued by local companies, utilities, and water districts. James also uses a national rather than a state-by-state price index to deflate his nominal interest rate series. Given the varied regional pattern of development across the United States, some variation among regions in the rate of inflation, even over several years, is to be expected. Thus, James' rates may be an unreliable guide to the pattern of interest rate differentials, particularly if comparisons are made between specific states. In the aggregate and over periods longer than a few years, however, such differences should wash out.

Besides disagreeing over the appropriate proxy for short-term rates, these researchers also differ in their methods of assessing the pattern of regional rate differentials. In his original article, Davis (1965) merely refers to a chart of regional rates to demonstrate the narrowing of regional differentials. While this narrowing is very evident for his less reliable net earnings series between 1870 and 1914, it is much less evident for his more reliable gross earnings series between 1888 and 1914. Smiley (1975) criticizes Davis for failing to measure regional rate convergence, as it is not obvious from Davis' gross rates that there is convergence. Smiley (1977) rejects a relative measure of dispersion used in Smiley (1975), and employs the standard deviation of rates by state to measure dispersion in each year.[5] He finds that this measure of dispersion fell from 2.80 percent in 1888 to 1.68 percent in 1913. The decline, however, was not even. After declining in the early years of this period, his measure of dispersion increases somewhat beginning in the mid-1890s. It turns down again around 1900-01. Using the same measure, Smiley (1981) shows that regional rate dispersion continued to decline until the end of the 1920s.

Like Davis, James (1976c) refers to a chart of his regional rates to demonstrate the narrowing of regional differences among his four regions (East, Midwest, South and West). As with Davis' chart of gross rates, this narrowing is not obvious, particularly if the first few years are ignored. In a footnote, however, James (1976c) does present an index of regional rate differentials. This index focuses on the divergence of regional rates from the eastern rate. The index, which is the square root of the sum of the squares of these differentials, shows that the regional dispersion of rates narrowed between 1888 and 1893, but then widened in the 1890s. By 1903, the index had narrowed again to just below its level in 1893; thereafter, it narrowed so that this average index had fallen from 3.74 percent in 1888 to 2.45 percent in 1911.[6] Thus, despite the differences in the methods of calculating the proxies for short-term interest rates, and assessing the pattern of regional rate differentials, a similar pattern appears in the series of all three researchers.

The same pattern is evident for interest rates in California. As Table 7-1 shows, the differential between the average rate as calculated by Smiley (1976) for California's country national banks and that calculated for New York City's national banks, decreased over the period 1888-1993, but not uniformly. After declining somewhat between 1888 and 1893, the differential increased in the mid-1890s. It declined again after 1900, and remained below 2 percent for most of the period 1902-1913. While the average differential for the first five years of the period was 3.58 percent, it was only 1.45 percent for the last five years.

Interestingly, the differential between the average rate for Wisconsin country national banks and the New York City rate shows a similar pattern. This differential was well above one percent for the years 1888-1900, with the exception of 1892, and was well below one percent for the years 1902-1913.[7] Moreover, the differential appears to have widened slightly in the latter 1890s. The reasons for this similarity are discussed below.

The differential between the rate for national banks in San Francisco and the New York City rate also narrowed over the period 1888-1913. After averaging 2.37 percent in the first five years of the period, this differential averaged only 0.37 percent in the last five years (see Table 7-1). To interpret this narrowing as a sign of an evolving capital market, however, is questionable. There were only two national banks in San Francisco in 1890. The number had risen to only four by 1900, and thereafter increased to just seven in 1905, and finally eleven in 1908. Thus, the San Francisco rate reflects the earnings of only two banks in the early years. The decline in this rate after 1901 may be due as much to the characteristics of the new national banks, which included some large, well established state banks that converted to national charters, as to any other factors such as risk, market power, or market demand.

Nevertheless, the small rate differential between New York City and San Francisco or Los Angeles national banks suggests that these cities were part of a national capital market by the 1900s at the latest. Since the differential between California country banks and San Francisco's banks does not experience the same decline, except perhaps in the last two years of the period, it appears that California's country banks were not as well integrated into the national market for short-term capital. Again, interpreting these differentials is complicated by the lack of national banks in San Francisco in the early years and the designation of Los Angeles as a reserve city in 1901, and the consequent redesignation of country national banks to reserve city banks.

The paucity of reserve cities in the developing regions of the United States in the beginning of this period, and the granting of this status to several cities during the period casts doubts on any analysis that is based on comparisons between reserve city rates and county bank rates for these regions. In the states included in the U.S. Comptroller's Region VI, for example, there was only one reserve city (Omaha) with any national banks before 1894, when Lincoln became a reserve city.[8] In 1901, Denver was the next city to become a reserve city in this region. In the South, there were only two reserve cities (New Orleans and Louisville) until 1895, when Savannah was designated a reserve city. In 1897, Houston was added, making only four reserve cities in Region III, which stretched from Texas to Virginia. In the vast Mountain-Pacific region, San Francisco was the sole reserve city until after 1900. The lack of reserve cities and the designation of new ones, as well as the changing number of banks in some reserve cities, casts doubts upon the conclusions drawn by James and Sylla from their analyses of the data for reserve city banks, which are discussed below.

A consensus now appears to exist among economic historians on the pattern of regional interest rate differentials during the nineteenth century. Research on recent regional interest rate differentials in the United States, however, suggests that economic historians may be wrong in inferring segmented capital markets from these differentials. Using a variety of rates for the period 1965-1977, Keleher (1979) finds that, despite regional differentials, interest rates moved in tandem with a national rate over these years. In a regression of each regional rate on the U.S. rate, a coefficient of unity is taken by Keleher as evidence that markets were integrated. Keleher criticizes economic historians for focusing on changing interest rate differentials to identify the integration of U.S.

capital markets. James (1976b) fortunately supplies the necessary ingredients for performing this test for the nineteenth century in the results of his cross-section time-series regressions of interest by state. (These results are discussed in more detail below.) Analysis of the statistics for the commercial paper rate, which can be interpreted as the U.S. market rate for short-term capital, shows that for both reserve cities and states, this coefficient did differ significantly from unity.[9] Accordingly, James' estimated bank loan rates by reserve city or by state did not move in tandem with the commercial paper rate. Thus, by Keleher's test, the United States did not have a unified capital market, though the statistics suggest that banks in the reserve cities are more likely to have been integrated into a national capital market than country national banks.

In contrast to the consensus on the pattern of interest rates, there remains considerable divergence among economic historians in their views on what explains this pattern. It is these divergent views that are the subject of the next three sections.

The Perfect Market Hypothesis

In an article questioning the existence of capital market imperfections, Stigler (1967) points out that differences in interest rates paid by borrowers could result from differences in the risk and transactions costs incurred by lenders. Stigler argues Davis (1965) is incorrect in inferring that U.S. capital markets were imperfect from the existence of regional interest rate differentials. Capital markets might have been perfect, but risk and transaction costs could have differed between regions, leading to a dispersion of regional interest rates. In a later article, Davis (1968) appears to respond to Stigler's criticism by discussing the role of both risk and information costs in the transfer of funds between regions. Davis concludes that differences in risk were not important in determining interest rates. The spread of the commercial paper market, however, did affect regional interest rates according to Davis, by reducing uncertainty discounts and transportation costs associated with moving funds between regions.

His evidence, however, is indirect. Davis argues that the narrowing of regional differences in interest rates, as measured by his net earnings series, was tied to the development of the commercial paper market. As commercial paper dealers penetrated each region, the differential between rates in that region and those in more developed regions fell. The commercial paper market reduced uncertainty and transactions costs associated with transferring funds from capital-surplus regions to capital-deficient regions. Thus, the cost of transferring capital declined with the extension of the commercial paper market, reducing interest rates in developing regions. Conversely, regional interest rates remained high in those regions where the commercial paper market was slow to penetrate. Davis cites the South as a prime example, attributing the high differential problem in average rates between the South and the East to the lack of penetration by the commercial paper market. Though Davis' argument is plausible, he presents no direct evidence of lower transactions costs.

By using a net earnings rate to measure regional rate dispersion, Davis argues he is allowing for differences among regions in the expected rate of losses on earning assets, and thus his rates are expected rates. But expected losses are not the whole story. The implication of Stigler's discussion is that lenders must consider not only the loss rate on loans, but also the variability of this loss rate. Davis dismisses the importance of this form of risk. As James (1978) points out, Davis is correct in ignoring differences in risk as long as lenders are risk neutral.[10] If lenders are in fact risk averse, they will require compensation, in the form of a higher rate, to make a loan where the variability of the loss rate, or the riskiness of the loan, is higher. Thus, loans in regions with more variability in loss rates will have higher interest rates, ceteris paribus. Davis does not measure the impact on interest rates of such risk. It is this omission that James and Smiley set out to remedy.

Beginning with the standard capital-asset pricing model, James (1974, 1976b) develops a bank portfolio choice model in which the market for bank loans is imperfectly competitive. A key assumption underlying James' model is that banks' owners and managers are risk averse rather than risk neutral. James argues that the small and closely-held nature of banks at that time justifies such an assumption. His model shows that the expected return on a bank's loan portfolio is a function of the riskless rate of return, the expected market yield, the covariance between the market yield and the loan rate, the variance in the market yield, the elasticity of the demand for loans, and the proportion of loans in the bank's portfolio. In his estimated model, the statewide average semi-annual gross real return on loans is a function of the New York commercial paper rate (the market yield), the loss rate on loans, the variance of the loss rate over the previous ten semi-annual periods, a monopoly power index, a business cycle index, and a seasonal dummy variable. Using multiple regression analysis, James estimates this model for the period 1893-1911 in three ways: a time-series analysis for each state; a cross-section time-series analysis for all states combined; and a cross-section time-series analysis for all reserve cities.

Of the variables James (1976b) includes in his empirical model, two show how banks were affected by losses and risk. As was discussed in Chapter 4 above, theoretically banks must adjust the rates they charge on loans for the losses they expect to incur on these loans. The expected loan yield, on which they base this portfolio decision, is equal to the loan rate charged less the expected rate of losses. James' model predicts that his loan loss rate will have a coefficient of one. In many of the states, James reports that this coefficient is positive and significant, but in some states, the loss rate has a significantly negative coefficient. Pooling all the coefficients, however, he finds that their distribution is consistent with the hypothesis that they were equal to unity.[11] The implication is that loan rates were higher in states where loan loss rates were greater, though James does not draw this conclusion out directly.

If banks' owners are risk averse, then loan rates will be higher where risk is greater, to compensate the owners for additional risk. James does not find solid support for this hypothesis. The coefficient of the variance of the loss rate is positive and significant in the time-series cross-section analysis of the pooled reserve cities, but negative and significant in that of the pooled states. When the states are estimated separately, only those in the South have consistently positive coefficients for this variable. In the West, only three out of twelve states have positive coefficients. James concludes that risk was not an important factor determining regional interest rates. He also concludes that reductions in risk differentials among regions were not sufficient to explain the narrowing that he finds for regional interest rate differentials, although he does not test this conclusion directly.[12]

Smiley (1976) also tests for the effects on interest rates of loan loss rates and the variability of these rates. His model, however, focuses on factors that affected the supply of loans, and hence the rate charged by banks. As Smiley notes, adequate data are lacking for a systematic treatment of demand factors. In Smiley's model, average interest rates by state are a function of average operating costs, transactions costs (distance by rail from New York), the expected loss rate (average loss rate over current and preceding four years), the variability of losses (the standard deviation of the loss rate over these five years, and the proportion of agricultural employment), and market power (the ratio of securities to loans plus securities). He estimates this model with a cross-section analysis of all states by year for the years 1888-1913.

The results he obtains with this model for the effects of losses and risk on bank behavior are similar to those obtained by James. In every year except 1900, Smiley finds that the average loss rate has a positive coefficient that is generally significant. In sixteen out of twenty-six years the coefficient is not significantly different from unity. In those years when it is different from unity, this coefficient has an interesting cyclical pattern being significantly greater than one in 1890-1891, and 1911-1013, and significantly less than one in 1898-1903. Thus, Smiley also finds that banks generally adjusted their loan rates to take account of expected loss rates, what Davis somewhat misleadingly terms uncertainty discounts. Smiley notes that the narrowing of regional rate differences could be due to the equalizing of loss rates among regions, though he does not test this directly.[13]

Like James, Smiley fails to find any solid evidence showing that risk affected loan rates. The coefficient of the standard deviation of the loss rate is never significantly positive, which Smiley attributes to the crudeness of the measure he uses. The coefficient of the percentage of agricultural employment, however, is significantly positive in seventeen out of twenty-six years, suggesting that loan rates in agricultural states were subject to risk premiums. The size of this risk premium is not very large, and Smiley argues this factor was not important in establishing interest rate differentials among states. Along the same lines, James (1978) argues that the uncertainty of cotton prices as compared to the prices of other crops may explain the importance he finds for risk in the states in the South.

One reason why James and Smiley do not find that risk was important may be their crude measures of risk. Their loss rate is the ratio of statewide losses to statewide loans plus discounts, which ignores intrastate variations in loss rates. This measure also presumes that all losses reported to the U.S. Comptroller of the Currency were on loans and discounts, and ignores losses on securities and other assets. Moreover, because aggregate losses are used, the impact of a single bank failure on the average loss rate can be substantial. Many banks failed because of worthless assets; losses in a particular year could be large due solely to the mismanagement of one or two banks. The use of total losses for each state may therefore overestimate the actual loan loss rates most banks were experiencing, and also exaggerate the variability of the loss rate.

A less obvious comment is that James and Smiley both implicitly assume the losses banks incurred were entirely local, when in fact banks may have been diversifying their loan portfolios across state lines. In which case, a narrowing of regional rate differences over time could have come about through wider geographic diversification of loan portfolios, as well as through greater similarity in the level and variability of regional loss rates. Wider geographic diversification could have come about through improved communications or through the use of institutions such as the commercial paper market. In fact, neither James nor Smiley evaluates loan loss rates or their regional variability to see if a narrowing in these factors, particularly the loan loss rate, contributed to the narrowing of regional interest rates. The next step would be to explain the changes in the loss rates and their variability. Smiley (1977) does find that the dispersion of interest rates estimated just with the loan loss rate and his gross average bank cost ratio using his cross-section regression equation becomes more highly correlated with the actual dispersion of interest rates over time. This result hints that loss rates may have been important factors in the narrowing of rates, but the high correlation is probably attributable to the cost ratio.

Risk appears to have played an important part in determining individual bank behavior in California. As Chapter 5 showed, banks with higher cash/deposit ratios, and presumably more risk averse management, had lower loan/asset ratios. Thus, James' assumption that nineteenth century bankers were risk averse is supported by the evidence for California.[14] A bank's capital position also affected its management's reaction to lending risk, at least in California. Banks with a higher capital/deposit ratio providing better protection against the risk of failure had higher loan/asset ratios. Neither James nor Smiley take these factors directly into account when analyzing the role of risk in determining interest rates. Changes in management risk aversion or regional variations in banks' capital positions could have produced differences in banks' reactions to risk both over time and across regions.

The cash/deposit ratio is only a relative measure of risk aversion, measuring differences in risk aversion among banks at any point in time. It cannot say much about changes in risk aversion over time since other factors are also changing. As communications and financial techniques develop, the cash/deposit ratio can be expected to fall without implying any change in risk aversion among banks' managements. Such a decline did occur in California between 1878 and 1908, which suggests financial arrangements were improving (see Table 5-3). Besides advances in communications, better correspondent relationships and the growing number of clearinghouses may have contributed to this improvement. In testing the impact of the commercial paper market on average interest rates of banks by reserve city, James pays no attention to the establishment and expansion of clearinghouses. Yet improved financial arrangements, by lowering cash requirements, may have led to lower deposit costs at the margin and hence lower loan rates. Smiley, however, may be capturing some of this effect through his average cost variable. In any case, James' dismissal of the impact of the commercial paper market is questionable in San Francisco at least, in view of the small and changing number of national banks in the city.[15]

In gauging the effects of risk on interest rates, James and Smiley ignore banks' capital positions. Yet this factor was important in determining California banks' behavior, and hence their reaction to risk. If all banks and all regions had the same capital position, this omission would be unimportant. In California, however, banks' capital positions varied both among the different types of banks and over time (see Table 5-3). More importantly, for James' and Smiley's conclusions about the importance of risk, are the regional differences that appear to have existed among banks' capital positions. Sylla (1975) reports the ratio of deposits (including note circulation) to capital (presumably just paid-up-capital) by region for the period 1850-1910. Surprisingly, the highest regional capital/deposit ratios between 1880 and 1910 are reported for the New England region, while the MidAtlantic and Mountain-Pacific regions typically had the lowest ratios (see Table 7-2). Non-national banks had lower average capital/deposit ratios than national banks in every region. The difference between these two types narrowed by 1910, indicating a similar pattern to that found for California's banks. While banks' capital positions in the long run may have been determined by management preferences, in the short run they were fixed. Since James and Smiley use short-run models, they should incorporate this factor into their empirical models. By ignoring bank capital, they may bias their results against finding risk to have been important.

Taking a very different approach to the role of risk in determining short-term loan rates, Rockoff (1977) finds that the rate of return to book capital, i.e., the rate of profit, in different regions was significantly and positively correlated with the regional rate of failure of national banks in each region. As regional rates of failure became more similar, Rockoff reports, the regional returns to national bank capital also became more similar, explaining part of the narrowing of regional interest rate differentials. The much smaller regional failure rates relative to the regional profit rates, however, lead Rockoff to doubt the importance of the risk of failure in determining profit rates directly. Nevertheless, he suggests that higher failure rates in some regions may have raised the cost of deposits to banks in those regions, leading to banks charging higher loan rates in those regions.

Though this may explain part of the discrepancy, an additional reason is that Rockoff's failure rate may seriously underestimate the risk of bank failure. His failure rate is only for national banks, yet many more state banks failed than national banks.[16] In California for example, state banks had a higher rate of failure in some periods than national banks (see Chapter 2). If investors looked to some extent at the failure rate for all types of banks, the riskiness of banking as compared to other investments may have appeared much higher than Rockoff's failure rate would indicate. Bank profit rates would have had to rise to compensate for this perception. Since the proportion of state banks was lower in the East, the use of the national bank failure rate underestimates the regional differentials in the risk of bank failure.[17]

The relationship between bank entry and the bank failure rate may also explain the discrepancy between profit rates and failure rates. The evidence for California presented in Chapter 6 suggests that bank entry over a three-year period was significantly reduced by a higher rate of bank failures over the preceding three years. After a financial panic, slower entry leading to relatively fewer banks may have driven loan rates and profit rates up in some regions. One problem with Rockoff's analysis is his use of data averaged over several long periods. A high failure rate in one year may have had an effect for several years, despite a low average failure rate over a longer period.

In sum, risk appears to have affected bank behavior, but the evidence does not always demonstrate that risk was important. California banks acted as if risk matters. Banks with low capital/deposit ratios and risk averse management had lower loan/asset ratios; bank entry was generally slower after periods of high bank failure rates. Rockoff shows regional bank profit rates were also associated with bank failure rates; the weakness of the reported relationship may reflect his method's underassessment of bank owners' perceptions of the risk of failure. Measurement problems may also explain the inconsistent results of other approaches. Though James and Smiley demonstrate that loan loss rates affected loan rates on a one-for-one basis, the variability of these loss rates was not found to be a consistently important factor explaining statewide interest rates. What is unclear from this research is how much of the pattern of interest rates can be explained by the pattern of loss rates. If loss rates became more similar among the states, what explains this growing similarity? While banks generally appear to have adjusted their loan rates for expected losses, the evidence suggests that banks did not have to adjust for risk in the form of the variability of loss rates. This failure, however, may be attributable to the crudeness of the measures of risk and the omission of any variable reflecting banks' capital position, which were not uniform across the states. In addition, no account is taken of changing information and transactions costs that might have permitted banks to diversify their portfolios and reduce their exposure to risk at lower cost over time. Thus, questions remain about the role of loan losses and risk in determining the regional pattern of interest rates.

The Market Power Hypothesis

Considerable effort has been devoted to evaluating the importance of banks' market power in explaining the pattern of regional interest rates. Three economic historians, James, Smiley, and Sylla, take aggregate approaches to this issue using states or regions for their unit of analysis. All three find some evidence suggesting that banks' market power did affect bank behavior. In a study of individual bank behavior in local bank markets in Wisconsin, however, Keehn (1972) finds that the level of concentration of banks in local markets did not consistently affect bank behavior.[18] The results obtained for individual banks in California in Chapter 5 above also show a weak and inconsistent relationship between bank behavior and local market concentration. Both studies also find the same pattern of inconsistency in the relationship between concentration and banks' loan/asset ratios. In Chapter 5 above, this similarity between California and Wisconsin was attributed to the pattern of bank entry. The evidence presented in Chapter 6 of this study demonstrates that bank entry was inhibited by market concentration although the extent to which this enabled banks to exploit any resulting market power appears to have been limited, since poor performance also stimulated greater bank entry. As it turns out, bank entry plays an important role in the explanations that James, Smiley and Sylla offer for the changing role of market power in determining the pattern of regional interest rates. This section reviews the evidence offered in support of the market power hypothesis, and discusses how the evidence for California supports this hypothesis.

Emphasizing the importance of banks' market power, Sylla (1969) employs a model of the individual bank similar to the model developed in Chapter 4 above, to establish the inverse relationship between a bank's market power and its loan/asset ratio. Instead of estimating the model with data for individual banks, he investigates the pattern of the aggregate ratio of loans to assets by region for the years 1870, 1875, 1880, 1885, 1890, 1900 and 1910. In 23 out of 41 year-region observations, country national banks had lower loan/asset ratios than reserve city national banks in the same region, which Sylla views as evidence of country national banks' market power. Of the 18 cases where country national banks had higher loan/asset ratios than reserve city national banks, 8 such cases occur in 1900 or 1910; Sylla argues this is evidence that the 1900 Gold Acts increased bank entry by lowering the minimum capital requirements for national banks, and hence increased competition among banks.[19]

Upon closer inspection of Sylla's evidence, this conclusion appears unwarranted. In three of the four regions where Sylla suggests market power should be most important (South, East North Central, and West North Central), the country bank loan/asset ratio exceeds the reserve city bank ratio in 1886, 1890, 1900 and 1910.[20] Sylla does note this and argues non-reserve city banks had to keep lower reserves.[21] In the remaining region, the Mountain-Pacific Region, the comparison is extremely unreliable since San Francisco was the only reserve city in this vast region until after 1900, and it had few national banks before 1900.

More convincing evidence of banks' market power appears to be the pattern of average profit rates, measured by the ratio of total net earnings to total capital and surplus of national banks in each region.[22] Sylla reports that the country banks' profit rate exceeded that of the reserve-city banks in 43 out of 53 region-year comparisons, a relationship that holds in all regions. There is, however, no evidence presented that shows a narrowing in the gap between these two groups after 1900, as one would expect given Sylla's emphasis on national bank entry after 1900. One problem with this approach is that the same set of data is being used to determine regional interest rate differentials (Davis' series) and to establish the existence of banks' market power. While the existence of banks' market power could account for both high profits and high loan rates, there is no independent test of the relationship between banks' market power and the rates charged on loans. There may be other factors involved. A second problem is Sylla's comparison of country and reserve-city banks. As was noted above, the paucity of reserve cities in the developing regions of the United States casts doubts on any conclusions drawn from such comparisons, at least prior to 1900.

While Sylla's evidence of banks' market power is largely indirect, James tests the effect of banks' market power directly. James' theoretical model of interest rate determination in imperfect capital markets incorporates a monopoly premium. He uses bank density, measured by the ratio of banks to population in each state, to evaluate the importance of this premium in the determination of interest rates. For the cross-section analysis of states with semi-annual observations during the years 1893-1911, he finds that increased bank density reduced interest rates.[23] In the cross-section time series analysis of reserve cities, the coefficient of bank density is also significantly negative, and larger than in the regression equation for the states. For individual states, time-series analysis shows bank density to have had the expected negative effect on interest rates in most of the states in the South and Midwest, but not in the West. James attributes the latter to the concentration of population in towns and cities in the West, a region that was otherwise sparsely populated, in contrast to more evenly populated regions such as the Midwest.

James concludes from his results that market power was the important factor explaining the pattern of regional interest rate differentials. He agrees with Sylla that bank entry resulting from the lifting of barriers to bank formations broke down banks' market power and led to a narrowing of the differentials. The important barriers, James argues however, were not the ones facing national banks that Sylla emphasizes, but rather were the ones facing state banks.[24] From the 1880s on, states generally introduced free incorporation laws and reduced minimal capital requirements for state banks, leading to the growth of state rather than national banks.

In concluding that "the erosion of local monopoly power was the principal reason for narrowing interest rate differentials," James glosses over potentially damaging flaws in his analysis.[25] Foremost, among these flaws is his statewide bank density variable, which ignores variations within the state in the concentration of banking. He uses the same statewide measure when analyzing reserve city interest rates. While one would expect market power to be more important for country banks than reserve city banks, the coefficient of bank density is substantially larger in the reserve city analysis (-7.635) than in the country bank analysis (-1.448).[26] These coefficients are surprising, especially when data for California's banks show that market concentration varied widely among California's counties throughout the period 1878-1908, and that the lowest values for the Herfindahl index occurred in Los Angeles County and San Francisco.[27] Market concentration also varied widely during this period among the Wisconsin markets Keehn studies.

Not only does statewide bank density overlook variations within states in market concentration, but it does not even appear to readily identify those states where banks' market power is supposed to have been important in determining interest rates. Goldsmith (1958b) provides data on banks per capita for 1900, derived from the same sources that James uses. As Table 7-3 shows, there was a wide disparity in bank density among states in 1900. The pattern is not what one would expect. While the states in the South generally had fewer banks per capita than states elsewhere, the region with the most banks per capita was neither the MidAtlantic nor New England, but instead was the West North Central. In fact, after the South, New England and the MidAtlantic had fewer banks per capita than any other region. Thus, James' bank density does not appear to be low in those regions where interest rates were high, except for the South.

His results are open to a different interpretation. For each state, banks per capita probably increased over the period, thus providing an indicator of financial development for any particular state. At any point in time, however, the indicator is probably less successful. Unfortunately, James presents only time-series results for each state, and cross-section, time-series results for all states combined, but does not provide cross-section results for all states combined at any point in time. The success of James' bank density variable may also reflect the impact of bank entry; rapid entry would increase bank density sharply at the same time that increased competition lowers interest rates. Thus, bank density may be a poor measure of differences in market power across states, but a good measure of changes in market power and financial development in any particular state.

Smiley (1977) also tests the market power hypothesis directly, but uses a different approach from James. Having established a theoretical link between a bank's market power and the ratio of securities to loans plus securities, Smiley then employs this ratio as a measure of market power in a regression explaining his statewide interest rates for the years 1888-1913. His model is similar to the one developed in Chapter 4 above, and produces the result that the ratio of a bank's securities to its loans plus securities varies directly with its market power. The model implies that banks with more market power had lower loan/asset ratios. He reports that this ratio has a significantly positive coefficient in the years 1892-1896, 1898, and 1900 and its coefficient is positive in all years before 1907, indicating to Smiley that banks possessed market power. Smiley takes the increase in the size of the coefficient in the 1890s to mean that banks' market power increased in the 1890s.[28]

Smiley also finds evidence of changing market power in national banks' average costs. His most important variable explaining interest rates by state is the ratio of gross expenses (operating expenses plus taxes) to loans plus securities for all the banks in each state. Its coefficient is significantly positive in all regressions. Smiley argues that as banks' market power increases, "the difference between average revenue . . . and average cost will increase."[29] Investigating the size of the coefficient of his cost ratio (expenses to earning assets), he concludes that banks' monopoly power decreased until the 1890s panic and depression, then increased through 1903, and subsequently decreased with a brief reversal in 1907-08. Smiley's explanation for this pattern is the changing rate of bank entry. Though he presents a table of entry rates for different regions that provides support for this hypothesis, he does not test it directly.[30]

While Smiley has gone further than Sylla or James in establishing when banks' market power increased or decreased, his evidence rests on somewhat weak theoretical foundations. Though it may be true that the gap between a bank's average revenue and average cost rises with the bank's market power, this does not mean that the ratio of gross expenses to earning assets increases with a bank's market power, as Smiley assumes, unless the bank's owners choose to take some of their monopoly profits in the form of salaries and other expenses rather than maximizing profits. A second problem is that Smiley includes both the securities/securities-plus-loans ratio and a measure of risk in his single equation explaining statewide interest rates. The evidence for California's banks indicates a strong relationship between risk and the loan/asset ratio which affects the significance of his estimated coefficients. There is also a potential simultaneous equation bias in Smiley's empirical model due to the dependency of the loan/asset ratio, and hence the securities/securities-plus-loans ratio, on the rate of interest charged by banks.

The flaws in the methods that James, Smiley and Sylla employ weaken the support their studies apparently provide for the market power hypothesis. The evidence for California does not strongly support this hypothesis either. As Chapter 5 above showed, local market concentration was not the most important variable affecting individual bank behavior in California; indeed, the effect of this variable on banks' loan/asset ratios was relatively small and somewhat inconsistent. Keehn (1972) obtains largely the same results for individual banks in Wisconsin. What is striking is that the pattern of inconsistency is similar in both states. In this similar inconsistency lies some support for the market power hypothesis. The results from California and Wisconsin suggest that local market concentration lowered banks' loan/asset ratios in the late 1890s, after having had the opposite effect around 1890. This finding would be consistent with banks' growing local market power during the 1890s. Growing local market power could partially explain the widening differential in these years between the average rate for national banks in New York City and the average rate for country national banks in both California and Wisconsin that was discussed above in this chapter. In this respect, the findings for California and Wisconsin support Smiley (1977) when he argues that the widening differentials among the states in the late 1890s was due to the increasing market power of banks.

Just as James, Smiley and Sylla argue that bank entry may explain the changes in banks' market power, so, too, in California, bank entry may be a factor in banks' changing market power. In particular, slower bank entry after the 1893 panic may have led to the existing banks possessing greater market power by the second half of the 1890s. A similar slowdown in bank entry in Wisconsin may also have contributed to an increase in banks' market power by 1900. With the results for only one state to interpret, Keehn (1972) draws a different, but not unreasonable, conclusion from the inconsistent results: in his view, the ease of bank entry in this period prevented banks from exercising any market power that local market concentration may have conferred on them.[31]

If bank entry can explain the changes in banks' market power, what explains the pattern of bank entry? The results reported in Chapter 6 above demonstrate that for California important factors were the local demand for banking services, local market concentration and risk of bank failure. These findings are important because they show that demand was important in determining the pattern of bank formations. Going further, they show that the pace of bank formations could fall behind demand, at least temporarily. Weak economic growth and memories of recent widespread bank failures slowed entry in the mid-1890s. When the economy began to recover in the late 1890s, existing banks benefitted from their position for several years before enough new banks were formed and existing banks expanded to restore equilibrium at competitive prices in the 1900s. This explains the widening and subsequent narrowing of the differential between the rate for California's country banks and the rate for New York City banks. The results also show that local market concentration inhibited bank entry to some degree, at least in the short run. But free entry limited the extent to which existing bankers could exploit any market power that concentration conferred, because entrepreneurs responded to profitable opportunities created by poor performance by forming new banks. Unfortunately, no detailed research on bank entry has been undertaken for any other state, so that there is no corroborating evidence. It seems likely, however, that further analysis would show that Wisconsin came from the same mold as California.

The results for bank entry in California strongly suggest that market demand and economic activity played an important part in determining the pattern of bank entry elsewhere in the country. Most of the research, however, has focused on regulatory restrictions, and only a little attention has been paid to the demand side. Based on just the rate of entry for national banks, for example, Smiley (1977) suggests that changes in the number of banks were due more to aggregate economic fluctuations than to changes in regulatory restrictions.[32] James provides some more substantial evidence. He finds that in some states changes in his bank density index (banks per capita) were a positive function of his measure of business cycle activity (an index of bank clearings outside New York City).[33] Thus, sketchy evidence for the United States as a whole and for some states also suggests that economic activity helped to determine the pattern of bank entry. Since downturns in economic activity were commonly triggered by financial panics, bank failures probably also played a role.

In seeking to explain the decline in banks' market power, to which they attribute the narrowing of regional interest rate differentials, James and Sylla concentrate on changes in the regulatory restrictions governing bank formations. Sylla emphasizes the change in the national banking laws in 1900, principally the lowering of the minimum capital requirements for national banks. He argues that the increase in the formation of national banks after 1900 was due to this change. According to Sylla, state chartered banks were inferior to national banks largely because they could not profitably issue bank notes, and deposits subject to checks were an imperfect substitute. Thus, Sylla believes that changes in the national banking laws were the primary determinants of changes in the pattern of bank formations, and hence of banks' market power.[34]

Unlike Sylla, James marshalls some statistical evidence to support his hypothesis that it was the entry of state banks which changed banks' market power. Accordingly, James (1976c) looks at changes in the regulations that affected the formation of state-chartered banks; in particular, he focuses on the minimum capital required for banks in each state. To establish the link between these capital requirements and interest rates, he regresses the minimum capital requirement for state banks in each state and the distance of the major city in each state from New York City on interest rates by state for 1909. He finds that interest rates were generally higher in states with higher minimum capital requirements. He also regresses the 1909 minimum capital requirements for each state on the change in interest rates between 1888 and 1911 in each state. He finds that lower minimum capital requirements were generally associated with a reduction in interest rates. Thus, James argues, lowered minimum capital requirements for state banks, rather than for national banks, led to the narrowing of regional interest rate differentials.[35]

The model of bank entry developed in Chapter 6 above provides an opportunity to test these hypotheses directly with data for California. A dummy variable, S, equal to unity for the periods 1902-1905 and 1905-1908, was introduced to test for an increase in entry after 1900. Its coefficient was positive but not significant, suggesting that changes in the national banking laws may have contributed to more entry, but did not result in significantly more entry in California after 1900, than before, ceteris paribus (see Table 7-4). Since minimum capital requirements for California's state banks were first introduced in 1895, bank entry should have been slower after 1895 according to James. A dummy variable, J, equal to unity for the periods 1896-1899, 1902-1905 and 1905-1908 had a coefficient that had the wrong sign (positive) and was insignificant (see Table 7-4), indicating that the increased capital requirements do not appear to have reduced bank entry in California. Of course, the two hypotheses are not mutually exclusive, since in California the lower capital requirements for national banks offset the increased requirements for state banks.

A more important reason for expecting there to be little relationship between changes in capital requirements and bank entry, at least in California, is the difference between the legal restrictions on entry and their enforcement. As was discussed in Chapter 2 above, the minimum capital requirements were an obstacle that was relatively easy to overcome prior to the 1909 Bank Act. Thus, the increase in the restrictiveness of California's banking law in 1895 was offset by a loophole in the law and the slack enforcement of this law after 1900.

One counter-example does not invalidate James' hypothesis, but California's history does raise some questions about James' evaluation of the relationship between minimum capital requirements and interest rates. Most notably, James has the wrong minimum capital requirement for California's state banks in 1895 (it was $25,000, not $5,000); the source of this error is the U.S. Comptroller's annual report for 1895.[36] One wonders how many other capital requirements are incorrectly reported by the Comptroller for 1895. How the correction of the California observation would affect James' results is impossible to tell; it eliminates the largest positive change of $20,000 in the minimum capital requirements for state banks. If there are further errors, the results might indeed change.

Another question is why James used the minimum capital requirements existing in 1909 rather than those existing in 1895 in determining the effects of minimum capital requirements on the change in interest rates between 1888 and 1911.[37] Although the minimum capital requirements were not raised in California, the 1909 Bank Act made California's banking regulation much more restrictive than it had been by imposing new restrictions and giving the newly-created Superintendent of Banks the power to enforce the law. If other states responded to the 1907 financial panic and its attendant bank failures in a similar fashion, it is likely that many of the states changed their minimum capital requirements for state banks in 1908 or 1909. Thus, the 1909 minimum requirements may well overstate the barriers to bank entry for the period 1888-1911 for some states, which may help to explain the low R2 that James reports for his regression equation explaining the change in interest rates. Moreover, the association between interest rates and minimum capital requirements James finds for 1909 may be an association between the effect of the 1907 panic on both interest rates and changes by the states in their minimum bank capital requirements.

While James' evidence gives some support to his hypothesis that minimum bank capital requirements for state banks affected interest rates, he does not estimate directly the link between entry and changes in these requirements, which is the basis for his hypothesis. Instead, he regresses the bank density coefficient for each state from his time series regressions by state on the minimum bank capital requirement for each state. He finds that bank density had a smaller effect the lower was the minimum bank capital requirement in 1909. This test raises a fundamental question about James' approach: how can James assume that the coefficient of bank density remains the same, when a variable he believes is crucial to determining banks' market power is changing? A better test might be to see if the size of this coefficient fell when minimum bank capital requirements were reduced in any state.

The results of such a test, however, are likely to be unconvincing. As this study's analysis of one state has shown, there were several factors determining bank entry, and minimum capital requirements appear to have been unimportant. What was important in determining entry into local markets was expected economic activity, the performance of existing banks, expectations about bank failures, and the concentration of banks. Whether the same factors were important elsewhere remains to be seen. It is likely, however, that in other states the barrier to entry posed by banking regulations is only partially reflected in the size of minimum bank capital requirements.[38] Moreover, the relationship between bank entry and bank regulation is not simply established; in some cases, better supervision may have increased entry by reducing expectations of bank failures.

The evidence reviewed here suggests that banks' local market power may partially explain the pattern of interest rate differentials, but many doubts about the importance of this factor remain. All studies that support this hypothesis, including this one, have their flaws. The direct evidence for California and Wisconsin indicates only a small effect on bank behavior, and hence only a small effect on interest rates. Though James' results provide the strongest support, his bank density variable is a questionable measure of banks' market power, and his results with this variable may reflect financial development over time as much as changes in banks' monopoly power.

Market Demand and Disequilibrium

Despite the potential importance of demand factors in the determination of regional interest rates on loans, only one study concludes that demand factors were important in explaining the pattern of regional interest rate differentials. Using a general equilibrium model, Williams (1974) finds that regional differences in the demand for capital explain the pattern of interest rate differentials between the Midwest and the East. According to Williamson, rapid growth in the Midwest in the 1870s combined with capital market imperfections to generate higher interest rates in the Midwest than in the East.[39] The differential between rates in these two regions narrowed in the 1880s and early 1890s, Williamson argues, because agriculture was generating a surplus of savings.[40] In the 1890s, the situation changed as industrialization accelerated in the Midwest, increasing the demand for funds.[41] Williamson's model comprises only three sectors: industry in the East, industry in the Midwest, and agriculture in the Midwest. Thus, his analysis can only contribute to explaining differentials between these regions. Nevertheless, his analysis suggests that demand factors may explain the widening of short-term regional interest rate differentials that James and Smiley report for the short-term market in the 1890s.[42] Williamson finds no evidence that expanded financial intermediation and institutional changes affected regional rate differentials. He dismisses Davis' suggestion that the failure of mortgage companies in the Midwest slowed the integration of the long-term capital market.[43]

Williamson's assumptions are often heroic and frequently questionable. His model reflects his views on the way a developing economy works. One feature of his model is the lack of any role for financial intermediaries; Williamson employs savings and investment functions that ignore financial intermediaries. It is not surprising under these conditions that perfect capital markets would have made little difference, since there appears to be no mechanism in the model for effecting the transfer of funds. This feature may also contribute to the problems others have found in the model. For example, Sylla (1977) points out that Williamson's simulated regional real rates of interest are unrealistic, and fail to show the convergence found in the actual rates.

While Williamson's major conclusion that a perfect national capital market would have hardly changed the course of U.S. economic development is highly questionable, his analysis does highlight the role of demand in determining the pattern of interest rates. What is surprising is that no other studies have found the demand for funds to matter at all. In James (1976b) a business cycle index has a negative coefficient, indicting that economic activity lowered interest rates. James does not comment on this finding, but a possible explanation is contained in the development of his model. Increased economic activity lowered banks' expected rate of loan losses, and for a given level of the New York commercial paper rate, this led to banks charging lower rates on loans. To capture variations in local loan demand, James includes deviations from the trend of farm revenues for 25 states, but he reports that this variable has a significant coefficient in only one state. Neither Smiley nor Sylla incorporate any aspects of loan demand into their analyses.[44] Employing a model similar to the one used in this study, Keehn (1972) finds that neither population growth nor assets per capital of Wisconsin counties had a significantly positive effect on banks' loan/asset ratios.

The results obtained in this study suggest that local demand did influence the banks' loan/asset ratios during the nineteenth century. Though the effect is not large, it does suggest that differences in loan demand could lead to differences in the rates charged on loans. Market demand also played an important role in determining bank entry. In California, the rate of bank entry into local markets was a function of both the growth of the market and the relative adequacy of the existing level of banking.

The importance of the latter indicates that disequilibrium existed in local banking markets in the short-run despite virtually free entry. An outward shift of a market's demand for banking services was not always followed immediately by the entry of new banks, because it took time to form new banks. Thus, the actual quantity of banking services supplied in the market (measured by bank assets) could lag behind the long-run level of banking services that would be supplied at competitive prices. With free entry and limited economies of scale (implying a horizontal long-run supply curve), market demand would determine this long-run level of banking services. Besides the time taken to organize a bank, other factors could reduce the pace of bank entry. Local market concentration and expectations about bank failures could combine to slow entry, and preserve higher local loan rates.

An important conclusion of this study is that demand factors are important in determining financial development. Other studies have treated this factor inadequately. As a result, their analyses can be misleading; their treatment of financial development in the South is an example. Davis, James and Sylla address the question of why rates in the South were slow to converge with rates in the developed regions of the country. All three find support for their hypotheses in the inadequate financial development of the South. Davis (1965) argues that it was the slow penetration of the commercial paper market that kept rates up in the South. James finds that the number of banks per capita had a significantly negative coefficient in most of the states in the South in his regression equation explaining interest rates by state.[45] He suggests that it was their spatial monopoly that gave banks in the South their monopoly power.[46] For Sylla (1972), the South's small share of the nation's bank deposits relative to its share of the nation's population indicate that the South's banking resources were inadequate, which he attributes to the national banking laws.[47]

Sylla argues that an efficient banking system would distribute bank deposits to match the distribution of population. Given the geographic shifts in population in the United States during the years 1850-1910, even an efficient banking system could not have produced equality immediately. A trend toward equality, however, does demonstrate that the banking industry was responding to demand. Sylla's calculations indicate a sharp increase in inequality between 1860 and 1870.[48] To achieve equality in the distribution of deposits and population, 40.3 percent of deposits needed redistributing in 1870, up from 18.3 percent in 1860 and 20.2 percent in 1850. Thereafter, this percentage fell; it was 33.8 percent in 1880, 25.5 percent in 1890, 25.6 percent in 1900, and 19.5 percent in 1970.

Sylla's approach deserves close attention for it purports not only to show the continued maldistribution of banking resources in the United States, but also to identify those regions with inadequate banking resources, in particular the inadequacy of banking in the South. Although population is a useful indicator of economic growth and regional differences in many instances, it is a poor measure of the demand for bank deposits. Since economic theory stresses the importance of income or wealth in the demand for deposits, a comparison of the regional distribution of bank deposits with the regional distribution of income is more appropriate.

Estimates of the regional distribution of income are available for the years 1880, 1900, and 1920. Table 7-5 presents these estimates along with the regional distribution of bank deposits and population. Column (7) gives the percentage of deposits requiring redistribution to obtain equality between the distribution of deposits and income. Column (6) gives the required percentage for equality between deposits and population. The difference between these two columns is dramatic. It suggests that by 1900 only 11.6 percent of deposits required redistribution, not 26.1 percent. Between 1880 and 1900, the U.S. banking industry appears to have reduced the maldistribution of deposits based on income, though the timing of this improvement cannot be determined. The maldistribution remained almost unchanged between 1900 and 1920, indicating that easier entry for national banks after 1900 did not improve the distribution of deposits.

The use of regional income shares as a basis for comparison (Column 7) suggests that the South was better served than the comparison based on population (Column 6) indicates. The South had less deposits per capita largely because it had the lowest regional income per capita.[49] When compared with the East North Central and the West North Central, it does not appear as deprived on the basis of Column 7 as it does on the basis of Column 6. The similarity among these three regions may explain why James finds that bank density had a significant effect for the states in all three of these regions. His failure to find a significant effect for bank density for states in the Mountain-Pacific region may reflect the adequacy of this region's banking resources, as indicated by its share of deposits (Column 7). While this static comparison of regional shares of income and bank deposits does not indicate the direction of causation between financial and economic development, it does suggest that the regional demand for financial services may have been important in determining the level of financial services in each region.

Though income or wealth is probably the most important demand factor, other factors may also help to explain the South's lower level of bank deposits. In general, an economy that is predominantly agricultural and rural, as the South's was, will have less demand for financial services than an economy that is commercial, industrial and urban. Rockoff (1975) finds that money per capita by state in 1850 and 1860 was a function not only of wealth per capita, but also of the proportion of a state's population that was urban. In 1860, the Southern states were typically the least urbanized of the states Rockoff analyses, although they were not generally the states with the lowest wealth per capita. In 1900, the Southern states were still the least urbanized, but by then were also relatively poor. In addition, the South's population was relatively illiterate, which may have contributed also to a relatively lower demand for financial services. If these demand factors were taken into account, banking in the South might no longer be termed inadequate.[50]

These features of the South's economy are nevertheless open to a different interpretation. James (1978a) finds that illiteracy contributed to the highest costs of operating banks in the South. Moreover, James views the rural and agricultural nature of the southern economy and its relatively illiterate population as contributing not to a lower level of demand for banking services, but to banks possessing spatial monopoly power and extracting monopoly profits by charging higher than market prices. Ransom and Sutch (1981) hold a similar view of the position of merchants in the provision of credit in the South. It was this local market power, based on barriers to state bank entry in southern states, that James argues caused interest rates to be higher and the level of banking resources per capita to be lower in southern states. Thus, James believes, as do Sylla and others, that structural factors slowed the South's financial development and this retarded development contributed to slower economic development.

In a largely unrestricted environment, banking in California does not appear to have either retarded growth or played a leading role in furthering economic growth. In the state as a whole, banking's development matched that of other advanced states. If banking did lag behind economic growth in California's local markets, entrepreneurs responded by forming new banks. A low level of bank deposits relative to the size and nature of the economy can indicate either poor performance by the existing banks or an economy growing faster than the capacity of local banks. An economy's banking system must in some sense be judged inadequate, if it cannot expand in response to this deficiency in banking resources. While Sylla may be right that the national banking laws were biased against regions such as the South and the West, liberal state banking laws enabled states like California and Wisconsin to achieve developed banking industries. In other states, banking laws were less liberal. In Texas, for example, state incorporated banks were prohibited between 1875 and 1905. In 1908, only three years after state-incorporated banking was authorized, there were as many state banks as national banks, though national banks still have five times the assets of state banks.[51] This rapid growth suggests the prohibition did lead to repression of the state's financial sector. James' emphasis on state banking laws appears to be appropriate, though the restrictions may be more complex than just minimum bank capital requirements. Even today, the cost of a state bank charter may substantially exceed the cost of raising the minimum capital. Moreover, other restrictions on financial activity, such as usury ceilings that can constrain financial development.[52] The emphasis on the negative effects of financial repression in current research on developing countries suggests that other restrictions may also be important. It is unfortunate that Williamson's model has not been extended to incorporate the South. Despite its flaws, it represents the only attempt at a comprehensive model of regional development that incorporates both demand and supply aspects of capital flows. Such a model might be able to distinguish between structural obstacles to southern development and those features of southern financial development that reflected the nature of its rural and agricultural economy.[53]

Conclusions

Capital markets have a crucial role to perform in a market economy, for it is through these markets that capital is allocated to the various sectors and regions of such an economy. Part of the process of economic development is the evolution of efficient capital markets that allocate capital to its most productive uses. One aspect of this evolution is the development of a national market for short-term capital. Considerable research has been devoted to discovering when and how this national market evolved in the United States, concentrating in particular on the narrowing of interregional interest rate differentials over the decades 1870 to 1910. Four hypotheses have been offered to explain the pattern of regional interest rates. Focusing particularly on the role of the banking industry, economic historians argue that the pattern can be explained by regional difference in risk and transactions costs, banks' market power, the demand for capital, and the adoption of financial innovations, specifically the penetration of commercial paper dealers. While these hypotheses are not necessarily mutually exclusive, economic historians tend to favor one hypothesis over the others. Even among proponents of a particular hypothesis, there are differences of opinion. Yet, this chapter's review of the evidence raises doubts about evidence supporting each hypothesis, and concludes that no single hypothesis dominates. For the present, a reasonable conclusion is that all four hypotheses are partly true, and hence many factors played a part in the evolution of a national short-term capital market in the United States.

Focusing on a single state, this study reveals the complexity of financial development, as many factors are found to have affected bank behavior. Banks' capital positions, bank managements' aversion to risk, local market demand, banks' local market power and bank regulation all appear to have influenced individual bank behavior to some degree; the most consistent factors were associated with risk and the form of a bank's charter. Market growth and perceptions of the existing banks' performance were major determinants of the pace and pattern of bank entry into local markets, but local market concentration and the risk of bank failure also affected bank entry. In finding that bank formations were a response to the inadequate level of banking services in local markets, this study shows banks were not generally formed in advance of local market growth. For the state as a whole, banking appears to have kept pace with the growth of the state's economy, and matched the development of banking elsewhere in the United States. Despite the relative laxity of state banking regulation in California, bank failures in California were not significantly higher than for the nation as a whole. California's history shows risk, market demand, banks' market power and bank regulation, all played a part in determining bank behavior, and therefore affected the pattern of interest rates.

In California, the relationship between bank behavior and bank regulation was more complex than the simplified formulations with which the role of bank regulation has been tested. Besides the rules and legislation governing banks' activities, the enforcement of these restrictions also determined the extent to which state-chartered banks were regulated. Other laws also affected banks' decisions: in California, property taxes and the methods of taxing banks also affected bank behavior. The competing national banking system added further complexity to banking regulation in California. In attempting to estimate the effects of regulation on bank behavior, economic historians must allow not only for the constraints imposed by these regulations, but also for the preferences of banks' customers. Californians' widespread dislike of bank notes was partially responsible for the slow start of national banking in California. The less diligent supervision of state banks after 1900 appears to have enhanced the reputation of national banks at the expense of state-chartered banks. Banking regulation did affect bank behavior, generally leading to lower loan/asset ratios in the case of the national banks. To attribute all the barriers to bank entry to minimum capital requirements, however, is an oversimplification, at least in the case of California; too many other factors are omitted.

In explaining bank behavior and the pattern of interest rates, this study did not incorporate information or transaction costs into the analysis. In general, other studies have also omitted these costs from their tests of the validity of the four hypotheses.[54] Instead, the importance of information and transaction costs has been inferred from the effects of the penetration of financial innovations, such as the commercial paper market, or from the failure of other factors to provide statistically significant results.[55] Yet, without information and transactions costs, risk, market demand, and market power would have contributed much less to the pattern of regional interest rates than they appear to have done. If borrowers could have readily and cheaply obtained funds from banks in other areas, banks could not have exercised local market power. If funds could flow easily and cheaply between local markets, restrictions on bank formations by themselves are not enough to give banks market power. If banks could have diversified their loan portfolios across regions at little cost, local loan risks would have ceased to determine the riskiness of banks' portfolios. Thus, the importance of risk, demand, and market power in determining regional interest rates must reflect the existence of information and transaction costs. It seems unlikely that these costs stayed the same across the country throughout this period. In which case, some of the narrowing of regional interest rates may be attributable to reductions in these costs, rather than to those other factors that are credited with causing a narrowing of regional rate differentials. Clearly, more research on this issue remains to be done.[56]

While part of the successful development of banking in California was due to the state's golden beginnings, much of this success is attributable to the relative freedom banking enjoyed in the state throughout most of the period. Relatively liberal banking laws enabled banking to develop with the state's economy, expanding its ability to generate financial capital as the economy's demand for finance grew. This freedom, however, did not lead to widespread or frequent bank failures by comparison with bank failures in the nation as a whole. These two features of banking's development together suggest that banking contributed to California's economic development, though not in the leading sector role that economic historians have ascribed to banking in other countries. In addition, there is little evidence of financial repression in California; even the distortions attributed to the national banking system were largely mitigated by the freedom of state-chartered banks. In other states, this was probably not so.[57] To determine the role that banking regulation played in economic development, further research is needed on bank behavior in states where economic development was less successful than California's. If this research is to be successful, it must take account of the many factors affecting bank behavior. In California during the period 1860-1910, banking regulation, risk, local market demand, and bank's market power all played a part in determining bank behavior.

Notes

1. Davis (1965), p. 357; Davis (1976), p. 17.
2. Smiley (1976), Table A4, gives the ratio of expenses plus taxes to private earning assets. Smiley (1977) compares his rates with Davis'.
3. James adjusts the Comptroller's national bank figures for losses plus premiums based on the proportion of premiums reported by the Comptroller in 1885, 1886, and 1887, James (1976b), p. 462. Smiley considers the proportion of premiums too small to require correction, Smiley (1975), p. 601.
4. James (1976b), p. 461.
5. Ironically, Davis also uses the standard deviation of rates in another article, and applies it to his net regional rates, but not his gross regional rates, over just three periods: 1869-79, 1880-99, and 1900-14; the standard deviation of these rates falls dramatically from 2.07 to 1.14 and then to 0.69. See Davis (1968), p. 21.
6. Footnote 6 in James (1976c) gives the following values for this index:

1888	3.737 percent	1903	2.748 percent
1893	2.955 percent	1908	2.341 percent
1898	3.353 percent	1911	2.451 percent

7. The average annual gross rate of return on private earning assets for New York City National Banks and Wisconsin Country National Banks, 1888-1913.

Year	(1) New York City	(2) Wisconsin	(2) - (1) WI - NYC
1988	6.03	7.79	1.76
1989	5.42	7.79	2.37
1890	5.88	7.63	1.75
1891	6.18	7.17	0.99
1892	5.17	6.60	1.43
1893	5.03	6.70	1.67
1894	5.22	6.60	1.38
1895	4.11	6.11	2.00
1896	4.71	6.21	1.50
1897	4.72	7.14	2.42
1898	3.89	6.16	2.27

1899	3.58	5.39	1.81
1900	4.19	5.75	1.56
1901	3.92	5.10	1.18
1902	4.23	4.85	0.62
1903	5.11	4.70	- .41
1904	5.56	5.01	- .55
1905	3.71	4.67	0.96
1906	4.58	4.93	0.35
1907	5.32	4.94	- .38
1908	5.13	5.10	- .03
1909	5.08	5.50	0.42
1910	5.69	6.13	0.44
1911	5.62	6.16	0.54
1912	5.78	6.35	0.57
1913	5.85	6.23	0.38

Source: Smiley (1976), Table A1.1 and A1.2.

8. Leavenworth apparently had no national banks. Smiley (1975) reports no earnings rate for this reserve city for the years 1888-1913.

9. For the regression of interest rates by state, the commercial paper rate's coefficient is 0.825, and the t-statistic for the null hypothesis that the coefficient is unity is 11.845. With 1788 observations, this coefficient is significantly different from unity at the one percent level of probability. For the regression of interest rates by reserve city, the commercial paper rate's coefficient is 0.951, and the t-statistic is 2.17. With 716 observations, this coefficient is significantly different from unity at only a five percent level. These results show that there is a very low probability that U.S. capital markets were integrated in the late nineteenth and early twentieth centuries. As one might expect, however, the evidence suggests that the reserve cities were probably more integrated into a unified capital market than were the states, which are aggregates of country national banks. See James (1976b), p. 460, for the regression results. An interesting test would be to divide James' interest rates into different periods and then test for any change in the unity of capital markets over time.

10. James (1978), p. 204, footnote 13.

11. James (1976b), p. 456.

12. James (1976b), p. 460.

13. Smiley (1977), p. 14.
14. Smiley (1977), p. 8, makes the same assumption that nineteenth century bankers were risk averse.
15. James (1976c), pp. 884-888.
16. U.S. Bureau of the Census (1976), Series X 741-755.
17. For the distribution of banks by type, see Board of Governors (1973).
18. Keehn (1972) uses two definitions of local markets: counties, and cities and towns. His results are reported in Keehn (1972), Tables 4-2 and 4-3, and Keehn (1980).
19. For more details on this Act, see Chapter 2 above, Robertson (1968) and Sylla (1975).
20. Sylla (1969), p. 676.
21. Ibid.
22. Sylla (1969), p. 679.
23. James (1976b), p. 460.
24. James (1976c).
25. See James (1976c), p. 897. To calculate the bank density index, James interpolates annual population estimates from U.S. Census data for each state. This procedure introduces another source of error in James' use of this variable in estimating his semi-annual time-series model. In many states, population growth is likely to have been uneven, especially in those states that were developing rapidly (see James (1976b), pp. 461-462). In fact, James' measure of market power reflects both demand and supply. Banks per capita reflect the need for additional banks in a state. In states where population is growing faster than the number of banks, banks per capita will fall, and bank earnings will rise.
26. San Francisco was the least concentrated county throughout the period with a value for the Herfindahl Index of 0.117 in 1878 and 0.065 in 1908. At the same time, there were many counties with only one bank, and numerous counties with a value for this index that was over 0.3.
27. James (1976b), p. 460.
28. Smiley (1977), p. 32.
29. Smiley (1977), p. 41.
30. Smiley (1977), Table 2.
31. Keehn (1972, 1980); the number of banks and the number of new banks in Wisconsin are given in Chapter 5 above.

32. Smiley (1977), p. 35.
33. James (1974), p. 511.
34. Sylla (1969, 1977).
35. James (1976c) does not estimate directly the importance of the changes in the minimum capital requirements for national banks. Elsewhere, James (1974), p. 510, he does find that a dummy variable for the post-1900 period is significantly positive in an equation explaining bank density for many states, but he attributes this result to the return of the U.S. economy to prosperity after 1900 because he also finds his business cycle index plays the same role.
36. The Comptroller was reporting the results of a survey of minimum capital requirements, and California's minimum may have been reported in error or misprinted (see U.S. Comptroller of the Currency, Annual Report, 1895/96). In a review of capital requirements for state banks, Barnett (1911), p. 37, reports California's 1895 minimum requirement correctly.
37. James (1976c), p. 894.
38. Barnett (1911), indicates states faced difficulties in enforcing their minimum capital requirements.
39. Williamson (1974), Chapter 6.
40. Ibid.
41. Ibid.
42. See the discussion above in Section 2 of this chapter.
43. Williamson (1974), pp. 130-132; Williamson cites Davis (1965), pp. 375; but, Davis makes no reference there to retardation of capital market development. However, Davis does conclude: "...the failure of these companies (mortgage banks) in the 1890s may have contributed to the retardation in development of a national long-term market." Davis (1965), p. 393.
44. Smiley (1977), p. 44, specifically states his model is a supply-side model.
45. James (1976b), p. 457.
46. See James (1978), p. 222, and James (1974), Chapter X.
47. Sylla (1972), p. 243.
48. Sylla (1972), pp. 239-241.
49. Brown and Reynolds (1973) make this point.

50. The predominance of agriculture in the economy of the South may have made bank lending riskier, leading to higher loan rates being charged by banks. Smiley (1977) finds that the proportion of the labor force in primary activities had a positive, and in some years significant, effect on interest rates by state. He attributes this positive effect to the greater risks inherent in a largely agricultural economy, as opposed to a diversified one. James (1976b) finds that risk was a significant, though not large, factor determining interest rates in southern states. See James (1978), p. 211 also.
51. Grant and Crum (1979).
52. Rockoff (1975) finds that the height of usury ceilings had a negative effect on the level of money per capita by state in 1850 and 1860.
53. The debate over the causes of the South's slow development during the post-Civil War period continues. See Walton and Shepherd (1981).
54. James, Smiley, and others have used distance from financial centers (variously defined), but the variable is not very meaningful, given the existence of the telegraph.
55. Davis (1965) and Keehn (1972).
56. One avenue for further research is the role of literacy. James (1974; 1978a) argues that the South's relative illiteracy raised the cost of operating a bank. One wonders if increasing literacy led not only to lower operating costs for banks, but also to more extensive use of financial services. Criticizing Davis (1975), Schwartz (1975) suggests various financial institutions that may have contributed to unifying U.S. capital markets. One important institution may have been the clearing house; in California, various clearing house associations were formed in the 1900s to improve banks' liquidity.
57. Texas may be one example.

Table 7-1
Average Annual Gross Rate of Return on Private Earning Assets
For California Country Banks, New York City Banks,
and San Francisco Banks
1888-1913

Year	California	New York City	San Francisco	Los Angeles	CA-NYC	SF-NYC	CA-SF
1888	9.70	6.03	7.70	-	3.67	1.67	2.00
1889	9.88	5.42	8.25	-	4.46	2.83	1.63
1890	9.77	5.88	8.05	-	3.89	2.17	1.72
1891	9.18	6.18	8.13	-	3.00	1.95	1.05
1892	8.03	5.17	8.37	-	2.86	3.20	-.34
1893	7.86	5.03	8.13	-	2.83	3.10	-.27
1894	9.18	5.22	8.11	-	3.96	2.89	1.07
1895	9.20	4.11	7.91	-	5.09	3.80	1.29
1896	8.29	4.71	7.54	-	3.58	2.83	0.75
1897	8.12	4.72	7.51	-	3.40	2.79	0.61
1898	9.21	3.89	7.10	-	5.32	3.21	2.11
1899	9.13	3.58	7.12	-	5.55	3.54	2.01
1900	9.32	4.19	6.95	-	5.13	2.76	2.37
1901	7.02	3.92	6.92	6.14	3.10	3.00	0.10
1902	7.79	4.23	6.48	7.01	3.56	2.25	1.31
1903	7.31	5.11	6.18	6.65	2.20	1.07	1.13
1904	6.72	5.56	5.53	6.16	1.16	-.03	1.19
1905	6.82	3.71	5.86	6.04	3.11	2.15	0.96
1906	6.48	4.58	5.34	5.69	1.90	0.76	1.14
1907	6.16	5.32	4.47	5.84	0.84	-.85	1.69
1908	6.22	5.13	5.78	5.92	1.09	0.65	0.44
1909	7.38	5.08	5.74	6.63	2.30	0.66	1.64
1910	6.89	5.69	5.07	6.08	1.20	-.62	1.82
1911	7.10	5.62	5.36	6.50	1.48	-.26	1.74
1912	7.09	5.78	7.01	6.21	1.31	1.23	0.08
1913	6.80	5.85	6.71	6.03	0.95	0.86	0.09

Source: Smiley (1976)

Table 7-2
Capital-Deposit Ratios by Region and Type of Bank
1880-1910

Type of Bank*	Region**						U.S.
	NE	MA	SO	ENC	WNC	M-P	
1880							
NB	1.18	.36	.74	.52	.48	.34	.55
Non-NB	.59	.35	.60	.24	.33	.27	.35
1890							
NB	.70	.29	.56	.38	.53	.34	.42
Non-NB	.19	.19	.50	.22	.44	.33	.27
1900							
NB	.44	.19	.33	.24	.29	.19	.25
Non-NB	.11	.16	.28	.15	.24	.15	.17
1910							
NB	.22	.16	.27	.19	.18	.17	.19
Non-NB	.08	.13	.27	.12	.16	.14	.14

* NB = National Banks and Non-NB = Non-national Banks
**For definitions of regions, see Table 7-5.
Source: Sylla (1975), Table II - 14, p. 81

Table 7-3
Number of Commercial Banks per 100,000 Inhabitants,
by States and Regions, 1900

State/Region	Banks	State/Region	Banks
Maine	14.2	Minnesota	28.6
New Hampshire	17.7	Iowa	51.1
Vermont	19.4	Missouri	21.7
Massachusetts	10.1	North Dakota	45.8
Rhode Island	14.0	South Dakota	50.0
Connecticut	11.4	Nebraska	48.1
New England	**12.3**	Kansas	32.9
		W. North Central	**35.4**
Delaware	12.4	Montana	20.2
Maryland	10.3	Idaho	23.5
District of Columbia	7.1	Wyoming	34.4
Virginia	8.5	Colorado	21.0
West Virginia	13.0	New Mexico	7.0
North Carolina	6.2	Arizona	16.4
South Carolina	10.1	Utah	13.9
Georgia	9.9	Nevada	22.7
Florida	7.1	**Mountain**	**18.8**
South Atlantic	**9.2**		
Kentucky	14.6	Arkansas	9.4
Tennessee	9.0	Louisiana	5.6
Alabama	5.7	Oklahoma	18.1
Mississippi	7.2	Texas	13.3
E. South Central	**9.4**	**W. South Central**	**11.5**
New York	10.6	Ohio	17.1
New Jersey	8.7	Indiana	19.1
Pennsylvania	12.0	Illinois	20.3
Middle Atlantic	**10.9**	Michigan	21.4
		Wisconsin	16.7
		E. North Central	**19.0**
Washington	19.3		
Oregon	18.4		
California	18.9		
Pacific	**18.9**	**Total United States**	**16.1**

Source: Goldsmith (1958b), Table D-14

Table 7-4
Legislative Changes and Bank Entry, 1884-1908: Regression Results

Dependent Variable	Independent Variable	Regression Coefficients	T-Values	Standardized Regression Coefficients
NET BS (R^2 = .13, SE = .398, F = 8.31)				
	CONSTANT	0.25	4.36	
	GRW3YR	0.61	5.34	0.28
	TD/W	-1.00	-2.46	-0.19
	HERFIN	-0.17	-2.37	-0.13
	FAILRT	-0.02	-1.63	-0.09
	WT	0.00	1.10	0.08
	S	0.08	1.40	0.08
NET TA (R^2 = .10, SE = .346, F = 6.60)				
	CONSTANT	0.23	4.66	
	GRW3YR	0.37	3.73	0.20
	TD/W	-1.21	-3.42	-0.27
	HERFIN	-0.21	-3.39	-0.19
	FAILRT	-0.02	-1.44	-0.08
	WT	0.00	0.97	0.07
	S	0.04	0.81	0.05
NET BS (R^2 = .12, SE = .399, F = 8.08)				
	CONSTANT	0.24	3.67	
	GRW3YR	0.65	4.88	0.30
	TD/W	-0.89	-2.23	-0.17
	HERFIN	-0.17	-2.32	-0.13
	FAILRT	-0.03	-1.62	-0.10
	WT	0.00	0.93	0.07
	J	0.05	0.86	0.06
NET TA (R^2 = .10, SE = .347, F = 6.54)				
	CONSTANT	0.22	3.93	
	GRW3YR	0.40	3.44	0.21
	TD/W	-1.16	-3.39	-0.26
	HERFIN	-0.21	-3.36	-0.18
	FAILRT	-0.02	-1.34	-0.08
	WT	0.00	0.90	0.06
	J	0.03	0.62	0.04

Table 7-5
Regional Distribution of Bank Deposits, Population and
Personal Income in the United States, 1880, 1900, and 1920*

Year	Region	(1) Deposits ($ millions)	(2) Deposits (percent)	(3) Population (millions)	(4) Population (percent)	(5) Income (percent)	(6) (2)-(4) (percent)	(7) (2)-(5) (percent)
1880	NE	161	11.3	4.0	8.0	11	+3.3	+0.3
	MA	708	49.5	11.8	23.4	33	+26.1	+16.5
	SO	105	7.3	15.3	30.4	16	-23.1	-8.7
	ENC	246	17.2	11.2	22.3	23	-5.1	-5.8
	WNC	98	6.8	6.2	12.3	11	-5.5	-4.2
	M-P	113	7.9	1.8	3.5	6	+4.4	+1.9
	U.S.	1431		50.3			+33.7	+18.7
1900	NE	507	9.3	5.5	7.1	10	+2.2	-0.7
	MA	2338	43.0	17.1	22.2	31	+20.8	+12.0
	SO	438	8.1	22.4	29.1	15	-21.0	-6.9
	ENC	1094	20.1	16.6	21.5	22	-1.4	-1.9
	WNC	586	10.8	11.2	14.5	13	-3.7	-2.2
	M-P	469	8.6	4.2	5.4	8	+3.2	+0.6
	U.S.	5433		77.1			+26.1	+11.6

Table 7-5 (continued)

Regional Distribution of Bank Deposits, Population and

Personal Income in the United States, 1880, 1900, and 1920*

Year	Region	(1) Deposits ($ millions)	(2) (percent)	(3) Population (millions)	(4) (percent)	(5) Income (percent)	(6) (2)-(4) (percent)	(7) (2)-(5) (percent)
1920	NE	4270	11.3	7.5	7.0	9	+4.3	+2.3
	MA	14400	38.2	24.6	23.1	30	+15.1	+8.2
	SO	4540	12.0	31.2	29.3	18	-17.3	-6.0
	ENC	6750	17.9	21.6	20.3	22	-2.4	-4.1
	WNC	4110	10.9	12.6	11.8	10	-0.9	+0.9
	M-P	3410	9.0	9.0	8.5	10	+0.5	-1.0
	U.S.	37680		106.5			+20.2	+11.2

*NE   = NEW ENGLAND (Maine, New Hampshire, Vermont, Massachusetts, Rhode Island, and Connecticut)

MA   = MIDDLE ATLANTIC (New York, New Jersey, Pennsylvania, Delaware, Maryland, and District of Columbia)

SO   = SOUTH (Virginia, West Virginia, North Carolina, South Carolina, Georgia, Florida, Alabama, Mississippi, Kentucky, Tennessee, Arkansas, Louisiana, Texas, and Oklahoma.

ENC = EAST NORTH CENTRAL (Ohio, Indiana, Illinois, Michigan, and Wisconsin)

WNC= WEST NORTH CENTRAL (Minnesota, Iowa, Missouri, Kansas, Nebraska, South Dakota, and North Dakota)

M-P   = MOUNTAIN PACIFIC (Montana, Wyoming, Colorado, New Mexico, Arizona, Utah, Nevada, Idaho, Washington, Oregon and California)

Sources: Column (1) - 1880 and 1900. Sylla (1975), Table A-5.

1920. U.S. Comptroller of the Currency, *Annual Report, 1920*, pp. 255-256.

Column (3) - 1880, 1890, and 1900. U.S. Bureau of the Census, *Historical Statistics of the United States, Colonial Times to 1970*, Part I, Series A 195-209.

Column (5) - U.S. Bureau of the Census (1975), Part I, Series F 287-296.

Bibliography

Akerlof, George (1970), "The Market for Lemons: Qualitative Uncertainty and the Market Mechanism," *Quarterly Journal of Economics*, v.84 (August 1970), pp. 488-500.

Alcaly, Roger E. and Richard W. Nelson, "Will Including Thrifts in the Banking Market Affect Mergers?" *Banking Law Journal*, v.97:4 (April 1980).

Alhadeff, David A. (1954), *Monopoly and Competition in Banking.* Berkeley: University of California Press, 1954.

_____ (1962), "A Reconsideration of Restrictions on Bank Entry," *Quarterly Journal of Economics*, v.76:2, (May 1962), pp. 246-263.

_____ (1963), "Bank Mergers: Competition Versus Banking Factors," *Southern Economic Journal*, v.29:3 (January 1963), pp. 218-230.

_____ (1967), "Monopolistic Competition and Banking Markets," in Robert E. Kuenne ed. *Monopolistic Competition Theory: Studies in Impact.* New York: John Wiley & Sons.

_____ (1974), "Barriers to Bank Entry," *Southern Economic Journal*, v.40:4 (April 1974), pp. 589-603.

Alhadeff, David A. and Charlotte P. Alhadeff (1975), "Bank Entry and Bank Concentration, *Antitrust Bulletin,* v. 20:3 (Fall 1975), pp. 471-484.

American Bankers' Association, *Proceedings of the Convention, Chicago, Illinois 1885.* New York: Bankers' Publishing Association, 1885.

Armstrong, L. and J.O. Denny (1916), Financial California: A Historical Review of the Beginnings and Progress of Banking in the State. San Francisco 1916.

Aspinwall, Richard C. (1970), "Market Structure and Commercial Bank Mortgage Interest Rates," *Southern Economic Journal,* v. 36:4 (April 1970), 376-384.

Austin, Douglas V. (1977), "The Line of Commerce and the Relevant Geographic Market in Banking: What Fifteen Years of Trials and Tribulations Has Taught Us and Not Taught Us About the Measure of Banking Structure" in *Bank Structure and Competition,* Federal Reserve Bank of Chicago, 1977, pp. 185-209.

Bain, Joe S. (1959), *Industrial Organization.* New York: John Wiley & Sons, 1959.

Barnett, George E. (1911), *State Banks and Trust Companies Since the Passage of the National Bank Act,* Washington, D.C.: U.S. Government Printing Office, 1911.

Bean, Walton (1968), *California: An Interpretative History.* New York: McGraw-Hill Book Co., 1968.

Bell, Frederick W. and Neil B. Murphy (1969), "Impact of Market Structure on the Price of a Commercial Banking Service," *Review of Economics and Statistics,* v.51 (May 1969), 210-213.

Bennett, Rex O. (1975), *Bank Location Analysis: Techniques and Methodology.* Washington, D.C.: American Bankers Association, 1975.

Benston, George J. (1972), "Economies of Scale of Financial Institutions, *Journal of Money, Credit and Banking,* v.4 (May 1972), pp. 312-341.

Benston, George J. (1973), "The Optimal Bank Structure: Theory and Evidence," *Journal of Bank Research,* v.4 (May 1972), pp. 220-237.

Berman, Peter I. (1974), "Socially Optimal Bank Structure," *Bank Structure and Competition,* Chicago: Federal Reserve Bank of Chicago, 1974.

Black, Fischer (1975), "Bank Funds Management in an Efficient Market," *Journal of Financial Economics,* v.2 (1975).

Blackford, Mansel (1973), "Banking and Bank Legislation in California, 1890-1915," *Business History Review,* v.97:4 (Winter 1973) pp. 482-507.

_____ (1977), *The Politics of Business in California,* 1890-1920. Columbus: University of Ohio Press, 1977.

Board of Governors of the Federal Reserve System (1943), *Banking and Monetary Statistics.* Washington, D.C., 1943.

_____ (1959), *All-Bank Statistics: United States, 1896-1955.* Washington, D.C. 1959.

Boczar, Gregory E. (1977), "Market Characteristics and Multibank Holding Company Acquisitions," *Journal of Finance,* v.1 (March 1977), pp. 131-146.

Breckenridge, R.M. (1898), "Discount Rates in the United States," *Political Science Quarterly,* v.13 (March 1898), pp. 119-142.

Broaddus, J. Alfred Jr. (1972), "Banking Market Structure and Bank Performance--A Theoretical Analysis," *Proceedings of a Conference on Bank Structure and Competition,* Federal Reserve Bank of Chicago, 1972, pp. 134-164.

_____ (1974), "A General Model of Bank Decisions," *Working Paper* 74-6, Federal Reserve Bank of Richmond, 1974.

Brown, William W. and Morgan O. Reynolds (1973), "Deb Peonage Reexamined," *Journal of Economic History,* v.33:4 (December 1973), pp. 862-871.

Brucker, Eric (1970), "A Microeconomic Approach to Banking Competition," *Journal of Finance,* v.25 (December 1970), pp. 1133-1141.

Buser, Stephen A., Andrew H. Chen, and Edward J. Kane (1981), "Federal Deposit Insurance, Regulatory Policy, and Optimal Bank Capital," *Journal of Finance,* v.35:1 (March 1981), pp. 222-240.

Cagan, Phillip (1965) Determinants and Effects of Changes in the Stock of Money 1875-1960. New York: Columbia University Press, 1965.

California Bankers' Association, *Proceedings of the Third Annual Convention,* San Francisco, 1894.

California State Board of Bank Commissioners, *Annual Reports, 1878-1908.* Sacramento, 1878-1908.

California State Board of Commissioners of the Building and Loan Associations, *Annual Report, 1900.* Sacramento, 1900.

California State Board of Equalization, *Biennial Reports,* 1885-1900. Sacramento, 1887-1901.

California State Commission on Revenue and Taxation (1906), *Report of 1906.* Sacramento, 1906.

_____ (1910), *Report of 1910.* Sacramento, 1910.

California State Superintendent of Banks, *Annual Report, 1910,* Sacramento, 1910.

Cameron, Rondo, ed. (1967). *Banking in the Early Stages of Industrialization: A Study in Comparative Economic History*. New York: Oxford University Press, 1967.

Cameron, Rondo, ed. (1972), *Banking and Economic Development*, New York: Oxford University Press, 1972.

Caughey, John W. (1970), *California: A Remarkable State's Life History*. Englewood Cliffs, New Jersey: Prentice-Hall, Inc., 1970.

Chandler, Lester V. (1938), "Monopolistic Elements in Commercial Banking," *Journal of Political Economy*, v.46 (February 1938), pp. 1-22.

Chandross (1971), "Bank Formations," *Journal of Bank Research*, 1971.

Cheng, Hang-Sheng (1980), "Financial Deepening in Pacific Basin Countries," *Economic Review*, Federal Reserve Bank of San Francisco (Summer 1980), pp. 43-56.

Cleland, Robert G. (1929), *The March of Industry*. Los Angeles, California: Powell Publishing Co., 1929.

Conzen, Michael P. (1975), "Capital Flows and the Developing Urban Hierarchy: State Bank Capital in Wisconsin, 1854-1895," *Economic Geography*, v.51:4 (October 1975), pp. 321-338.

_____ (1977), "The Maturing Urban System in the United States, 1840-1910," *Annals of the Association of American Geographers*, v.67:1 (March 1977), pp. 88-108.

Cooke, Thornton (1909), "The Insurance of Bank Deposits in the West," reprinted in George E. Barnett, *State Banks and Trust Companies Since the Passage of the National Bank Act*. Washington, D.C.: U.S. Government Printing Office, 1911, pp. 261-352.

Cross, Ira B. (1927), *Financing an Empire*. San Francisco: S.J. Clarke, 1927.

Crosse, Howard, *Management Policies for Commercial Banks,* Englewood Cliffs, NJ: Prentice-Hall, 1962.

Crumb, Jr. (1935), "Banking Regulation in California," unpublished Ph.D. dissertation, University of California at Berkeley, 1935.

Dana, Julian (1947), A.P., *Giannini, Giant in the West: A Biography,* New York: Prentice-Hall, 1947.

Davis, Lance E. (1965), "The Investment Market, 1890-1914: The Evolution of a National Market," *Journal of Economic History,* v.25 (September 1965), pp. 355-399.

_____ (1968), "Capital Immobilities, Institutional Adaptation, and Financial Development: the United States and England, an International Comparison," *Zeitschrift Fur Die Gesamte Staatswissenschaft,* v.124 (1968), pp. 14-34.

_____ (1975), "The Evolution of the American Capital Market, 1860-1940: A Case Study in Institutional Change," in William L. Silber (ed.) *Financial Innovation,* Lexington, Mass.: D.C. Heath and Co., 1975.

De Vries, Barend A. (1981), "Economic Development and the Private Sector," *Finance & Development,* v.18:3 (September 1981), pp. 11-15.

Duro, Lorraine and Robert Ware (1972), "Potential Competition and the Strategy of Entry," in *Bank Structure and Competition,* Federal Reserve Bank of Chicago, 1972.

Edwards, Franklin R. (1964), "Concentration and Competition in Commercial Banking: A Statistical Study." *Research Report No. 26,* Federal Reserve Bank of Boston, 1964.

Edwards, Linda N. and Franklin R. Edwards (1974), "Measuring the Effectiveness of Regulation: The Case of Bank Entry Regulation," *Journal of Law and Economics,* v.17:2, (October 1974), pp. 445-460.

Edwards, Franklin R., and Arnold A. Heggestad (1973), "Uncertainty, Market Structure and Performance: The Galbraith-Caves Hypothesis and Managerial Motives in Banking," *Quarterly Journal of Economics*, v.87:3 (August 1973), pp. 455-473.

Fand, David I. (1954), "Estimates of Deposits and Vault Cash in the Nonnational Banks in the Post Civil War Period in the United States: 1876-1896," unpublished Ph.D. dissertation, University of Chicago, 1954.

Fankhauser, W.C. (1913), *A Financial History of California: Public Revenues, Debts and Expenditures*. Berkeley: University of California Press, 1913.

Federal Reserve Bank of Atlanta (1982), "Line of Commerce: Battle Over Banking," *Economic Review*, Federal Reserve Bank of Atlanta (April 1982).

Federal Reserve Bank of Boston (1972), *Policies for a More Competitive Financial System*. Proceedings of a conference held in June, 1972. Federal Reserve Bank of Boston, Conference Series No. 8, Boston, 1972.

_____ (1981), "Changing Commercial Bank Structure in New England: 1976-1979," *Research Report 66*, Federal Reserve Bank of Boston (September 1981).

Fraser, Donald R. and J. Patrick McCormack (1978), "Large Bank Failures and Investor Risk Perceptions: Evidence From the Debt Market," *Journal of Financial and Quantitative Analysis*, v.13:3, (September 1978), 527-532.

Fraser, Donald R and Peter S. Rose (1972), "Bank Entry and Bank Performance," *Journal of Finance*, v.27:1, (March 1972), pp. 65-78.

Friedman, Milton and Anna Schwartz (1963), "Money and Business Cycles," *Review of Economics and Statistics*, v.45 supple., (1963).

Fry, Maxwell J. (1980), "Savings, Investment, Growth and the Cost of Financial Repression," *World Development,* v.8 (1980), pp. 317-327.

Galbraith, John A. (1963). *The Economics of Banking Operations.* Montreal: McGill University Press, 1963.

Gerschenkron, Alexander (1962). *Economic Backwardness in Historical Perspective.* New York: Frederick A. Praeger, 1962.

Gilbert, R. Alton (1974), "Measures of Potential for De Novo Entry in Bank Acquisition Cases: An Evaluation," Federal Reserve Bank of Chicago, *Bank Structure and Competition,* 1974, pp. 159-170.

Gilbert, Gary (1974), "Predicting De Novo Expansion in Bank Merger Cases," *Journal of Finance,* v.29:1 (March 1974), pp. 151-162.

Glassman, Cynthia A. (1973), "Banking Markets in Pennsylvania," in *Changing Pennsylvania's Branching Laws: An Economic Analysis.* Federal Reserve Bank of Philadelphia (1973), pp. 19-42.

Goldsmith, Raymond W. (1958a), *Financial Intermediaries in the American Economy Since 1900.* Princeton: Princeton University Press, 1958.

_____ (1958b), Supplementary Appendices to *Financial Intermediaries in the American Economy Since 1900.* New York: National Bureau of Economic Research, 1958.

_____ (1967), "Financial Structure and Economic Development," *Economic Development and Cultural Change,* (April 1967), pp. 257-268.

_____ (1969), *Financial Structure and Development.* New Haven: Yale University Press, 1969.

_____ (1975), "The Quantitative International Comparison of Financial Structure and Development," *Journal of Economic History,* v.35:1 (March 1975), pp. 216-237.

Good, David F. (1973), "Backwardness and the Role of Banking in Nineteenth-Century European Industrialization," *Journal of Economic History,* v.33:4 (December 1973), pp. 845-850.

Graddy, Duane B. and Reuben Kyle, III (1979), "The Simultaneity of Bank Decision-Making, Market Structure, and Bank Performance." *Journal of Finance,* v.34:1 (March 1979), pp. 1-18.

Grant, Joseph M. and Lawrence L. Crum (1978), *The Development of State-Chartered Banking in Texas.* Austin, Texas: Bureau of Business Research, University of Texas, 1978.

Greenbaum, Stuart (1974), "Entry, Control and the Market for Bank Charters," *Journal of Finance,* v.29 (May 1974), pp. 527-535.

Greenbaum, Stuart, and Robert Taggart (1975), "Bank Capital Adequacy," in Bank Structure and Competition, Federal Reserve Bank of Chicago, 1975.

Gurley, John G. and Edward S. Shaw (1955), "Financial Aspects of Economic Development." *American Economic Review,* v.45 (1955), pp. 515-38.

_____ (1956), "Financial Intermediaries and the Saving-Investment Process," *Journal of Finance,* v.2:2 (May 1956), pp. 257-76.

_____ (1957), "The Growth of Debt and Money in the United States 1800-1950." *Review of Economics and Statistics,* v.39 (1957) pp. 250-62.

_____ (1960). *Money in A Theory of Finance.* Washington, DC: Brookings Institute, 1960.

Guttentag, Jack M. and Edward S. Herman (1967). "Banking Structure and Performance." *The Bulletin,* v.41:43, New York University, Graduate School of Business Administration, Institute of France, (February 1967).

Hallagan, William S., "Sharecontracting for California Gold," paper presented at the 1977 Western Economic Association Meetings, (June 1977).

Hannan, Timothy (1978), "Limit Pricing and the Banking Industry," *Research Paper* No. 32, Federal Reserve Bank of Philadelphia, (March 1978).

Hanweck, Gerald (1971), "Bank Entry into Local Markets: An Empirical Assessment of the Degree of Potential Competition Via New Bank Formation," Federal Reserve Bank of Chicago, *Bank Structure and Competition*, 1971, pp. 161-172.

Hawke, John D. Jr. (1981), "Competitive Factors: Review of 1980 Fed Decision," *Legal Times of Washington*, (February 23, 1981), pp. 26-36.

Heggestad, Arnold A. (1977). "Market Structure, Risk and Profitability in Commercial Banking," *Journal of Finance*, v.32 (September 1977).

Heggestad, Arnold A. and John J. Mingo (1977), "The Competitive Condition of U.S. Banking Markets and The Impact of Structural Reform," *Journal of Finance*, v.32:3, (June, 1977), pp. 649-661.

Hirschman, Albert O. (1958). *The Strategy of Economic Development*. New Haven, Connecticut: Yale University Press, 1958.

Hodgman, Donald R. (1963), *Commercial Bank Loan and Investment Policy*. Champaign: University of Illinois Press, 1963.

Horvitz, Paul M. (1958). "Concentration and Competition in New England Banking." *Research Report No. 2*, Federal Reserve Bank of Boston, 1958.

Hutchison, ed. (1946). *California Agriculture*, 1946.

Irving Trust Co. (1977), *Capital Securities Issued: Commercial Banking*. New York: Irving Trust Co., 1977.

James, John A. (1976), "A Note on Interest Paid on New York Bankers' Balances in the Postbellum Period," *Business History Review*, v.50 (Summer 1976), pp. 198-202.

_____ (1976b), "Banking Market Structure, Risk, and the Pattern of Local Interest Rates in the United States, 1893-1911," *Review of Economics and Statistics,* v.58 (November 1976), pp. 453-462.

_____ (1976c), "The Development of the National Money Market, 1893-1911," *Journal of Economic History* v.36:4 (December 1976), pp. 878-897.

_____ (1976d), "Portfolio Selection with an Imperfectly Competitive Asset Market," *Journal of Financial and Quantitative Analysis,* v.11 (December 1976).

_____ (1978), *Money and Capital Markets in Postbellum America,* Princeton, New Jersey: Princeton University Press.

_____ (1978a), "Cost Functions of Postbellum National Banks," *Explorations in Economic History,* v.15 (April 1978), pp. 184-195.

Kareken, John H. (1981), "Commercial Banking as a Line of Commerce: An Appraisal," *Quarterly Review,* Federal Reserve Bank of Minneapolis, (Winter 1981), pp. 7-13.

Kaufman, George G. (1966), "Bank Market Structure and Performance: The Evidence from Iowa," *Southern Economic Journal,* v.32 (April 1966), pp. 429-439.

_____ (1975), "Preventing Bank Failures," in U.S. Congress. Senate Banking, Housing and Urban Affairs, *Compendium of Major Issues in Bank Regulation,* Washington, D.C.: Government Printing Office, pp. 787-814.

Keehn, Richard H. (1972), "Market Structure and Bank Performance: Wisconsin, 1870-1900," unpublished Ph.D. dissertation, University of Wisconsin-Madison, 1972.

_____ (1974), "Federal Bank Policy, Bank Market Structure, and Bank Performance: Wisconsin, 1863-1914," *Business History Review,* v.48:1 (Spring 1974), pp. 1-27.

_____ (1975), "Bank Market Structure and Individual Bank Performance: Some Evidence from Wisconsin, 1870-1900," paper presented at the 1975 Western Economic Association Conference.

_____ (1980), "Market Power and Bank Lending: Some Evidence from Wisconsin, 1870-1900," *Journal of Economic History,* v.40:1 (March 1980), pp. 45-52.

Keehn, Richard H. and Gene Smiley (1976), "Mortgage Lending by National Banks, 1890-1914," paper presented at the 1976 Western Economic Association Meetings, (June 26, 1976).

Keleher, Robert E. (1979). "Regional Credit Market Integration: A Survey and Empirical Examination." *Working Paper Series,* Federal Reserve Bank of Atlanta, (February 1979).

Klein, Michael A. (1970), "Imperfect Asset Theory and Portfolio Theory," *American Economic Review,* v.60:3 (June, 1970), pp. 491-494.

_____ (1970), "A Theory of the Banking Firm," *Journal of Money, Credit and Banking,* v.3 (May 1971), pp. 205-218.

Knox, John J. (1903; 1969), *A History of Banking in the United States.* New York: B. Rhodes and Co., 1903. Reprinted New York: Augustus M. Kelley, 1969.

Kuznets, Simon, Ann Ratner Miller and Richard A. Easterline (1960), *Analyses of Economic Change,* Vol. II of *Population Redistribution and Economic Growth: United States, 1870-1959.* Philadelphia: The American Philosophical Society.

Lester, Richard A. (1939). *Monetary Experiments,* Princeton University Press, Princeton, NJ, 1939.

Lewis, K.A. and Yamamura, K. (1971), "Industrialization and Interregional Interest Rate Structure, the Japanese Case: 1889-1925," *Explorations in Economic History,* v.7 (Summer, 1971), pp. 473-499.

Lindow, Wesley (1963), "Bank Capital and Risk Assets," *National Banking Review,* v.1:1, (Sept. 1963).

Lister, Roger C. (1979), "The Expansion of Banking in the Metropolitan Areas of the Southwest," *Voice,* Federal Reserve Bank of Dallas, (June 1979), pp. 1-9.

Littlefield, James E., G. Jackson Burney and William V. White, (1973), *Bank Branch Location.* Chicago: Bank Marketing Association, 1973.

Lockhart, Oliver C. (1921), "The Development of Interbank Borrowing in the National System," *Journal of Political Economy,* v.29:2 (February 1921), pp. 138-160 and v.29:3 (March 1921), pp. 222-240.

Mandle, J.R. (1974), "The Plantation States as a Sub-Region of the Post-Bellum South," *Journal of Economic History,* v.34 (September 1974), pp. 732-738.

Mayer, Thomas (1975), "Preventing the Failure of Large Banks," in *Compendium of Major Issues in Banking Regulation,* US Congress. Senate Committee on Banking, Housing, and Urban Affairs, Washington, DC, 1975.

Mayor, Thomas H. and John T. Fraser (1976), Government Printing Office, "An Analysis of Factors Used to Determine the Public Need for New Banks," *Southern Economic Journal,* v.43:1, (July 1976), pp. 818-826.

McCall, Alan S. and Manfred O. Peterson (1976), "The Impact of De Novo Commercial Bank Entry," Federal Deposit Insurance Corporation, Division of Research, *Working Paper No. 76-7,* 1976.

McKinnon, Ronald (1973), *Money and Capital in Economic Development*. Washington, DC: The Brookings Institute, 1973.

_____ (ed.) (1976), *Money and Finance in Economic Growth and Development*. New York and Basel: Marcel Dekker, 1976.

McKinnon, Ronald I. and Donald J. Mathieson (1981), *How to Manage a Repressed Economy*. Princeton, NJ: International Finance Section, Princeton University, 1981.

McWilliams, Carey (1971), *Factories in the Field*. Santa Barbara and Salt Lake City: Peregrine Publishers, 1971.

Meyer, Paul (1976). "Price Discrimination, Regional Loan Rates, and the Structure of the Banking Industry." *Journal of Finance,* v.22:1 (March 1967), pp. 37-48.

Miller, Stephen (1975), "A Theory of the Banking Firm: Comment," *Journal of Monetary Economics,* v.1:1 (January 1975).

Mingo, John J. (1975), "Regulatory Influence on Bank Capital Investment," *Journal of Finance,* v.30:4, (September 1975).

Moore, Basil J. (1968). *An Introduction of the Theory of Finance*. New York: The Free Press, 1968.

Moses, Bernard (1892), "Legal Tender Notes in California," *Quarterly Journal of Economics,* v.7 (October 1892), pp. 1-25.

Mote, Larry R. (1979). "Empirical Delineation of Banking Markets," paper presented at the Midwest Finance Association's 28th Annual Meeting, (April 1979).

Motley, Brian (1982), "Consumption, Saving and Asset Accumulation," *Economic Review,* Federal Reserve Bank of San Francisco (Winter 1982), pp. 37-54.

Motter, David C. (1965), "Bank Formation and the Public Interest," *National Banking Review,* v.2 (March 1965), pp. 299-350.

Motter, David C. and Deane Carson (1964), "Bank Entry and the Public Interest: A Case Study," *National Banking Review*, v.1:4, (June 1964), pp. 469-512.

Nash, Gerald (1964), *State Government and Economic Development: A History of Administrative Policies in California, 1849-1933*. Berkeley: University of California Press, 1964.

Nosari, Eldon J. (1975), "An Empirical Investigation into the Determinants of National Bank Entry," *Mississippi Valley Journal of Business and Economics*, v.10:3 (April 1975), pp. 25-35.

Nutter, Warren G. and John H. Moore (1976). "A Theory of Competition," *Journal of Law and Economics*, v.19:1 (April 1976), pp. 39-65.

Olmstead, Alan (1976), *New York City Mutual Savings Banks, 1819-1861*. Chapel Hill: University of North Carolina Press, 1976.

Olmstead, Alan and Victor Goldberg (1975), "Institutional Change and American Economic Growth: A Critique of Davis, and North," *Explorations in Economic History*, v.12 (1975), pp. 193-210.

Orgler, Yair and Benjamin Wolkowitz (1976). *Bank Capital*. New York: Van Nostrand Reinhold, 1976.

Osborne, Dale and Jeanne Wendell (1978), "The Main Fault with Traditional Research on Banking Competition," *Research Paper, No. 7805*, Federal Reserve Bank of Dallas, (September 1978).

_____ (1981), "A Note on Concentration and Checking Account Prices," *Journal of Finance*, v.36:1 (March 1981), pp. 181-186.

Pakonen, R. Rodney (1970), "Branch Regulation and Its Effect on Commercial Bank Entry," Federal Reserve Bank of Minneapolis, *Staff Report SR-4*, (January 1970).

Peltzman, Sam (1965), "Entry in Commercial Banking," *Journal of Law and Economics*, v.8 (October 1965).

_____ (1965), "Bank Entry Regulation: Its Impact and Purpose," *National Bank Review,* v.2 (December 1965).

_____ (1970), "Capital Investment in Commercial Banking and its Relation to Portfolio Regulation," *Journal of Political Economy,* v.78:1, (January/February 1970).

Perloff, H.S., et al. (1960), *Regions, Resources, and Economic Growth,* Baltimore, 1960.

Phillips, Almarin (1976). "A Critique of Empirical Studies of Relations between Market Structure and Profitability," *Journal of Industrial Economics,* v.24 (June 1976).

_____ (1967). "Evidence on Concentration in Banking Markets and Interest Rates." *Federal Reserve Bulletin,* (June 1967), pp. 916-926.

Phillips, C.A. (1920), *Bank Credit.* New York: Macmillan, 1920.

Pierson-Doti, Lynne (1978). "Banking in California: Some Evidence on Structure, 1878-1905." Unpublished Ph.D. dissertation, University of California at Riverside, 1978.

Plehn, Carl C. (1897), "The General Property Tax in California," *Economic Studies,* American Economic Association, v.2:3 (June 1897), pp. 119-198.

_____ (1899), "The Taxation of Mortgages in California, 1849 to 1899," *Yale Review,* v.8 (May 1899), pp. 31-67.

Powlison, K. (1931), *Profits of the National Banks,* Boston, 1931.

Pringle, John J. (1974a), "The Imperfect Markets Model of Commercial Bank Financial Management," *Journal of Financial and Quantitative Analysis,* v.9 (January 1974), pp. 69-87.

_____ (1974b), "The Capital Decision in Commercial Banks," *Journal of Finance,* v.24:3, (June 1974).

_____ (1975), "Bank Capital from the Perspective of Shareholder Interests-Implications for Bank Regulation," in *Compendium of Major Issues in Bank Regulation*, U.S. Congress, State. Committee on Banking. Housing and Urban Affairs, Washington, DC: 1975.

Ransom, Roger L. and Richard Sutch (1981), "Credit Merchandising in the Post-Emancipation South: Structure, Conduct, and Performance," in Gary M. Walton and James F. Shepherd (eds.), *Market Institutions and Economic Progress in the New South, 1865-1900*. New York: Academic Press, 1981, pp. 57-81.

Redlich, Fritz (1968), *The Molding of American Banking*. Second Edition, New York: Johnson Reprint Co., 1968.

Rhoades, Steven A. (1977). "Structure-Performance Studies in Banking: A Summary and Evaluation," Board of Governors, Federal Reserve System, *Staff Economic Studies*, No. 92, 1977.

Riefler, W.W. (1930), *Money Rates and Money Markets in the United States*. New York: Harper and Brothers, 1930.

Robertson, Ross (1968). *The Comptroller and Bank Supervision*. Washington, DC: The Office of the Comptroller of the Currency, 1968.

Rockoff, Hugh (1975), "Varieties of Banking and Regional Economic Development in the United States, 1840-1860," *Journal of Economic History*, v.35:1 (March 1975), pp. 160-181.

_____ (1977), "Regional Interest Rates and Bank Failures, 1870-1914," *Explorations in Economic History*, v.14 (1977), pp. 90-95.

Rodkey, R.G. (1928), *The Banking Process*. New York: Macmillan, 1928.

Rose, John T. (1977). "The Attractiveness of Banking Markets for De Novo Entry: The Evidence from Texas," *Journal of Bank Research*, v.7 (Winter 1977), pp. 284-293.

Rose, Peter S. and Donald R. Fraser (1976). "The Relationship between Stability and Change in Market Structure: An Analysis of Bank Prices," *Journal of Industrial Economics,* v.24 (June 1976), pp. 251-266.

Scherer, F.M. (1970), *Industrial Market Structure and Economic Performance.* Chicago: Rand McNally, 1970.

Schwartz, Anna J. (1975), "Comment: The Evolution of the American Capital Market, 1860-1940: A Case Study in Institutional Change," in William L. Silber (ed.) *Financial Innovation,* Lexington, Mass.: D.C. Heath and Co., 1975.

Scott, John T. (1977), "Price and Nonprice Competition in Banking Markets," Federal Reserve Bank of Boston, *Research Report No. 62,* 1977.

Scott, Kenneth E. (1975). "In Quest of Reason: The Licensing Decisions of Federal Banking Agencies." *University of Chicago Law Review,* v.42:2 (Winter 1975), pp. 42-103.

_____ (1977), "The Dual Banking System: A Model of Competition in Regulation," *Stanford Law Review,* v.30:1 (April 1977).

_____ (1980), "The Patchwork Quilt: State and Federal Roles in Bank Regulation," *Stanford Law Review,* v.32 (April 1980), pp. 687-742.

Shaw, Edward S. (1973), *Financial Deepening in Economic Development,* New York: Oxford University Press, 1973.

Shull, Bernard (1963), "Commercial Banks as Multiple-Product Price-Discriminating Firms," in Deane Carson, (ed.), *Banking and Monetary Studies,* Homewood, Illinois: Richard D. Irwin, 1963, pp. 351-368.

Silber, William L. (1975), "Toward a Theory of Financial Innovation," in William L. Silber (ed.), *Financial Innovation.* Lexington, Massachusetts: D.C. Heath and Co., 1975.

Smiley, Gene L. (1973), "The Evolution and Structure of the National Banking System," unpublished Ph.D. dissertation, University of Iowa, 1973.

_____ (1975), "Interest Rate Movement in the United States, 1888-1913," *Journal of Economic History,* v.35 (September 1975), pp. 591-620.

_____ (1976), "Revised Estimates of Short Term Interest Rates for National Banks for States and Reserve Cities, 1888-1913," Working Paper, Department of Economics, Marquette University, Milwaukee, Wisconsin 53233 (October, 1976).

_____ (1977), "Risk, Market Structure, and Transactions Costs in the Development of the National Short Term Capital Market, 1888-1913." Working Paper, Department of Economics, Marquette University, 1977.

_____ (1981), "Regional Variation in Bank Loan Rates in the Interwar Years," *Journal of Economic History,* v.41:4 (December 1981), pp. 889-901.

Smith, W.P. (1965), "Measures of Banking Structure and Competition," *Federal Reserve Bulletin,* v.51 (September 1965), pp. 1212-1222.

Southworth, Shirley Donald (1928), *Branch Banking in the United States.* New York: McGraw-Hill, 1928.

Spellman, Lewis J. (1976), "Economic Growth and Financial Intermediation," in Ronald I. McKinnon (ed.), *Money and Finance in Economic Growth and Development.* New York and Basel: Marcel Dekker, 1976, pp. 11-34.

Stigler, George J. (1961), "The Economics of Information," *Journal of Political Economy,* v.69:3 (June 1961), pp. 213-225.

_____ (1964), "A Theory of Oligopoly," *Journal of Political Economy,* v.72 (1964), pp. 44-61.

_____ (1967), "Imperfections in the Capital Market," *Journal of Political Economy,* v.75 (June 1967), pp. 287-292.

Stolz, Richard W. (1975), "Local Banking Markets and the Relation Between Structure, Prices, and Nonprices in Rural Areas," *Staff Report No. 11,* Federal Reserve Bank of Minneapolis, 1975.

_____ (1976), "Local Banking Markets, Structure, and Conduct in Rural Areas." In *Proceedings of a Conference on Bank Structure and Competition.* Chicago: Federal Reserve Bank of Chicago, 1976, pp. 134-48.

Sylla, Richard (1969), "Federal Policy, Banking Market Structure, and Capital Mobilization in the United States, 1863-1913," *Journal of Economic History,* v.29 (December 1969), pp. 657-686.

_____ (1972), "The United States, 1863-1913," in R. Cameron, (ed.) *Banking and Economic Development: Some Lessons in History,* New York: Oxford University Press, 1972, pp. 232-262.

_____ (1975), *The American Capital Market, 1846-1913.* New York: Arno Press, 1975.

_____ (1977), "Financial Intermediaries in Economic History: Quantitative Research on the Seminal Hypotheses of Lance Davis and Alexander Gerschenkron," in R.E. Gallman, ed., *Recent Developments in the Study of Business and Economic History: Essays in Memory of Herman E. Krooss,* Greenwich, Connecticut, 1977.

Throop, Adrian W. (1975), "Capital Investment and Entry in Commercial Banking, "*Journal of Money, Credit and Banking,* v.7:2 (May 1975).

United States Bureau of the Census (1975), *Historical Statistics of the United States, Colonial Times to 1970.* Bicentennial Edition, Parts 1 and 2, Washington, DC: Government Printing Office, 1975.

United States Census Office, *Abstract of the Eleventh Census of the United States, 1890*. Washington, DC: Government Printing Office, 1896.

United States Census Office, *Abstract of the Twelfth Census of the United States, 1900*. Washington, DC: Government Printing Office, 1903.

United States National Monetary Commission, (1909), *Special Reports From the Banks*, Washington, DC: Government Printing Office, 1909.

United States Office of the Comptroller of the Currency, *Report of the Comptroller of the Currency*, annual volumes 1870 through 1914.

Vojta, George (1973), *Bank Capital Adequacy*, New York: First National City Corp. 1973.

Walton, Gary M. and James F. Shepherd (eds.) (1981), *Market Institutions and Economic Progress in the New South, 1865-1900*. New York: Academic Press, 1981.

Watkins, L. (1929), *Banker's Balances*, Chicago, 1929.

White, Eugene N. (1981), "State-Sponsored Insurance of Bank Deposits in the United States, 1907-1929," *Journal of Economic History*, v.41:3 (September 1981), pp. 537-557.

_____ (1982), "The Political Economy of Banking Regulation, 1864-1933," *Journal of Economic History*, v.42:1 (March 1982), pp. 33-40.

Williamson, Jeffrey, G. (1974), *Late Nineteenth-Century American Development: A General Equilibrium History*. Cambridge: Cambridge University Press, 1974.

Willis, Parker B. (1937), *The Federal Reserve Bank of San Francisco*. New York: Columbia University Press, 1937.

Wood, John H. (1975), *Commercial Bank Loan and Investment Behaviour*. Wiley Monographs in Applied Econometrics, edited by A.A. Walters. London and New York: John Wiley & Sons, 1975.

Wright, Benjamin J. (1910), *Banking in California: 1849-1910*. San Francisco: H.S. Crocker, 1910.

Wright, Colin (1967), "Interest Elasticity of Consumption," *American Economic Review*, v.57:4 (September 1967), pp. 850-855.

Yeats, A.J. (1974a), "A Framework for Evaluating Potential Competition as a Factor in Bank Mergers and Acquisitions," *Journal of Money, Credit and Banking*, v.6:3, (August 1974).

Yeats, A.J (1974b). "Further Evidence on the Structure Performance Relation in Banking." *Journal of Economics and Business*, (Winter 1974).

Index